Your Official America Online® Guide to Internet Living

Your Official America Online® Guide to Internet Living

Jennifer Kaufeld

AOL Press

IDG BOOKS WORLDWIDE

Foster City, CA • Chicago, IL • Indianapolis, IN • New York, NY

Your Official America Online® Guide to Internet Living

Published by
IDG Books Worldwide, Inc.
An International Data Group Company
919 E. Hillsdale Blvd., Suite 400
Foster City, CA 94404
www.idgbooks.com (IDG Books Worldwide Web site)

ISBN: 0-7645-3431-9

Printed in the United States of America

10 9 8 7 6 5 4 3 2 1

1B/ST/RR/ZZ/FC

Distributed in the United States by IDG Books Worldwide, Inc.

Distributed by CDG Books Canada Inc. for Canada; by Transworld Publishers Limited in the United Kingdom; by IDG Norge Books for Norway; by IDG Sweden Books for Sweden; by IDG Books Australia Publishing Corporation Pty. Ltd. for Australia and New Zealand; by TransQuest Publishers Pte Ltd. for Singapore, Malaysia, Thailand, Indonesia, and Hong Kong; by Gotop Information Inc. for Taiwan; by ICG Muse, Inc. for Japan; by Intersoft for South Africa; by Eyrolles for France; by International Thomson Publishing for Germany, Austria and Switzerland; by Distribuidora Cuspide for Argentina; by LR International for Brazil; by Galileo Libros for Chile; by Ediciones ZETA S.C.R. Ltda. for Peru; by WS Computer Publishing Corporation, Inc., for the Philippines; by Contemporanea de Ediciones for Venezuela; by Express Computer Distributors for the Caribbean and West Indies; by Micronesia Media Distributor, Inc. for Micronesia; by Chips Computadoras S.A. de C.V. for Mexico; by Editorial Norma de Panama S.A. for Panama; by American Bookshops for Finland.

For general information on IDG Books Worldwide's books in the U.S., please call our Consumer Customer Service department at 800-762-2974. For reseller information, including discounts and premium sales, please call our Reseller Customer Service department at 800-434-3422.

For information on where to purchase IDG Books Worldwide's books outside the U.S., please contact our International Sales department at 317-596-5530 or fax 317-596-5692.

For consumer information on foreign language translations, please contact our Customer Service department at 800-434-3422, fax 317-596-5692, or e-mail rights@idgbooks.com.

For information on licensing foreign or domestic rights, please phone +1-650-655-3109.

For sales inquiries and special prices for bulk quantities, please contact our Sales department at 650-655-3200 or write to the address above.

For information on using IDG Books Worldwide's books in the classroom or for ordering examination copies, please contact our Educational Sales department at 800-434-2086 or fax 317-596-5499.

For press review copies, author interviews, or other publicity information, please contact our Public Relations department at 650-655-3000 or fax 650-655-3299.

For authorization to photocopy items for corporate, personal, or educational use, please contact Copyright Clearance Center, 222 Rosewood Drive, Danvers, MA 01923, or fax 978-750-4470.

Library of Congress Cataloging-in-Publication Data

Kaufeld, Jenny. Your official America Online guide to Internet living / Jennifer Kaufeld.

  p. cm.

ISBN 0-7645-3431-9 (alk. paper)

1. Internet (Computer network) 2. America Online (Online service) I. Title.

TK5105.875.I57 K385 1999
025.04-dc21

99-051999

is a registered trademark or trademark under exclusive license to IDG Books Worldwide, Inc. from International Data Group, Inc. in the United States and/or other countries.

is a registered trademark of America Online, Inc.

ABOUT IDG BOOKS WORLDWIDE

Welcome to the world of IDG Books Worldwide.

IDG Books Worldwide, Inc., is a subsidiary of International Data Group, the world's largest publisher of computer-related information and the leading global provider of information services on information technology. IDG was founded more than 30 years ago by Patrick J. McGovern and now employs more than 9,000 people worldwide. IDG publishes more than 290 computer publications in over 75 countries. More than 90 million people read one or more IDG publications each month.

Launched in 1990, IDG Books Worldwide is today the #1 publisher of best-selling computer books in the United States. We are proud to have received eight awards from the Computer Press Association in recognition of editorial excellence and three from Computer Currents' First Annual Readers' Choice Awards. Our best-selling ...For Dummies® series has more than 50 million copies in print with translations in 31 languages. IDG Books Worldwide, through a joint venture with IDG's Hi-Tech Beijing, became the first U.S. publisher to publish a computer book in the People's Republic of China. In record time, IDG Books Worldwide has become the first choice for millions of readers around the world who want to learn how to better manage their businesses.

Our mission is simple: Every one of our books is designed to bring extra value and skill-building instructions to the reader. Our books are written by experts who understand and care about our readers. The knowledge base of our editorial staff comes from years of experience in publishing, education, and journalism — experience we use to produce books to carry us into the new millennium. In short, we care about books, so we attract the best people. We devote special attention to details such as audience, interior design, use of icons, and illustrations. And because we use an efficient process of authoring, editing, and desktop publishing our books electronically, we can spend more time ensuring superior content and less time on the technicalities of making books.

You can count on our commitment to deliver high-quality books at competitive prices on topics you want to read about. At IDG Books Worldwide, we continue in the IDG tradition of delivering quality for more than 30 years. You'll find no better book on a subject than one from IDG Books Worldwide.

John Kilcullen
Chairman and CEO
IDG Books Worldwide, Inc.

Steven Berkowitz
President and Publisher
IDG Books Worldwide, Inc.

*Eighth Annual
Computer Press
Awards ≥1992*

*Ninth Annual
Computer Press
Awards ≥1993*

*Tenth Annual
Computer Press
Awards ≥1994*

*Eleventh Annual
Computer Press
Awards ≥1995*

IDG is the world's leading IT media, research and exposition company. Founded in 1964, IDG had 1997 revenues of $2.05 billion and has more than 9,000 employees worldwide. IDG offers the widest range of media options that reach IT buyers in 75 countries representing 95% of worldwide IT spending. IDG's diverse product and services portfolio spans six key areas including print publishing, online publishing, expositions and conferences, market research, education and training, and global marketing services. More than 90 million people read one or more of IDG's 290 magazines and newspapers, including IDG's leading global brands — Computerworld, PC World, Network World, Macworld and the Channel World family of publications. IDG Books Worldwide is one of the fastest-growing computer book publishers in the world, with more than 700 titles in 36 languages. The "...For Dummies®" series alone has more than 50 million copies in print. IDG offers online users the largest network of technology-specific Web sites around the world through IDG.net (http://www.idg.net), which comprises more than 225 targeted Web sites in 55 countries worldwide. International Data Corporation (IDC) is the world's largest provider of information technology data, analysis and consulting, with research centers in over 41 countries and more than 400 research analysts worldwide. IDG World Expo is a leading producer of more than 168 globally branded conferences and expositions in 35 countries including E3 (Electronic Entertainment Expo), Macworld Expo, ComNet, Windows World Expo, ICE (Internet Commerce Expo), Agenda, DEMO, and Spotlight. IDG's training subsidiary, ExecuTrain, is the world's largest computer training company, with more than 230 locations worldwide and 785 training courses. IDG Marketing Services helps industry-leading IT companies build international brand recognition by developing global integrated marketing programs via IDG's print, online and exposition products worldwide. Further information about the company can be found at www.idg.com. 1/24/99

About the Author

Jennifer Kaufeld has written (or cowritten with her husband, John, also a computer book author) four books about America Online, including the *America Online® For Dummies® Quick Reference* (published by IDG Books Worldwide). After being dragged kicking and screaming into the world of computers, she now spends her copious free time reviewing educational software for homeschoolers and home education journals, speaking on the educational use of computers and software, and presiding over the Greek and English lessons in the family home school.

Credits

IDG Books Worldwide

Acquisitions Editor
Kathy Yankton

Development Editor
Michael Christopher

Technical Editor
Matt Converse

Copy Editor
Ami Knox

Project Coordinators
Linda Marousek
Joe Shines

America Online Techincal Editor
Jenn Thompson

Cover Design
DKG design, LLC

Graphics and Production Specialists
Mario Amador
Stephanie Hollier
Dina Quan
Ramses Ramirez

Quality Control Specialist
Chris Weisbart

Book Designer
Evan Deerfield

Cover Design
Clark Creative Group

Proofreading and Indexing
York Production Services

Illustrator
Mary Jo Weis

To my Best Friend, who captured my heart, my imagination, and my loyalty.

Preface

Welcome to *Your Official America Online Guide to Internet Living*. Now more than ever before, the Internet contains vast reservoirs of information and assistance for the various aspects of your everyday life. To reach them, however, you need to know that they're there. You also need to be able to sift through the other stuff to get to exactly what you want.

That's where this book comes in. *Your Official Guide to Internet Living* takes you through and beyond the basics. Each chapter focuses on a different task you can do online, spending less effort and less time than if you did the same thing on paper, in the car, or on the phone.

On the other hand, are these the only things you can do online? Of course not — any book claiming to include "everything" would be hopelessly incomplete as soon as the first draft was done. Instead, think of this book as providing you a jumping-off point.

When you're finished with this volume, you'll know enough searching tricks to track down pretty much anything you want to find online. You'll also recognize the benefits of using your online connection to save time for the things that really matter. Would you like to spend the day driving from one car lot to another, looking for ideas on your next auto replacement? Or, would you rather spend one hour searching for a car online, isolate one or two cars that fit your family, and then load up the gang in your current vehicle for a day of picnicking and kite flying?

I don't know about you, but your kids would probably prefer the picnic. I know mine would.

About This Book

This book helps you use your online connection to do the things you're already doing every day, every month, and every year. Hungry? Order lunch or dinner from a local restaurant through your online connection. Need to redecorate a room? Glean ideas online and save petrol at the same time.

If you're like most of my readers, you lead a very full life. Squeezing in one more thing might fill your plate too full. This book helps you look at your obligations differently. Will it eliminate the jobs you need to perform in the various areas of your life? Well, no. I wish I could help you there, but I can't.

What it will do, though, is help you to look at your to-do list in a new way. Instead of jumping into the car to track down an item, you can save hours (not to mention a few dollars here and there) by searching for it online and then purchasing it right there. Here's one of *my* success stories:

While I was writing this book, it occurred to me that Christmas was not too far off. I wanted to purchase a couple of bears and a set of bear outfits for my small daughter. The closest toy store carried about half of what I wanted. To find the rest I needed to hop onto the beltway and search every Toys R Us in the area, since I was looking for specific outfits and only this toy store carried them in our area. (Ever seen a bear dressed like a ballerina? It's a hoot.)

In desperation, I used my online connection and searched EToys.com. Within fifteen minutes, I found the toys. In this particular instance, EToys carried every item in the series, so I was able to place my order and turn back to my project without ever leaving the computer (except for that quick dash in search of my credit card). And instead of losing an entire afternoon or more driving around the city, I finished that segment of my shopping in record time.

You can do that, too. More than half the battle is won when you know where to go to find what you need, and you're holding a good amount of that information in your hands right now.

Using the AOL Software

I assume that you either already use America Online as your online service, or you have the software installed somewhere on your system. If neither of these assumptions apply to you, then you first need a copy of the software! One quick call to the America Online sales staff at 1-800-827-6364 will send a copy of the latest version of the AOL software winging its way to you via postal mail.

If the software is already installed on your system but you haven't signed up for an AOL account, double-click the AOL.exe icon to start the software. Look for it in the America Online folder on your hard drive if you don't see the green and blue AOL icon on your desktop. (If you do find the icon on your desktop, double-click it and save yourself some rooting time.) The software leads you through the signup process.

The Parts

How do *you* use the Internet? For some tasks, such as checking the weather or the news, you can use it every day — or even several times a day. Other activities and events of your life may lead you to online resources once a week, once a month, or even once a year, such as at tax time.

To best accommodate these lifestyle differences, this book is organized into sections that reflect how you use America Online. For topics that come up daily, such as news gathering and money management, turn to Parts I and II. Further on, as you work your way through the book, you'll find travel topics, purchasing pointers, and even job search sites in Parts III through VII.

Although you can read this book from cover to cover, you don't need to begin at Chapter 1 and read straight through to the end. If you find a part or individual chapter that interests you, dive right in and read the rest of the book once you've satisfied your immediate curiosity.

Part I: Your Everyday AOL. Part I contains the chapters you'll turn to again and again. They discuss the ways you can use your online connection over and over, every day. Topics range from checking the news to finding local merchants.

Part II: Dollars and Cents Management. Part II talks about the financial side of your life. Whether you need help balancing your checkbook or you'd like to delve into online investments, look to these chapters for guidance on dozens of related topics — budgeting, online banking, taxes, and mortgages, to name just a few.

Part III: Professional Life and Training. When you're thinking about changing your own job, defining your career, or you need to bring someone alongside to help you, these chapters point you in the right direction. Also look here for suggestions on finding online training and education.

Part IV: Home Is Where the Art Is. Use the tips in Part IV to create your personalized castle. These chapters talk about finding a home or apartment, and then altering, decorating, and landscaping your abode.

Part V: Buying the Easy Way. To find gifts for the important people in your life, use your online connection. Use it also to help you evaluate your options and decide on a specific big-ticket item for yourself or your family. Pick up other items you've always wanted in any of the online auctions. In short, check out the many convenient, cost-saving ways to shop online.

Part VI: Going There from Here. Plan your vacation, your business trip, or your next sojourn across town with help from your online connection. This section also gives you ideas for learning about other countries without ever leaving your computer.

Part VII: Pursuing Life's Passions. Plunge deeper into the interests you already have using your AOL connection, and add to your knowledge. At the same time, meet people who enjoy the same things you do. These chapters explore the pleasures of fitness, pets, photography, cooking, games, and sports.

Conventions

Computer book authors, in attempts to make the intricacies of their subjects a bit clearer, use all sorts of print tricks. This book is really no different. Within these pages you'll see several techniques designed to highlight points and simplify instructions, from typeface changes to cool art in the margins.

Commands

Because this is an America Online Internet Guide, the book doesn't require you to do advanced finger calisthenics when you want to access an online area or open a Web site. You do, however, need to type Keywords or Web addresses every now and then. When you might otherwise trip across those instructions, look for the words in **bold**. They tell you exactly what to type into the browser bar text box at the top of your screen.

Icons

The icons guide you through the murky spots, point out things you should notice, and generally ensure you a safe and informative reading experience.

Tip: When you see a Tip icon, look for some timely information to help you with the steps or topic at hand. Tip icons also give you time and money-saving advice, or tell you how you can do something better via the suggested option.

Note: Information that merits remembering appears next to a Note icon. Look to the Note icons to provide additional information that increases your knowledge or facility with the topic at hand.

Find It Online: Looking for something in particular? The Find it Online icon points your way to specific sites of interest, and includes methods for locating a site you need.

Cross-Reference: When more information appears elsewhere in the book, a Cross Reference icon points it out. Use this icon to jump to related information, as well.

Caution: The Caution icon warns you of possible unpleasant consequences. When you see one of these, proceed slowly and carefully, lest you need to retrace your steps or complete some task all over again.

Sidebars

Once in a while you might happen upon a sidebar, a couple of paragraphs that give some extra information about the topic at hand (or even a related topic). You'll know them when you see them — these sections appear in gray boxes to distinguish them from the rest of the text.

Before You Go On . . .

Of course, I hope that this book gives you the information you need to make your online experience even more useful and productive. Over the past several years, I've transferred many portions of my life to the Internet and no longer waste time that used to be spent utilizing pencil and paper, conducting library research, waiting on hold, or scrounging at the mall. I wish you the same progress I've had in lowering my holiday shopping stress, finding that important document *before* the meeting, and crunching the numbers online. (*Was there life before EToys.com?*)

If you have any comments about this book, I'd enjoy hearing from you. Getting e-mail from a reader always brightens my day — it's nice to know when the book helps someone, and what readers think. You can generally find me online at AOL screen name JSKaufeld.

# Acknowledgments

With the chapters finally off my desk, I get to relax a moment, take a long breath, and think about the people who helped pull this project together. I'm not sure who actually reads this part, but it's a lot of fun to write.

First, hats off to the teams at America Online and IDG Books. Andy Cummings, my acquisitions editor, took one of his many visions and created a reality with the patience and vibrance that are his hallmarks. Kathy Yankton, Andy's Counterpart on the West Coast, made sure I got beta materials when I needed them. Thanks to her, I've Got Pictures!

John Dyn, the Man In Charge Of A Lot Of Things at America Online, took time out of his incredible schedule to guide the project and offer ongoing feedback. Thank you!

Michael Christopher, my development editor, deserves the tastiest milk and cookies I can buy for his wonderful sense of humor, willingness to talk as long as it took, and incredible ability to evaporate my stress. I actually looked forward to your calls.

Ami Knox, my copy editor gets a round of applause. And without the IDG production department, we'd have to send out this book on floppy disk. I appreciate the magic you do.

Back at AOL, thanks to Matt Converse for his technical editing. With you at the project's technical helm, I know the various instructions operate the way I said they would. As always, working with you is a joy. Also at America Online, Janine Smith patiently answered a myriad of questions about AOL's You've Got Pictures feature.

And finally, one more huge thank you to the community members who offered hugs all around as deadlines approached. John, your day-by-day encouragement kept me going. Sandy, I'll take that massage now. Steve, thanks for the hours of conversation via AOL Instant Messenger. Derek, your "Hey guys! I wrote this yesterday. Listen to these lyrics!" made me smile when I needed it most. And kids, get your shoes on. It's time for a day at Chuck E. Cheese.

Contents at a Glance

Contents

Part V: Buying the Easy Way   251

Part VI: Going There from Here   299

Chapter 28: Saving on Vacation Reservations 300

Chapter 29: Mapping Your Way Around 310

Chapter 30: Packing Your Briefcase 318

Chapter 31: Cruising AOL Worldwide 328

Chapter 32: Learning About a Country 336

Jump Start

Your America Online account allows you to do many things online, faster and better than if you did them any other way. You can track your favorite sports team. Watch for upcoming IPOs. Take a course in accounting. Learn about antiques. Develop puzzle and game skills of all kinds. Or find the perfect accessory for any room in your house.

In fact, practically anything you already do you can do online with less hassle. And quite often you'll save money at the same time.

Dipping into the Offerings

From your computer, you can complete dozens of tasks in ways that lighten your daily workload. Whether you need a ZIP code or an e-mail address, or you want to know whether your upcoming flight is on schedule, you can find the answers fast via your AOL account. Let me give you a few examples.

Track That Airline Flight

When it comes to airline flights, whether you're boarding or picking up a passenger, it's nice to know if the flight will be on time. With an online flight tracker, you know in advance, *before* you leave for the airport.

Here's how to track a flight:

1. Use Keyword: **Flight Tracker** to open the Flight Tracker in your browser window, as shown in Figure JS-1.

Tip

If you'd like to see an interactive graphic that shows an instrument panel and the plane actually moving over a topographic map (see Figure JS-3), click the Graphical Version button after you enter the flight number in Step 2.

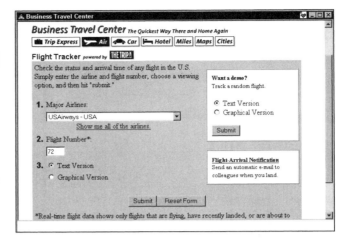

Figure JS-1. Use the Flight Tracker to view your flight status.

2. Select the correct airline from the drop-down list. Then type the flight number and click the Submit button to see the flight's status.

3. The flight information appears in the browser window, as shown in Figure JS-2.

Figure JS-2. Flying high with an expected on-time arrival.

Screen shot of Business Travel Center showing Flight Tracker

Figure JS-3. When the information is presented this way, you know exactly where the plane is.

Order from the Registry

Instead of driving to the mall, you can order a bridal gift from a bride's registry and have it sent directly to her without ever leaving home. Just type Keyword: **Wedding**. Weddingline, at www.weddingline.com, allows you to access gift registries from Macy's, Rich's, Lazarus, Goldsmith's, Stern's, and other retailers 24 hours a day.

See Your Seats Before Ordering Tickets

See where you'll be sitting during the concert with Topcentre (www.topcentre.com) or Ticketmaster (www.ticketmaster.com). These vendors show you venue layouts so you know exactly where seat CC578 is *before* you arrive for the show.

Send E-Mail Greeting Cards to Friends, Free!

Send e-mail greeting cards to a friend, at no cost to you whatsoever. Pick the card, write a sentiment, and send the greeting. The Internet greeting system then drops a message into his or her e-mail box. Your friend then sees a message that tells him or her you sent an online greeting, and provides a link in the message. Your friend then clicks the link to visit the site and read the card. No stamps, no ink, and nothing for your friend to download into his or her computer.

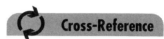

Cross-Reference

Turn to Part VI for online travel tips. In particular, Chapter 30 talks about business travel.

Cross-Reference

Chapter 26 offers additional suggestions for saving time and energy during the gift-giving seasons of your life.

Cross-Reference

Chapter 4 tells you more about online entertainment options.

Jump Start

Find free online greeting and post cards at these sites:

▶ Great Greetings at `www.greeting-cards.to`

▶ Free Web Greeting Cards at `www.free-web-cards.com`

▶ All Occasion Online Greeting Cards at `www.women.com/postcards`

▶ Free Online Postcards at `www.ynot.com`

Send Virtual Flowers to Someone You Love

When the real thing just won't do, send virtual flowers. They never fade, never wilt, and they're perfect for any occasion. A bouquet of virtual flowers, sent via e-mail, brightens a friend's day, cheers a lonely college student, and tells your partner you love 'em.

Think of a virtual floral bouquet as a cross between an electronic postcard and flowers from your local floral shop. These photographs of stunning floral arrangements and plants are free to send — you pick the bouquet, type a message, enter the recipient's e-mail address, and send it on its way. When your friend receives a message in his or her e-mail box that flowers are waiting, he or she uses the included Web address to view the flowers and message you sent.

Find virtual flower shops at Shawna's Virtual Flowers, `drew.netusa1.net/~shawna/virtual`, or the Virtual Florist, `www.virtualflorist.com`.

Order Food

It's your turn to buy lunch, and you have a project due at 2 p.m. Before you experience a meltdown, jump onto AOL and order lunch for the office from Food.com. Open the Food.com Web site (`www.food.com`), as shown in Figure JS-4, to find out which restaurants serve in your area.

Figure JS-4. Order meals online for the office or home.

Find the ZIP Code You Need

When you're ready to send that letter, but you don't know which ZIP code to use, go to Keyword: **Zip Codes** to open the U.S. Postal Service Web site. From there, clicking the ZIP Code Look-Up and Address Information button opens an area that gives you several ZIP Code options.

Which Word Did I Really Mean?

When that word on the tip of your tongue doesn't sound exactly right, check it against the online dictionary or thesaurus before you type it into a letter or document.

Keyword: **Dictionary** opens the Merriam-Webster Dictionary, and Keyword: **Thesaurus** opens the Merriam-Webster Thesaurus. And if your term is highly specialized, Keyword: **Dictionaries** opens a window full of links for other dictionaries. Check those computer, medical, or science terms through the Dictionaries window.

Create Your Own Web Page

Take ten to fifteen minutes of your time and create your own Web page that tells people who you are, what makes you tick, or the things you like to do. Keyword: **123 Publish** opens a window with ready-made templates that make Web page creation a breeze — choose from over 50 possibilities, including the following:

My Business Page	Our Genealogy Page
My Love Life	My Newsletter
About My Faith	My Recipes
My Web Profile	My Sports Page
Our Baby Announcement	My Favorite TV Shows

Once your page is finished, you can preview it by clicking the Preview button. To save your page and add it to AOL Hometown, America Online's free Web storage system, click Save.

Check the Weather Forecast

Check within a matter of seconds to see whether your city is due for rain or shine. Click the My Weather button to see your city's forecast for the next few days. Want to see another city? Use Keyword: **Weather** to open the National Weather window, and then type the city name or ZIP code into the text box and click the Search button.

Keep an Eye on Your Bank Balance

Sign up with your bank's online banking Web site, and you can check your balances, pay bills, or transfer funds 24 hours a day. Keyword: **Banking** gives you an introduction; for in-depth information, turn to Chapter 6.

Download Your Tax Forms

Forget that late-night run to the library. Jump online and download all the tax forms you need to file your taxes this year. Whether you need the 1040EZ or the state form for Vermont, you'll find it at Keyword: **Tax**.

Look for a New Job

Feeling burned out? Need a change? Monster.com, at www.monster.com, lists more than 150,000 jobs waiting for takers. Find out whether they have a listing with your name on it.

Increase Your Knowledge

Knowledge means power. If you know, you can do. When that urge to learn something new strikes you, hop online and check into one of the hundreds of online courses available. Some of them offer college credits, whereas others offer continuing education units. Others exist simply for the sake of learning itself, which is motivation enough for thousands of online learners just like you.

Use Keyword: **Courses** to open AOL's Courses Online window, where you can browse through continuing education and collegiate offerings.

Get Driving Directions

Planning on a visit to a new area, whether across town or across the country? You can tell the Maps & Directions site where your journey begins and ends, and it presents you with door-to-door driving directions. Use Keyword: **Mapping** to open the site.

Access the Real Estate Listings

Check out the real estate listings by typing Keyword: **Looking**. Clicking the Search over 1.3 million homes link loads the Realtor.com Homes for Sale Web site. From this site, you can search through more 1 million house listings, including listings near your home or far away.

Note

See other AOL members' Web pages at AOL Hometown (Keyword: **Hometown**).

Cross-Reference

Chapter 3 tells you more about finding weather news and forecasts online.

Note

If you don't have Adobe Acrobat Reader, you'll need that to read the forms. Find it at www.adobe.com, or click the Acrobat Reader button in the Tax Forms & Schedules window.

Spiff Up Your Surroundings

Cross-Reference

Need a more detailed federal schedule than one of the 1040 forms? Chapter 8 tells you where to find them.

Paint the walls. Rearrange the furniture. Purchase a new accent item or two. Create a desktop water fountain for that bare tabletop. No matter what direction you go, AOL can help you decorate without breaking your back or destroying your bank account. Use online resources to design the furniture layout, order the wallpaper, and answer all your questions. Then sit back and wait for the pieces to arrive.

Cross-Reference

Monster.com is one of several online job banks. Chapter 14 tells you about the others, and also lists some other places you might want to look online.

Start with the Design-A-Room Web site (at www.designaroom.com). This unique resource lets you "try things on" by helping you arrange the furniture you already have (or want to purchase). First establish the room size, and then select furniture to go inside. Move the pieces around, try different combinations — in short, play with the arrangement until you figure out what might work best for you — all without straining a single muscle.

Build Your Foreign Language Vocabulary

Cross-Reference

Turn to Chapter 17 for more information on online classes.

When toddlers pass the 300-word vocabulary mark, they're suddenly a lot more fun to talk to. Granted, they don't ask questions like "Which way to the train station?" but the same could generally be said for foreign language learners.

Cross-Reference

Chapter 29 tells you how to get all kinds of maps and directions, whether you want a segment of a city, an urban overview, or a state map.

You can quickly enhance your basic vocabulary with a software package or two. How about a program that emphasizes holiday words in Spanish? Or maybe an introduction to Russian? AOL contains files to help with French, Spanish, Greek, Japanese, Arabic, Chinese, Vietnamese, Hebrew — you name it, the files are ready and free for the download. Use Keyword: **Download Center** to open the Download Center window, and go from there.

Check Out Those Foreign Words and Phrases

Every now and then you get stuck for a word. Maybe it's "windshield wiper" in French — *pare-brise essuie-glace*. Perhaps you need a specific phrase to make a thought complete. When the need for a specific noun or verb arises, turn to the foreign language dictionaries for help.

Use Keyword: **Foreign Language** to open the window. Click the book graphic to open the Dictionaries by Language window, where you can select the language you want to research. Each language lists at least one or two online dictionary resources for that language.

Eat Healthy

A healthful diet means more than munching rabbit food. If your idea of healthy cuisine means carrot sticks and raw broccoli, then the online food areas for the health-conscious could open your eyes.

The Dieting and Nutrition area (at Keyword: **Dieting**) leads you to some excellent collections of low-fat and generally healthy meal suggestions online. Click the Nutrition tab to see folders on nutrition and health, kids' nutrition, healthy fast food, and more. You can also link-up to several healthful food areas online via Keyword: **Healthy Eating**. Many of the individual forums (especially the women's areas) offer a small health and diet section. And through the Healthy Eating window you can visit them all, without memorizing a host of keywords to get you there.

And Finally . . .

Now that you've had a small taste of the kinds of topics covered in *Your Official America Online Guide to Internet Living*, pick a chapter and dive in! Or start at Chapter 1 and progress through the topics in numerical order. This is your guide. The choice is up to you.

CHAPTER

1

KEEPING UP WITH
THE LOCALS

Chapter 1
Keeping Up with the Locals

IN THIS CHAPTER

How to find your Digital City online

What local chat rooms are good for

Where to locate business addresses

How to find enough food online for the entire gang

What's important to the residents of your city? Go online and find out where they eat, shop, and play! And while you're at it, use your online connection to track down long-lost friends, locate businesses by the goods or services they provide, find out the latest doing of area newsmakers, and more, either locally or nationally.

Finding Your Digital City

If you live near or in a major metropolitan area in the United States, America Online probably offers a *Digital City* for your area. Much more than places for the locals to meet, Digital Cities offer entertainment calendars, restaurant recommendations, traveler's tips, and much more.

To find a Digital City for the area you're interested in, follow these steps:

1. Click the Local channel button. The Digital City window blazes to life.

2. Click the button for any city you like that appears on the map. That city's Digital City site opens in the browser window, as shown in Figure 1-1.

Figure 1-1. News, sports, entertainment — it's all here, customized for your neck of the woods.

3. From the Web site that appears, click your way through the hyperlinks that interest you. Each Digital City site offers hyperlinks to several departments full of useful local information.

The Digital City departments keep you up-to-date on your city's happenings:

Tip

While you peruse your Digital City Web site, click the Local Links link. Look for it in the Local Tools section. One of the best kept secrets on this particular service, this section provides links to all the local stuff you want to find online. Looking for links to local history, a health club close to home, or your state's constitution online? Drop by the Local Links and check there first.

▶ **Entertainment:** Learn about the best local restaurants, upcoming events, and hopping nightlife.

▶ **People & Personals:** Meet other people from your city. Whether you're looking for someone to write to or a possible romance, this department connects you with local people.

▶ **Live Chat:** Shoot the breeze with other city denizens. Populated day and night, these chat rooms introduce you to neighbors you'd probably never meet otherwise.

▶ **Sports:** Keep your finger on the pulse of homestyle college and pro sports with this department.

▶ **News & Issues:** Who's making news in your part of the world? Read local stories and post your views on-line for other members to read. When a tiny town in your state rocks the nation's headlines, you'll find the story in the Digital City News department.

Locating Lost People

Find that friend you haven't seen since graduation with a little help from the Web-based White Pages, and save yourself a trip to the local library research desk. Keyword: **White Pages** opens the AOL White Pages Web page, which should resemble the one shown in Figure 1-2. Type the person's last name, first name, and city (if you know it) into the text boxes. Then select state and country from the drop-down list (if you know them), and click the Find button.

The window displays the addresses it finds for that particular name. If you specify no state or province, the system searches all states and shows you the list of matches. When you find the person you're looking for, click the linked name and address to see a page of linked services, including a neighborhood map and driving directions from the address you enter to the person's home address.

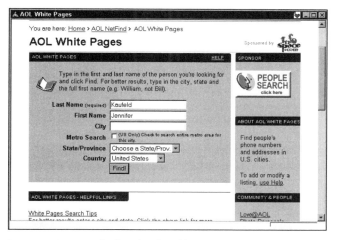

Figure 1-2. Locate that long lost friend here.

Other options linked to the person's page include

▶ **Neighborhood Services:** Links to local pharmacies, department stores, home stores, and gas station addresses.

▶ **Schools & Colleges:** Get maps and information about local schools, whether you want the Web site for the elementary school around the corner or data on a local college that interests you.

▶ **Government:** Connect to local, state, and federal Web sites that serve the address you found.

▶ **E-mail a greeting:** Send a free greeting card via e-mail to your newly located friend.

▶ **Add to address book:** Create an entry for your friend and add it to an online address book. Unlike the E-mail address book, which only holds e-mail addresses, this database provides room for name, address, e-mail, employer information, several phone numbers, ICQ ID, and AOL Instant Messenger ID. Plus, you get a notes section into which you can jot down any relevant information — for example, how you know this person in the first place!

▶ **Search for e-mail address:** If you don't know the person's e-mail address, this link attempts to give you a valid one. However, your best bet is to take that new phone number you found, pick up the phone, and ask for it.

Tip

If your phone number is unlisted, you won't find an entry for yourself in the online White Pages.

▶ **Search for public records on the person:** If the mood strikes you and it fits your budget, you can purchase a public record for the person you found. It lists any known past addresses, phone numbers, professional licenses, and so on. The information is most useful if the person happens to live in Florida or Texas, as several of the options, such as inclusion of a spouse's name, apply only to Florida or Texas residents.

You might want to check your own listing to see if it's current. Enter your own name and see if the system offers you an outdated address. Here's how to change it if your address is incorrect:

1. Open the White Pages Directory with Keyword: **White Pages**.

2. Type your own name and city into the text boxes, and select your state and country from the drop-down lists. Click the Find button.

3. Your information should appear in the Web browser. Click the Update link next to your name. The Edit Your Listing screen appears.

4. Enter your e-mail address. The system uses this to confirm your update request.

5. Check the box that says you are authorized to modify the database information for this name and address.

6. Use the name and address text boxes to alter your name and address entry; refer to Figure 1-3 for an example.

7. Ensure that your phone number is current. Your phone number must be included if you want your name and address in the Web directory.

8. To include your listing in the E-mail Directory, enter your e-mail address into the E-Mail Address text box.

9. The next section, Optional Information, gives you room to include all sorts of things: your age, maiden name, employer, a business phone number, the name of your high school or college, info on any military affiliation, and mention of any hobbies that pique your interest. Just remember — whatever information you include will appear when anyone else pulls up your name and address in the Directory.

10. When you've finished making your changes, click the Update/Remove button. The Confirm changes to a White Pages listing screen appears, telling you to reply to the e-mail message you will soon receive to confirm the suggested changes to your entry.

11. Look for an AOL White Pages verification e-mail in your mailbox. If the information in the e-mail message is correct, reply to the message to activate the changes to your listing. If the information is incorrect, close the message window without replying and enter the new information again into the update screen. In other words, you need to return to Step 1 and do the whole thing over again.

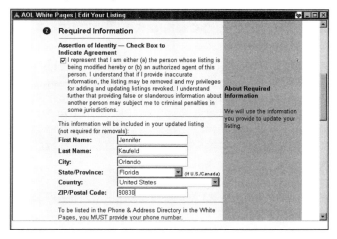

Figure 1-3. Update your information in the White Pages Directory.

On the other hand, if you get a sense of "being watched" by revealing all this information to anyone who just happens to type in your first and last name, you can delete your own record from the database. Here's how to wipe yourself completely out:

1. Type in your own name and city, and click the Find button.

2. When your record appears, click the Delete link. A Delete Your Listing window appears, showing the name and address about to be axed.

3. Enter your AOL e-mail address as a confirmation.

4. Click the Delete button. A message window appears, telling you that you must reply to the e-mail you receive to successfully delete the address.

5. The system sends you an e-mail message to confirm your deletion.

6. Click the Read button on the tool bar and open the message called AOL White Pages verification.

7. If the address is correct and you truly want to delete it from the system, click the Reply button and then the Send Now button to wing the message back to the Web site and complete the deletion process.

Tracking Down Goods and Services

When you absolutely have to leave your computer to carry on your life, first use your online connection to find the businesses you need and protect your fingers from newsprint stains. The AOL Yellow Pages locates everything from music instructors to schools, online. The system not only gives you the address but also provides driving directions if you need them. What service!

To find your local merchants, follow these steps:

1. Use Keyword: **Yellow Pages** to open the AOL Yellow Pages site.

2. Enter the kind of business you're looking for (dry cleaner, post office, interior decorator) into the Business Category text box, or use the exact business name, if you know it, in the Business Name text box.

3. Type in the city and select the state from the drop-down list. Then click the Find button to display your options, as shown in Figure 1-4.

4. Depending on the scope of the category you entered into the field, you might see a list of individual businesses and their addresses or you might see a whole page of topical links. If you entered *music* as a category, for example, the results might include subcategories such as Compact Discs – Retail, Music Boxes, Music Dealers, and so on. Click the link that most closely matches what you're looking for to continue searching.

Figure 1-4. Find directions to that music store before you hop into the car.

5. The results appear in an All Listings screen. Each listing offers a map and driving directions; some list a fax number.

6. Click the map link to see the business location or the Fax# link to see the expanded business listing complete with a fax number and a map. Click the driving directions link and fill in your address in the resulting form to get door-to-door directions.

Online Options to Make Your Life Easier

Considering today's hectic schedules, the more you can get done without fighting traffic and parking shortages, or enduring thirty minutes on hold, increases your daily productivity. Utilize these online services to their full potential and save yourself some time.

Order Food to Make That Meal Special

The next time you plan an Asian, German, Hispanic, Italian, Kosher, or Middle Eastern meal, you can have the ingredients sent directly to your door. Onlinefood.com offers individual meal components, gift baskets, and practically everything in between.

Cross-Reference

Onlinefood.com requires a $25 minimum purchase in various categories before you can finish your order. If your order doesn't meet the minimum, the site provides a list of your various purchase categories.

To open the Onlinefood.com site, follow these steps:

1. Type `www.onlinefood.com` into the browser bar text box and click the Go button. The browser opens, and Onlinefood.com loads, as shown in Figure 1-5.

Figure 1-5. Order your ingredients and beverages online.

2. Click the tab that corresponds to your meal theme; now you see a list of links.

3. Click the link for the ingredients you want, such as pasta, beverages, or meats.

4. That category's items fill the window, as shown in Figure 1-6. Click any item's Info link to learn more about it. Clicking an item's Buy link includes one in your online shopping cart.

5. Once you include an item in your shopping cart, a list of the cart's contents appears along the left side of the screen (see Figure 1-7).

6. When you have as many items as you want, click the shopping cart icon to begin the checkout process.

7. The checkout window shows your item list; if you like it the way it is, enter your zip code into the text box and click the Proceed button. To remove an item or two, click the Edit Cart button.

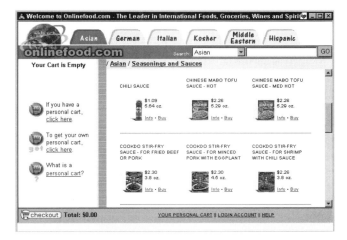

Figure 1-6. Choose from a large item assortment.

Figure 1-7. Your selected items appear along the window's left side.

8. Fill in your name and address, credit card information, and select a shipping option. When you're ready, click the Submit Order button to send your order on its way.

Select Office Meals Delivery from the drop-down menu entitled What Service Do You Want, and then fill in your street, city, state, and ZIP code. Click the Search Restaurants button, and your available selections appear on screen. Select a restaurant, place your order, and the food wings its way to you via the nearest delivery van.

Find that ZIP code

The mailman's on his way, you can't find the phone book, and you need to address a whole pile of letters. Turn to the ZIP Code Look-Up feature to locate the data you need. In addition, if you need to know how much postage to place on an envelope before it goes out the door, the U.S. Postal Service Web Site, at www.usps.com, provides that information in a handy table, plus a whole lot more.

> ▶ Click the ZIP Codes button to check the ZIP code for any given address. Of the options listed, you probably want the City/State/ZIP Code Associations section.
>
> ▶ Click the Rate Calculator button to find domestic and international postage rates.
>
> ▶ Click the StampsOnline button to purchase stamps online, which the Postal Service will send to you via regular mail.
>
> ▶ Track delivery of Express Mail and Priority Mail Global Guaranteed packages with the Track/Confirm button.

Coming Up Next . . .

Now you can log onto the Internet and read up-to-the-minute newspapers and magazines from anywhere in the world, all available — literally — at your fingertips. You can also keep up with what's going on in the business world too. Find out how to get daily updates, do corporate research, and locate all kinds of business information, all coming up in the next chapter.

CHAPTER

2

KEEPING UP WITH
THE NEWS

Chapter 2

Keeping Up with the News

IN THIS CHAPTER

Scan news headlines for quick updates

Perform detailed searches via prime news sources from all over the world

Customize your browser to deliver exactly the news you want to read — business, world events, or sports

Track IPOs and keep up-to-date on your favorite industry

Relax with your favorite magazines, online

Find your favorite political cartoons — fast

Personalize your own comics page and start every day with laughter, the best medicine

Forget folding that huge paper over your knees, wiping newsprint off your shirt, and scanning the small print for a likely story. The digital world brings news straight to your own monitor — in many cases, the very newspapers you love to read will appear in online editions.

This section helps you find your favorite news sources. When you locate an online version you really like, you can mark it as a favorite place and read articles on the site day after day. Of course, it's hard to rest in the sunshine with a 17-inch monitor propped up on your lap. So, if you miss the portability of paper, each of these online editions offers subscription information too.

Scanning the Headlines

The easiest way to get the news once you sign on is by clicking the Top News button in the Welcome window. The News channel opens, as seen in Figure 2-1, and you can click your way to your favorite news sections from there. Using Keyword: **News** takes you to the same place.

Figure 2-1. Begin your reading adventures with the News channel.

Watch the news ticker in the upper-right corner of the News window for the nation's top stories, and click one that looks interesting. You can also click any of the headline links below the ticker to read an article.

Once in a while, perusing an entire online edition is both relaxing and informative. When the urge strikes, check out these areas to fill your news quota:

▶ **The New York Times on America Online:** Offering everything the nation expects from *The New York Times*, this AOL version covers international and national news, science, technology, entertainment, and a host of other topics. Use Keyword: **NYT** to see for yourself.

▶ **Chicago Tribune AOL Edition:** Get all the news from the Windy City. The Trib window uses its own news ticker; you can watch the news and sports headlines flash, then click one you like. Although most news stories are available through the Tribune online area (at Keyword: **Tribune**), the window also contains a link to chicagotribune.com, the paper's Web site.

▶ **USA Today:** Glean the nation's top stories from the USAToday.com Web site. Organized just like the popular

Tip

Bookmark any sites that particularly pique your interest by including it in your favorite places list.

print version, this site is easy to navigate. Click the News, Sports, Money, Life, or Weather buttons to access those portions of the site, and then click any underlined link to read the full associated story. Major news items appear in the main browser window when the site loads. Find it at www.usatoday.com.

If you prefer news that lands closer home, a quick Internet search will find online versions of nearby city newspapers, or perhaps even that of your own hometown. Here's how to locate local news:

1. Use Keyword: **Netfind** to open the AOL.com search system.

2. Type **newspapers** into the Search the Web text box and click the Search button in the browser window, as shown in Figure 2-2.

3. Click the AOL.com Online Newspapers link in the Matching Sites list.

4. Scroll down the list of papers in the Online Newspaper Directory window, shown in Figure 2-3, and click any link that looks interesting.

Each link leads to that newspaper's online Web site, which generally features national and local news for your reading pleasure.

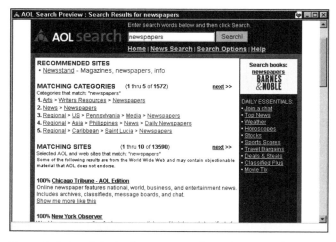

Figure 2-2. Search for local newspapers online with AOL Search.

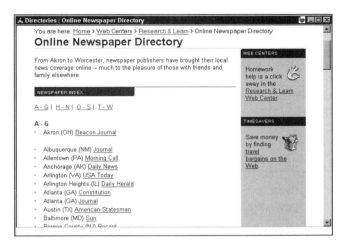

Figure 2-3. Select your favorite newspaper from the list.

Digging Deeper

When a topic really intrigues you, sometimes the daily news articles provide less information than you might like. This is especially true when a topic remains in your mind after the news stories die down. What do you do then?

You have a couple of online options. First, if the topic was of worldwide interest (or occurred outside the United States), you can try the international news sources. Use Keyword: **Intl News** to open the International News window, as seen in Figure 2-4. This window contains links to newspapers around the world; whether you want to read opinions from Africa or need write-ups from Uzbekistan, this is the place to visit.

Once the International News Window appears, look in the item list for folders containing worldwide news sources. Then do the following.

Although the area doesn't say so, you can also use the search window to read international stories about a particular topic. Type a search term such as "auto" into the text field, instead of a country name, and the search engine returns all the international stories it can find about autos. Of course, some articles may be more relevant to your needs than others, but the search engine gives you a good start.

Figure 2-4. International News provides more information about topics of worldwide interest.

▶ Open the Foreign Newspapers folder in the item list. It contains folders for each continent; a peek inside any folder, such as Central American Newspapers, reveals a folder for each individual country's newspapers. Double-click any folder to open it, and then double-click any link to open that newspaper's Web site.

▶ The Wire Updates by Country folder in the item list allows you to select news items for particular countries. Double-click the Wire Updates folder to open the News Stories by Country window, and then double-click the folder that contains the target country's news articles (countries are arranged in alphabetical order). Double-click any news entry to read the story.

▶ The News Stories by Country window also sports a Search button. Click it to open a search window, and then type the country name into the text box and click the List Articles button.

▶ Open the Wire Updates by Region folder to read integrated news stories separated into areas such as the Pacific Rim, South & Central Asia, or Europe. Instead of being separated by country, each individual region's folder opens to a list of news articles from that area of the world. Use this option when you want an overview of a region's current news and don't want to select each country individually.

▶ Near the bottom of the item list, the AOL's Foreign News Sources link opens a window that lists the news areas for various international AOL services: AOL U.K., AOL France, AOL Germany, AOL Australia, and AOL

Canada. Double-click one of the entries to open the AOL news window for that particular international version of AOL.

For stories a little closer to home, find in-depth coverage with AOL's News Search feature (Keyword: **News Search**). When the News Search window opens, type a word or two to tell the search engine what you're looking for. Then click List Articles to see news stories about that topic from the past 30 days, as seen in Figure 2-5.

The search engine returns up to a maximum of 250 stories for each search, no matter how many might be available in the database. Choose a search term that's as narrow as possible for the most efficient search. A search term such as "Cubs," for example, will return fewer possibilities than a term such as "baseball."

Figure 2-5. Search for recent news stories on any topic, from anywhere in the world.

Making the News Your Own

Personalize your corner of the newsworld with My News. Here, you can specify exactly what news, sports, business news, or extras — such as This Day in History or a Warner Bros. Hip Clip (cartoon) — you'd like to see each day. Personalization takes a couple of minutes, but you get to choose from more than 1,500 customizations.

Here's how to make My News work for you:

1. Use Keyword: **My News** to open My News into your browser (see Figure 2-6).

2. Click the Personalize This Page button in the top-left corner of the browser window. If you're not already registered, the site leads you through a few questions first so you can register as a member.

Tip

Look for fun options, like daily multimedia and sound, under the Daily Briefing links. To view the featured videos, you need to have RealPlayer installed on your system. Click the download the player link on My News Front Page in the Daily Briefing section to lead you through the RealPlayer download.

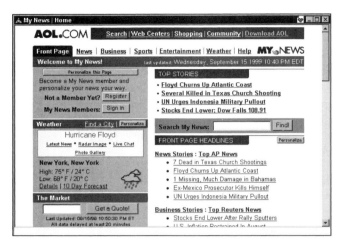

Figure 2-6. With My News you can have your news delivered just the way you want it.

3. Once you register, the site presents you with an Edit My News screen. This is where the fun begins.

4. The window's list begins with selections under Front Page. As you scroll down the window, you see sections called News, Business, Sports, Entertainment, and Weather.

5. Each section lists several lines of linked text, such as My Picks — Weather. Click any link to customize that portion of the software.

6. Have fun! You can even include your favorite Web sites under each heading. Look for the My Picks — Personal Sites links to fill in your faves.

7. When you've finished customizing, click the Return to Your new Front Page link to view your handiwork.

Checking Out Business World Events

In addition to all the above, you can read business news online any time of the day, too. Opening a few key windows gives you access to general business news or targeted articles about a specific company, depending on your interests. For example, you can check ongoing business news with Keyword: **Business News**, which carries daily stories about technology, industry, international business, and the economy. Figure 2-7 shows the

Business News window; click any department button to read
that topic's latest news stories.

Figure 2-7. Track the ups and downs of capitalism through Business News.

If you know exactly what you want but can't find it, use the
Business News Search system to locate an elusive news story.
Here are the steps:

1. Open the Business News window with Keyword:
   Business News.

2. Enter the subject or company name into the Business
   News Search text box.

3. Make sure the by subject radio button is active. If not,
   click it to search by subject.

4. Click the Go button. The News Search window opens,
   displaying the latest news stories about your topic, as
   seen in Figure 2-8.

Figure 2-8. Find that business story with a news search.

To get market information at the same time you access news stories, open the Business News window and enter the company's
trading symbol into the Business News Search text box. Then

Tip

Go directly to the News
Search window with
Keyword: **News Search**.

click the By ticker symbol radio button, and click the Go button.
The system churns for a second or two, and then presents the
company's Investment Snapshot window. Click any of the hyperlinked articles in the News Headlines list box to read recent
stories about the business. Of course, this option only works
for publicly traded companies, since privately held companies
don't have a trading symbols.

Daily Updates from Business Week

Business Week Online brings you business commentaries,
international business news, and news from various specific
sectors of the business world. Keyword: **BW** opens the main
Business Week Online window, sporting buttons linked to its
various departments and main stories, as shown in Figure 2-9.

Figure 2-9. Business Week Online brings news and commentary to your screen.

For a day-by-day update and breaking business bulletins, check
Business Week Online's Daily Briefing section, at Keyword:
BW Daily. Here you can read the Online News Flashes,
catch up on worldwide market updates, and check out
the Stock of the Week.

News in Your Mailbox

Here you can also design a News Profile that scours the news services and drops business stories directly into your e-mail box. In addition to being incredibly helpful to busy people, the News Profiles can be customized to accept (or reject) certain terms and phrases. With a little tweaking, the feature gives you exactly what you want — whether you're tracking a whole industry or you have your eyes on a particular company or two.

To create a business News Profile, follow these steps:

1. Use Keyword: **News Profiles** to open the News Profiles window (see Figure 2-10).

2. Click the Create Your News Profiles button. The Screen name's News Profile window opens. AOL gives each new profile a number as you create it; click in the Create a title for your news text box and enter your own title, such as Business News or an industry name.

3. Click Next. Your News Profile appears as a name instead of a number in the new window that presents itself on screen.

4. The next several screens ask you to list terms you want to see in the news stories you receive, any words you require in each news story that comes to your mail box, and terms you don't want to see. Enter your terms (you can always alter them later) and click Next.

5. Step 5 asks you to select news sources for the profile. Options include Reuters Alert, AP Business Wire, and the PR NewsWire, among many others. Highlight any news source you want, and click the Add button to add it to your selections. When you're finished, click the Next button.

6. A summary window appears, recapping the name of your News Profile, the search terms you entered, and the news sources you selected. If all this looks okay, click the Done button. To change anything in the list, click the Prev button to move backward screen by screen.

7. After you click the Done button, a dialog box appears to inform you that AOL has successfully created your personal News Profile. Click OK to close the dialog box.

Tip

Hoover's gives you basic company financial information for free. To see detailed reports and statistics, you need to become a member of their service (membership is $14.95 per month).

Figure 2-10. News Profiles delivers the news your way.

The Up and Comers

Turn your attention to the new publicly held companies, as well as those about to release initial public (stock) offerings (IPOs). Find out who's going public, view public company profiles, and glean other corporate tidbits from Hoover's Online, including company News Alerts, as seen in Figure 2-11.

To see Hoover's Online IPO Central, use Keyword: **IPO**. Click any company's hyperlinked text to show information for that corporation. Enter a company's name or trading symbol into the Find an IPO text box and click Go to see the company's IPO.

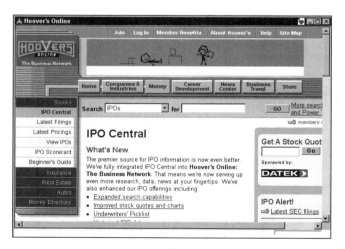

Figure 2-11. Research companies about to go public in Hoover's IPO Central.

Industry Information

Whether the aerospace industry interests you or technology makes you twitter, you'll find plenty of pertinent articles in AOL's Industry News area (Keyword: **Industry News**). This area organizes articles by industry topics into separate folders, such as Automobile, Business Equipment, and Chemical. In total, the area highlights 22 different industry segments. If you follow one or two industries avidly, open their individual folders and then mark them as favorite places.

If you are interested in technology, for example, double-click the Technology folder. The Technology folder opens into a window with technology press releases from various companies, enabling you to read about their strategic partnerships, new products, and quarterly profits. If a huge topic rocks the industry, look at the top of the list for a folder with the latest news on that subject. Otherwise, browse through the window's items for news stories that pertain to your interest.

Individual Industry windows also sport a button called Be Part of Your Business Community. Clicking that button opens the Professional Forums window, where you can meet others who share your work interests and goals.

Cross-Reference

Find out how to read the news online in Chapter 3.

Tip

International political cartoons, or historical cartoons, give you a great glimpse into the culture of the time or area they portray.

2

Keeping Up with the News

Giggling with the Comics

At last we get to the important part of online newspapers!

If a picture's worth a thousand words, a four-panel comic is worth at least a medium-sized entry from the Encyclopedia Brittanica, right? Dip into online comics for a bit of refreshment on days when you need a chuckle or want to smile along with your favorite political cartoonist.

The online areas and Web sites in this section focus on the funnies. Find one or two you really like and mark them as Favorite Places so you can visit them quickly. Although not exactly equivalent to television soap operas, some of the daily comics will pull you into their story lines if you read them for a few days.

Tracking Down Political Cartoons

Take a look at current news stories through the eyes of the artists. Political cartoons tell the news story (and the cartoonist's opinion) at one glance. Of course, it helps to understand the cartoons if you have at least a passing acquaintance with the stories they lampoon, which is where the online news articles come in.

Peeking at the Back Page

If you want one or two political cartoons to start your day, you might want to begin with The Back Page, part of AOL's News Channel. Keyword: **Back Page** opens the screen and displays the daily Mike Keefe cartoon, as seen in Figure 2-12. To see more of Keefe's work, either click one of the InToon.com links in The Back Page window or use Keyword: **InToon** to open the InToon.com Web site. The site offers archived Mike Keefe cartoons as well as other diversions, such as U.B.A. Cartoonist, where you create your own cartoons, and Talking Heads, a collection of animated celebrities who spout various political (and not so political) statements.

Figure 2-12. Don't miss The Back Page and its daily political cartoon.

You need to download a free Shockwave player to view much of the InToon.com site (except for the Mike Keefe cartoons, which is what brought you here to begin with). To download Shockwave into your computer, do the following:

1. Use Keyword: **InToon** to open the InToon.com Web site, if you're not already there (see Figure 2-13).

2. Click on the Talking Heads or U.B.A. Cartoonist button, whichever intrigues you.

3. Scroll down the window until you see a statement saying you need the free Shockwave Plugin or Active X Control to use that portion of the Web site.

4. Click the blue Get Shockwave button. The Macromedia Web Player Download Center site appears in your browser window.

5. If you have Windows 95/98, click the yellow Click Here To Install/Autoinstall Now button under Step 1 in the Macromedia window.

   If you have a Windows version other than 95/98, click the Need a Different Web Player link at the bottom of the Step 1 section. Find your operating system (Win3.1, Mac PPC) in the grid, and click the corresponding Go link, and *then* click the yellow Download Now button.

6. Several dialog boxes appear as the program downloads into your system. The first dialog box asks you to click Next to continue. Click Next.

7. The second dialog box asks you to register your version of Shockwave. Enter your first and last name and Internet e-mail address (your AOL screen name followed by @aol.com) into the text boxes. Click Next.

8. The third dialog box asks if Macromedia can automatically update your version of Shockwave as they improve the program. If you're comfortable with that, click Next. If not, click to uncheck the statement okaying the updates, and then click Next.

9. The fourth dialog box shows the download progress. When the program finishes downloading, a dialog box congratulates you on your installation. Click OK.

10. To return to the original Macromedia window, click Return to Previous Site. A movie should play in the Macromedia Download Player window to show that the software is installed.

Congratulations! You're now the proud owner of the Shockwave player. Click the back arrow on the browser bar twice to return to the InToon Web site and load a Talking Head or two or create your own comics in U.B.A. Cartoonist.

Figure 2-13. Make your own cartoons at Intoon.com.

Toons from Papers Around the Nation

Drop into the nation's online newspapers to view a variety of political cartoons. Although each online area or Web site varies a little in construction, you'll find links to each newspaper's political cartoons in the Opinion section for that paper.

> ▶ Jeff MacNelly brings his view of the world and Chicago to your screen when you visit the Chicago Tribune on AOL. Use Keyword: **Tribune** to open the Chicago Tribune window, and then look for the Jeff MacNelly cartoons link in the Opinion section's item list.

> ▶ The New York Times on America Online showcases several political cartoonists — Tony Auth, Pat Oliphant, and Tom Toles, to name a few. See their latest cartoons by using Keyword: **NYT** and then clicking the Opinion link. Once in Opinion, clicking Political Cartoons near the top of the window takes you right to the good stuff.

> ▶ Chuckle at several political cartoons from around the nation at USA Today's Web site. Type **www.usatoday. com** into the browser bar to open the site, and then click the Opinion link to get to the USA Today Cartoons link. USA Today features cartoons from several papers, so not all of them are to-the-date current. And depending on where you live, you might have seen one of them in your home town paper.

For a change of pace, as well as a selection most cartoon junkies only dream of, take a look at PoliticalCartoons.com. Located at `www.politicalcartoons.com`, this site features cartoonists from all over the world. Figure 2-14 gives you a glimpse of the available cartoonists. Select from American cartoonists from coast to coast, or broaden your horizons with cartoonists from Canada, Switzerland, Jerusalem, Singapore, Dublin, or Bulgaria.

A click on any cartoonist's link loads the most recent political cartoon, and offers links to the cartoonist's Web site, and an e-mail link as well, for viewers who want to send comments directly to the cartoonist. Also, from each artist's Web site you can often view cartoons from the past, or explore some of their other professional endeavors; for example, the Dry Bones Web site (from the Jerusalem Post) contains a multiscreen explanation of a Jewish holiday, along with illustrations by the Post's political cartoonist.

Figure 2-14. Pick a cartoonist, any cartoonist, from PoliticalCartoons.com.

Reading Magazines Online

Quiet evenings and rainy afternoons were made for reading. Eventually you'll run out of newspapers, but you can still take advantage of those down times, even if your subscription to The

Best Magazine of All lapsed last month. Within a few moments of clicking on AOL, online versions of your favorite magazines can be made to appear, ripe for reading.

Best of all, no matter where your interests lie, you'll find a magazine for you. AOL offers online magazines that cater to almost everyone, from rock music enthusiasts to home improvement gurus to computer aficionados. Online magazines also focus on families, sports lovers, and arts and crafts practitioners, artists of all persuasions, and business people. Pick a topic and you'll probably find an online magazine that caters to it.

Reading magazines online provides a great way to preview a publication you think you might want to order. And with over 100 magazines available online, finding a future favorite should be easy. However, be aware that while many articles from the current print version appear online, most magazines don't post every single article from the printed pages. If you want to read the letters to the editor, for example, you probably need to buy a copy for yourself.

These magazines also provide a wealth of information for the situational reader — the person who needs specific information about a particular topic . . . and needs it now! Planning to take the family hiking for the first time? You might want to check out *Backpacker Magazine*, as shown in Figure 2-16, and see which trails the magazine recommends. If you find you enjoy hiking, *Backpacker Magazine* might then become a regular stopping point in your online jaunts.

Likewise, when you want to upgrade that computer, take a look at *Family PC Online* or *PC Computing* for recommendations before you replace or upgrade the machine you have. These magazines regularly review new technology, and tell you what you might (or might not) want to consider for your home.

Figure 2-15. Backpacker Magazine, one of over 100 magazines online, offers camping and hiking tips.

Magazines to Match Your Moods

AOL provides a couple of different ways to find online magazines. Of course, if you know which magazine you want you can always use the magazine's name as a keyword — Keyword: **Rolling Stone** opens the RollingStone.com Web site, for example. That trick works 99 percent of the time. It even works for some magazines that don't appear in the regular magazine lists, like *Soap Opera Digest* (Keyword: **SOD**) and *Playbill Online* (Keyword: **Playbill**).

If you're not sure of the magazine's name, or you want to browse the selections, follow these steps to locate online titles:

1. Open the Newsstand window with Keyword: **Newsstand**. It appears on screen looking just like Figure 2-17.

Figure 2-16. Begin your search for magazines in the Newsstand window.

2. The item list on the right side of the window contains various publications that pertain to news. Scroll down the list box and double-click any that appeal to you. The magazine's online area or Web site opens.

3. If you had a topic other than news in mind, click the drop-down list on the left side of the window. Most of the AOL channels appear in the drop-down list.

4. Select a channel from the list. That channel's magazine selection appears in the item list.

5. Continue browsing from channel to channel, opening any magazine that looks interesting.

Most magazine areas contain current articles, an archive of past articles, and downloadable software, projects, or documents in a library (depending on the magazine's topic). Click any link or button that looks interesting in the magazine's window; you might find something worth exploring.

Another option for finding magazines is to access the channel newsstand directly from the individual channel windows. Many of the channel windows highlight an online magazine or two, or the window contains a Newsstand department button that leads to that channel's available magazines. Click the Newsstand button to open the channel's newsstand window, and then select a magazine from the item list on the right side of the window.

Nearly every channel offers several online magazines. Here's a channel-by-channel overview:

▶ **Computing:** Look to the Computing channel for titles like such as *C|Net News*, *Computer Shopper*, *Interactive Week*, *MacWorld* Online, *PC Computing*, and *PC Week*. These, along with other titles, keep you up-to-date on computing trends, hardware, and software.

▶ **Entertainment:** The Entertainment channel brings you online versions of *Teen People*, *Rolling Stone*, *Premiere*, *Spin*, *Stereo Review*, and *Video Magazine*. From people to politics, you can find magazines to fit your mood here (see Figure 2-18).

Figure 2-17. Get the lowdown on new movie releases in Premiere Online.

▶ **Families:** Family and home topics abound in the Families channel newsstand. This channel spotlights online versions of magazines such as *Better Homes and Gardens*, *Redbook*, *Family PC*, *Home Office Computing*, *Seventeen*, *Victoria*, and *Woman's Day*.

▶ **Games:** Check out the Games channel newsstand for links to Marvel Comics, Antagonist Inc., and C|Net's Gaming News (open the Gamer's Forum item to see the C|Net link).

▶ **Interests:** One of the largest magazine listings online, the Interests channel includes such offerings as *Big Twin, Boating Online, Car & Driver, Country Living's Gardener, Flying Magazine Online, Home Magazine, House Beautiful, Popular Photography, Rebecca's Garden, Road & Track,* and *Town & Country*.

▶ **Lifestyles:** Drop into the Lifestyles channel newsstand for online versions of magazines like *Cosmopolitan*, *Country Living*, *Ladies' Home Journal*, *Good Housekeeping*, and *Marie Claire*. Also look in this window for the Jewish Community Newsstand and the Christianity Online Newsstand.

▶ **News:** When your taste runs to news, turn here for the scoop. Online magazines in this newsstand window include *Time.com, The NY Times, Atlantic Monthly, Congressional Quarterly,* and *The Christian Science Monitor*.

Tip

Go directly to a channel's newsstand by using the channel name, along with **Newsstand**, as a keyword. Thus, Keyword: **Families Newsstand** opens the Families channel magazine listing.

▶ **Sports:** Where would sports fans be without stats? Find those and much more in the Sports channel newsstand, which features mags such as *The Sporting News*, *Ski* and *Skiing*, *Field & Stream*, and *GOLF Magazine*. See Figure 2-19 for a peek at The Sporting News.

▶ **Business News:** Most of the WorkPlace channel magazines settle here. Think of the Business News newsstand as a cross between the News channel and the WorkPlace channel. Look in this area for *Bloomberg Personal*, *Business Week*, *Money.com*, *Family Money*, *Financial Times*, *The National Review*, and *The Nation*.

Figure 2-18. Sports magazines like The Sporting News keep you on top of the game.

Coming Up Next . . .

Just as you can use AOL to peruse headlines from around the world, or read an assortment of news and business articles, or magazines, or comics assembled every day specifically for you, you can preview the weather, too. Just check out the next chapter — full details ahead.

Chapter 3

Checking Weather at Home and Abroad

IN THIS CHAPTER

Catch up with local weather before it catches up with you

Read all the latest U.S. weather stories

Get weather maps from around the world, 24 hours a day

No matter where you live, local weather probably shows up somewhere on your personal radar screen. Spend a few moments commiserating with the rest of the world — see whether it's likely to snow in Switzerland or rain in Romania. Or bring the whole topic a little closer home. What will the weather be like where you live? What about your planned weekend excursion? This section tells where you can find the online answers to your pressing precipitation questions.

Daily Drizzle or Sunshine

A quick click on My Weather in the Welcome window opens the Weather window for your city, as seen in Figure 3-1. Here you can view a five-day extended forecast; either glance at the icons in the middle of the window that show sun, rain, clouds, or snow, or read the Your Regional Forecast information in the text box.

Tip

The AOL Canada Weather window, at Keyword: **CDN Weather**, presents a set of weather icon definitions in addition to a look at Canada's weather. Click the Learn button to view the icon lineup.

Figure 3-1. Will it rain on your picnic? Check Your Local Weather to see.

Also look in this window for updated local information, including temperature, winds, and barometric pressure. Not sure what barometric pressure is? Click any of the weather terms next to the listing and a small definition window appears, explaining what the clicked term means and why it could be important to you.

If you'd rather use a keyword to see your local weather, try **Weather**. When the National Weather window appears, enter your city or ZIP code into the Search for local weather text box, and click Search. Double-click the item that appears in the small Search Results window, and the Your Local Weather window appears like magic.

National Forecasts

While you're checking for sunny skies, take a peek at national weather forecasts and see the trends as they develop. The Keyword: **Weather** opens the National Weather window, which sports a colorful national weather map as seen in

3

Checking Weather

Figure 3-2. To view a slideshow of the nation's weather, click the map itself. Updated at 8 a.m. and 6 p.m. ET, the slideshow gives an overview of the day's highs and lows.

Figure 3-2. Try Keyword: *Weather* to see the nation's weather at a glance.

Read daily weather news stories when you click the Weather News button. The Weather News window opens, listing several daily news stories that pertain to current (and some forecasted) conditions.

The Satellite, Radar, and Map Images button opens the Weather Images window, which provides a wealth of current national weather information. From this window you can view satellite and radar images, which are updated throughout the day. Click the Maps tab in the window, shown in Figure 3-3, for the current and extended forecast maps that make this area such a wealth of information.

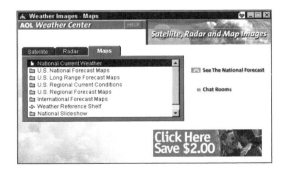

Figure 3-3. Check out the current radar or open a national forecast map.

Choose from national and regional forecast maps, extended U.S. forecast, and even international forecast maps. Opening any map folder reveals an impressive list of maps to choose from. View a map showing national rainfall amounts, low temperature forecasts for the current day, or a thunderstorm outlook. To navigate through the maze of windows until you actually reach a map, keep double-clicking folder icons until you reach a group of icons that look like sheets of paper with the corners folded down. Double-click any sheet icon and a map opens on screen.

Earthwatch Weather On Demand presents storm updates and satellite images at their site, `www.earth watch.com`.

International Weather News

See what the weather around the world is up to by checking international weather. AOL has two international weather areas. One is presented by the News channel team, and focuses on international weather as it affects travelers. The other, brought to you by the International channel, takes a more cultural tack.

To check worldwide weather through the National Weather window, follow these steps:

1. Use Keyword: **Weather** to open the National Weather window.
2. Click the World Weather button. The World Weather Information window opens.
3. Double-click any entry in the item list to open it.

If you want a visual display of Asian or European travel conditions, open either continent's Travel Weather Forecast Map. For more detailed information, double-click the World Cities Travel Forecast Table folder. Inside you'll find a list of travel forecasts by area, from the Caribbean to Russia. Opening any of these files shows five-day forecasts for various destination cities within that area.

When you check weather through the International channel, you see the various weather windows for AOL's international services. Use Keyword: **Intl Weather** to open the Worldwide Weather window. Click one of the four buttons in the window to see U.K. Forecasts, Canadian Forecasts, German Forecasts, or French Forecasts. The item box along the right side of the window lists links to Web sites such as the Weather Channel and World Forecasts.

If you like, you can use individual keywords to open the international service weather windows. Keep in mind that several of these windows will appear in the country's native language:

▶ See the German forecast with Keyword: **Wetter**.

▶ Keyword: **Meteo** opens the AOL France weather window.

▶ View the Aussie forecast with Keyword: **Au.weather**, as shown in Figure 3-4.

▶ Britain's and Ireland's weather forecasts appear when you use Keyword: **UK weather**.

Figure 3-4. Check the forecast Down Under.

Coming Up Next . . .

There's more to entertainment than weather watching. The next chapter explores other entertainment options, such as local movies, concerts, and video rentals. Plus, with AOL's new Calendar feature, your calendar can now notify you of upcoming music and video releases, concert dates, and much more.

CHECKING LOCAL
ENTERTAINMENT

Chapter 4

Checking Local Entertainment

Concerts. Movies. Good books. Time with friends. How we spend our free time tells a lot about what we consider important. Whether your idea of a great evening includes a classical concert, the latest movie, or dinner with friends, you can use your online connection to make the most of those after-work hours.

Attending Scheduled Events

As we all know, schedules make the world go round. With a good schedule in hand, your daughter doesn't get stranded at ballet class while you take the Cub Scout to his den. Schedules keep you from making dinner dates with two different families on the same night. They also tell you about events other people are involved in, so you can find an interesting lecture, conference, or opening to attend when it fits in.

My Calendar

Using the My Calendar online scheduler keeps everything in one place, and it allows you to include other people in your plans easily. When you set up events on your calendar, you can

- ▶ Mark an event to repeat daily, weekly, monthly, yearly, or a certain combination of days each week.

- ▶ Invite other people to your event via an e-mail message sent by the My Calendar software. You specify the e-mail addresses for the friends and colleagues you want to invite, and AOL sends a My Calendar Notification message to the list with your event name in the subject line.

- ▶ View events one day a time, a week at a time, or for the entire month, simply by clicking the tab at the bottom of the calendar screen.

- ▶ See what events are taking place in your area, such as upcoming CD releases, classical music, and local concerts. Click the Event Directory tab.

- ▶ Use the Event Directory to program religious and national holidays into your calendar. If your family tracks the national holidays of Brazil or the Islamic feast days, My Calendar makes it easy.

- ▶ Keep your eye on that upcoming Initial Public Offering when you add IPO releases to your calendar. Look in the Event Directory in the financial section.

- ▶ Place current local weather forecast icons on your calendar pages. Click the Weather link in the Event Directory.

Tip

If you miss an event (a "chat" even, that is!) that you wanted to attend, download the transcript from the AOL Live area. Transcripts become available a few days after the events occur.

▶ Use the Event Directory to track recent book releases, and buy promising titles online.

Open My Calendar by clicking the My Calendar button on the Welcome screen or by using Keyword: **My Calendar** (see Figure 4-1).

Figure 4-1. Use My Calendar to keep track of appointments, holidays — even upcoming CD releases.

AOL Live

Find a list of scheduled live events at AOL Live (Keyword: **AOL Live**). Although My Calendar's Chat section shows you the next few days' top chats, you can plan further in advance (as well as take a look at more scheduled chats) through the AOL Live window. AOL Live hosts guest speakers who are celebrities, authors, scientists, newsmakers, and more.

Video Reviews, Releases, and Rentals

Miss that movie when it hit the theaters? Find out what others think about it, learn when copies hit the stores, and rent one yourself — all online.

Reading video reviews online can tell you whether you want to bring the movie home in the first place. In addition to steering you away from duds, the reviews can also alert you to videos you may have overlooked in the past. Keyword: **EW** opens the Entertainment Weekly Web site; click the Video link to read a raft of reviews for current and past video releases.

Once you have a list of potential weekend videos ready to go, visit an online area or two to streamline your search. Netflix, at www.netflix.com (shown in Figure 4-2), offers DVD rentals — you rent the DVDs online, receive them in the mail, keep them for a week, and then mail them back when you're finished.

Tip

Dropping into the Home Video forum online, at Keyword: **Home Video**, gives you one-stop shopping for video reviews, as well as DVD and video purchasing options.

Figure 4-2. Rent DVDs online, and they arrive in your mailbox in a couple days.

To locate video rental stores in your area, first open the AOL Yellow Pages with Keyword: **Yellow Pages**. Then type **video rental** and your city into the appropriate text boxes, select your state from the drop-down list, and click the Find button. Up comes a list of video rental stores in your area, and may include maps, driving directions, and fax numbers.

To make the video your very own, order it online from one of these vendors:

▶ **DVD Express:** Order DVDs, send an e-mail gift certificate, or preorder upcoming releases at www. dvdexpress.com.

▶ **Reel.com:** Purchase videos and DVDs at www.reel.com. The site also includes video and DVD reviews at the site.

▶ **800.com:** This site, at www.800.com, sells movies in DVD and VHS format as well as music, games, and electronics.

4

Checking Local Entertainment

Asterisks next to an event
entry show that tickets may
be purchased online for
that event.

Purchasing Tickets Online

Whether you're headed to the latest rock concert, a sporting event, or the hot new movie topping the charts, buy your tickets online and save yourself the hassle of long lines and busy signals. Then pick those tickets up at the theater or have them mailed to you, and you're set for a night on the town.

Live Events

Buy tickets online through Tickets.com (`www.tickets.com`). Whether you want to see the latest touring rock band, an NFL game, or a touring ballet company, you can find tickets through Tickets.com. In addition to online sales, the company also offers tickets in online auctions. The site offers an easy-to-navigate list of upcoming events.

Ticketmaster, the special event clearinghouse, offers everything from soccer tickets to museum admissions from the Ticketmaster Online Web site at `www.ticketmaster.com`. To browse the site for tickets by event, click one of the links in the featured sections: Concerts, Sports, Arts, and Family events. Then browse the items in the text box or click the alphabet letter that begins the name of the event you want.

Ticketmaster Online also offers a personalization service called My Ticketmaster. With it you can check the view from your potential seats before you purchase the tickets. And, you can customize the Ticketmaster offerings so that you see only the concerts and events most likely to interest you.

Movie Tickets

You can purchase tickets online through Moviefone.com. Also, use Moviefone to find out what movies are playing in your area, complete with theater addresses and viewing times. Either search for theaters near you, or search by movie title, star, or viewing time.

Go to the Moviefone site, at `www.moviefone.com` (or Keyword: *Moviefone*), and then enter your ZIP code so the system can find theaters close to your home (see Figure 4-3). Then click the Go button to see a list of theaters near you.

Clicking any theater's name shows the current movies and times.

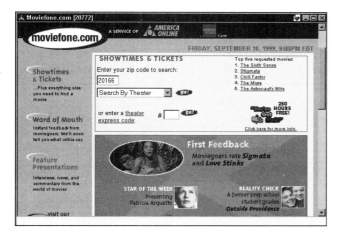

Figure 4-3. Order tickets online for that new flick.

If the movie time appears in bold black type, you need to purchase tickets at the theater. Not every theater offers Moviefone tickets yet.

Of course, you can always turn to the AOL Yellow Pages (Keyword: **Yellow Pages**) for restaurant and nightlife suggestions.

Catching Local Flavor

When the dining and nightlife urge hits, look online for leads to the best restaurants and clubs in your area. From new favorites to old standbys, their names, addresses, and reviews reside in your Digital City.

To find a new favorite in your neighborhood:

1. Click the Local channel button. The main Digital City window appears.

2. Click the button for your city to open its Digital City site.

3. Click the Dining link to see a list of great restaurants in your area. If you already know about the featured restaurants, click the Make your own recommendations link to read what other local dining denizens have to say.

4. Click the Nightlife link to view your city's best evening spots. Several of the top ten nightclubs in this area offer maps to get you there. If none of the featured spots interest you, scroll to the bottom of the screen to read other local residents' recommendations.

4

Checking Local Entertainment

Coming Up Next . . .

Now that you know some of the cool ways to relax in your
locale, turn to the next chapter for ideas on managing money
so you can pay for that night out. Balancing your checkbook,
while not on most people's top ten list of favorite things to do
on a Saturday afternoon, helps you to know when you can
play and when you should stay home.

PART

II

DOLLARS AND
CENTS MANAGEMENT

Chapter 5

Balancing Your Checkbook

IN THIS CHAPTER

How to balance your checkbook numbers online

Open the right account for you

Save a little here and there

Having trouble making those monthly numbers come out right? Perhaps you're one of those people who don't bother to balance the checkbook at all; instead, you keep a running estimate in your head. Turn to this chapter for online help in checkbook management — you need it badly!

Making the Numbers Balance

Balancing your checkbook brings with it a couple of inviting side effects: You always know exactly how much money you have, and you know within a few days if the bank made an error in your accounts. Even with the advent of high technology (or perhaps because of it), banks make occasional errors. Fixing any such problem is much easier if you mention it the month after it occurs than if you wait until the following February, when you're compiling your financials for tax time.

For a step-by-step guide to balancing your checkbook, visit Learn2.com. This site offers a checkbook tutorial in their 2torial collection. To actually balance the checkbook, you need a pencil, your checkbook, a calculator, and your bank statements. If you like, you can balance the checkbook while you read through the instructions, but your best bet might be to read through the entire process once, collect what you need, and then give it another go with information in hand.

To see the Balance Your Checkbook 2torial, follow these steps:

1. Type the Learn2.com Web address, `www.learn2.com`, into the browser bar and click the Go button. The Learn2 site loads into the browser.

2. Type **Balance Checking** into the What do you want to Learn2 text box, and click the Go button.

3. The search returns over 25 matches. Click the top link of the pile, Learn2 Balance Your Checkbook Intro.

4. The Learn2 Balance Your Checkbook 2torial appears, as seen in Figure 5-1.

5. The tutorial opens at the introduction. Read through the introduction, and click the Step1 link at the bottom of the screen.

6. Read through the steps, clicking the Step link at the bottom of each screen to go on to the next step.

7. When you're finished, the 2torial gives you the option of seeing all steps at once. This gives you a version you can print easily, so that you have the instructions when you aren't online and need to balance the checkbook.

Tip

As you browse through the search returns for balancing your checkbook, you might also be interested in the Business & Money Learnlets link. One of the Learnlets tips talks about possible bank errors in your checking account.

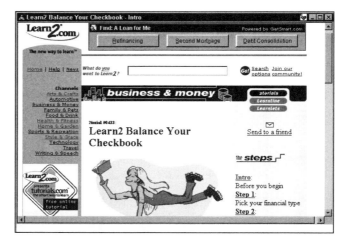

Figure 5-1. You're on the way to a perfect balancing act with Learn2.com.

Balance your checkbook online with the Consumer Credit Counseling Service Account Balancer. You can find the CCCS Account Balancer at `www.cccsintl.org`. When the main Consumer Credit Counseling Services site opens, look for the Account Balancer link in the main window.

Enter the amounts into the online form and click the My Account Balancer button to see the results. If your checks and other withdrawals equal your deposits and money left over, you're okay.

If you're looking for a checkbook balancing program, and Quicken didn't come with your computer, you might take a look at Simply Balanced. This shareware program helps you balance your checkbook. You use it for 45 days free, and if you like it you pay the $19.95 fee.

Opening and Closing an Account

There's more to checking accounts than meets the eye. Some accounts limit the number of checks you can write each month, whereas others require minimum balances to avoid charges. Taking a realistic look at your financial picture and your spending habits before you make any quick account moves will probably end up saving you money in the long run.

MoneyWhiz, a site dedicated to financial information, offers several articles on the ins and outs of checking. Many of these articles are part of their Whz-101 financial education series. To reach them, do the following:

1. Use Keyword: **TheWhiz** to open the AOL TheWhiz.com window.

2. Click the Banking button. The MoneyWhiz site opens, displaying the banking section shown in Figure 5-2.

3. Skim the articles in the banking window. If none currently apply to checking, use the search engine to locate the stories you need.

4. Type **checking account** into the Search text box, and then click the Search button to see a list of relevant articles.

Here's a sampling of TheWhiz.com articles that might interest you:

▶ **Lower your bank fees:** Gives you the scoop on some new bank fee structures that might affect you.

▶ **What free checking really means:** Where does the bank make money with "free" checking? Find out here.

▶ **You and your checking account:** Choose an account based on how you spend money, rather than trying to make your habits fit a specific account.

▶ **Whz-101: Check out of your checking account:** What you need to know if you close your bank checking account.

▶ **High yield checking accounts:** Increase the money you make by choosing a specific type of checking account.

The CCCS site also contains solid financial information on fair credit reporting, consumer scams, and consumer credit law. Look for these links in the Consumer Info section.

Find Simply Balanced at www.somtel.com/ ~barrym/sb/help/ sb.html.

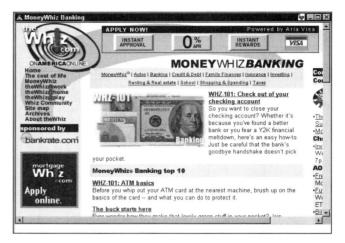

Figure 5-2. Find checking and banking articles to ease your mind at TheWhiz.com.

Saving in the Long Run

What's the best way to save what you have? Believe it or not, the little things *do* add up. Checking your bank statements carefully to cut extra costs, prepaying debt, and similar tricks make a difference when you practice them month after month.

Check the Personal Finance Credit & Debt area (Keyword: **Debt**) for some excellent ideas. The item list contains links to articles such as Best Investment: Pay Debt and Top Five Financial Myths, both articles produced by TheWhiz.com. Also look here for a series of articles called 12 Steps to Being Debt Free, which discuss credit card and bank account management. Step 12 in the series, Virtually All of Your Expenses are Optional, might change how you look at the things you buy (see Figure 5-3).

Figure 5-3. Read about debt and savings strategies here.

Drop by TheWhiz.com (at www.thewhiz.com) and read some of their Credit & Debt articles. They discuss ways to reduce your spending in areas like online bill paying, how to stay out of debt, and a guide to credit cards. The Credit & Debt Archive link, at the bottom of the Credit & Debt screen, leads to formerly featured goodies.

Here are other ways to save a penny here and there:

▶ **Use your own ATM machine.** Many times, other banks charge a fee for using their machines, even if those machines sport a sign that says they accept your ATM card. Then, on the other end, your bank may charge a fee for the transaction as well, which means you get hit twice.

▶ **Prepay your mortgage.** Even though it doesn't seem like a lot, sending extra money to your mortgage company takes money off the balance of the loan, which reduces your total loan obligation as well as the amount of total interest you pay over the life of the loan.

▶ **Pay more than the minimum on credit cards.** If you can't pay off the entire balance each month (which is by far the preferred plan), at least pay more than the minimum. Credit card minimum payments are designed to draw out the repayment as long as possible — that's one way the company makes its money.

➤ **Balance your checkbook.** Knowing exactly how much you have in the bank tends to guard against overdrawn checks, which can be expensive. Even if you have some type of overdraw guarantee in place, the bank charges you for covering your overdrawn check. Thirty or so minutes a month to balance your checkbook can drastically reduce the number of checks you bounce.

Coming Up Next . . .

Not too long ago you had to physically appear at your bank to conduct business (and — trust me on this — real people actually waited on you). Then, banks discovered telephone transactions. Now, you can conduct almost the entire range of banking transactions on the Internet. So delve into the world of online banking — the next chapter talks about locating your current bank online, setting up an account, and various online transactions.

C H A P T E R

6

BANKING ONLINE

Chapter 6

Banking Online

We knew it would happen sometime. As banks become more interested in keeping their customers happy, they implement new programs to lessen the stress and inconvenience of banking. Establishing an online account, whereby you can transfer funds, pay bills, and complete other transactions, gives you access to your banking information at your fingertips, 24 hours a day, without leaving your house.

Setting Up an Account

Beginning your online banking experience is as easy as typing some numbers into a form and clicking the Register button. Although each bank customizes its sign-up form to meet its own needs, the general format is usually the same.

To register as an online banking client, you first need to find out if your bank offers services online. If they do, you're well on your way to online banking success. If not, and if you really want to participate in online banking, you need to establish an account with a bank that does offer an online option.

Find out if your bank offers online banking by opening the Banking & Loans window and then accessing the bank list for your state. Here's how:

1. Use Keyword: **Banking** to open the Banking & Loans window. In addition to large national banks that offer online options, this window also contains a drop-down list that lets you locate online banking centers by state, as shown in Figure 6-1.

2. Use the State Banking Centers drop-down list to locate your state, and then click the Go button.

3. Your state's Banking Center window opens, showing some buttons that link you to the online banking windows of specific banks. To locate your local bank, look in the item list.

Double-click your bank's name to open their online banking information window.

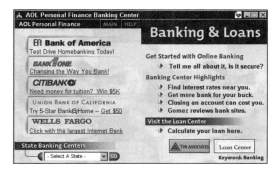

Figure 6-1. Determine which banks in your state offer online access.

Also look at Wells Fargo and KeyBank for online banking tutorials — they're both accessible through Keyword: **Banking**.

Once you reach your bank's window, you want a button or link that says Online Banking, Enroll Now, or something similar. Most of the sites are pretty self-explanatory; mouse around until you find something that looks like what you want.

To enroll with your bank as an online customer, you probably need a few numbers. One bank requires your social security number, your ATM card number, and your e-mail address. That's it. Fill in that information, click the Enter button, and you're enrolled.

On the other hand, another bank requires your social security number, mailing information, and account numbers. Then you need to print the form, sign it, and fax or mail it to the institution. As you can see, banks vary widely in the documentation they require in order to activate a customer's account online.

Transacting Online

Several banks offer online demos that show you various facets of banking over the Internet with that institution. If your bank doesn't offer a demo, use Keyword: **Home Banking** and click the Home Banking button to walk through Bank of America's demonstration. Although each bank's presentation varies a little bit, the basics — transfer balances, pay bills, get information — remain the same no matter which institution you use.

With an online account, you can do the following, all in the comfort of your home:

- ▶ View current account totals
- ▶ Balance your checking account
- ▶ Transfer funds
- ▶ Pay monthly bills
- ▶ Pay one-time bills
- ▶ View bank credit card accounts

Once you're set up with an account, you generally access it with a social security number and password. Then look for links or buttons that match what you want to do — for example, click the Pay Bills link to open that section of the site and begin the bill-paying process, as shown in Figure 6-2.

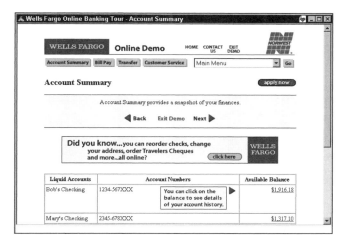

Figure 6-2. Pay bills, transfer funds, or check those accounts with Wells Fargo Bank.

Most sites walk you through each step of your transactions, and you complete one type of transaction before jumping to another. In other words, if you begin by paying bills, you send everything that needs to be paid before you leave that area of the site and transfer money from one account to another.

Getting the Scoop

Find out what others say about the online banking boom by reading a few of the articles available online. MoneyWhiz does a particularly good job of discussing online banking's convenience and security.

Located at Keyword: **TheWhiz**, MoneyWhiz posts many articles about life and finances (see Figure 6-3). Click the Banking link to see several articles about the ins and outs of banking. To browse the archived articles, click the Banking archive link in the Resources list. These articles talk about online banking, its safety, and how to jump on board.

Figure 6-3. Research online banking at MoneyWhiz.

As you explore possible banking options, you'll notice that the costs vary with online banking. Many banks offer some free online services; others charge a small monthly fee if clients want to pay bills from their online account. Is it worth it? For some people, the ability to save time by banking online qualifies as nothing short of a gift, and no price would be too high for the convenience.

You also might want to visit The AOL Banking Center for additional information (Keyword: **Banking**). Click the Tell me all it about, is it secure? button to see the broad brush strokes of banking online. A window opens with sections that talk about getting started with your online banking account, the safety of online banking, and general questions and answers.

Coming Up Next . . .

Many households seem to avoid dealing with a basic budget, perhaps because the whole process can seem so intimidating. But it need not be — the next chapter tells you where to find budgeting help online, whether you're just starting out, you see college expenses in the near future, or you've already established a nest egg of your own.

CHAPTER

7

SETTING UP A
FINANCIAL BUDGET

Chapter 7

Setting Up a Financial Budget

Budget. To many people, budget is a four-letter word. They think of committing their finances to paper about as eagerly as they look forward to their next root canal. However, maybe you find that your month drags on long after the money is gone. Perhaps you wonder where the money goes. You might even like to find some extra cash here and there for your next vacation.

A budget can help with all that. Instead of constricting your cash flow, a budget can actually open up the bottlenecks by telling you where your money is currently going, so you can then make informed decisions about where you *want* it to go. It is, after all, yours. A budget can help you make it work to meet your goals.

Budgeting Basics

Budgeting is one of those light bulb topics. Once you see how it helps you get what *you* want, the *aha* moment occurs and you're well on your way. Several money management sites offer online budgeting help, from informational articles to hypothetical budgets based on your income.

Read a couple of how-to articles to help you on your way. MoneyWhiz, which you can find at Keyword: **The Whiz**, offers several good articles on reducing debt and using credit cards wisely. In addition, MoneyWhiz also does periodic financial "makeovers" that show you how they designed budgets for specific people with troubled finances.

For budgeting and debt information, read through several stories in the Credit & Debt area:

1. Use Keyword: **The Whiz** to open the MoneyWhiz (also known as theWhiz.com) window.
2. Click the Credit & Debt button to access the Web site.
3. The Credit & Debt area shows you its top ten stories. To see more, click the Credit & Debt archive link near the bottom of the browser screen.

The Personal Finance Credit & Debt area (Keyword: **Debt**) offers credit card calculators so that you can see how a change in credit card rate effects your balance. Also take a look at the calculators if you're thinking of getting a new credit card. The calculators compare airline cards, rebate cards, and low rate cards. Click the Calculators button in the Credit & Debt window to work through the numbers for yourself, as shown in Figure 7-1.

While you visit the Credit & Debt window, look in the item list box for useful budgeting resources. 12 Steps to Being Debt Free links you to a set of suggestions from Ric Edelman, a financial planner. The twelve articles in the window that appears talk about reducing debt, setting goals, and tracking expenses — all good budgeting concepts.

Find It Online

Visit Home Budgeting Online, at www.homebudgeting.com, for a list of financial links that discuss credit, insurance, banking, savings, and investing. The Money Links section reveals links to sites such as Quicken Financial Network, Credit.com, and the Investment FAQ.

Tip

Money.com walks you through budget making steps in their Making a Budget Tutorial. Find it at www.pathfinder.com/money/101/lessons/2/intro.html. First read through the sections, then take the quiz at the end to see how well you understand the budgeting concepts (see Figure 7-2).

Figure 7-1. Find debt reduction resources in Credit & Debt.

Also take a look at the Dig Yourself Out of Debt folder. Brought to you by those Foolish Investors at The Motley Fool, these financial wizards take a lighthearted look at debt reduction, and make you smile even as they present solid budget and debt reduction advice.

Finally, Calculate the Real Cost of Your Debt shows you a nifty debt calculator. Enter a loan amount, the term (number of months or years), and the interest rate, and the calculator gives you the monthly payment as well as the total interest you end up paying.

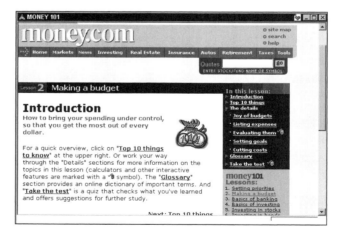

Figure 7-2. Online tutorials guide you through the basics.

As financial counselors will tell you (and the credit card calculators reemphasize), paying off your debt in full each month is the best way to use a card. After all, the bank is already making money from the merchant in the form of a three to four percent charge to the store every time you use the card. Any interest they get from you is extra profit.

Designing Your Own

The first step in creating your own budget is to grab a piece of paper and a pencil, or open a spreadsheet, and jot down where your money goes each month. How much do you currently pay for housing? What about dinners out, clothing, and insurance? If you currently spend nothing in the entertainment categories, a good budget will show you how to include them. On the other hand, if you eat a restaurant dinner each and every night, your first set of figures will show an entertainment amount that could use a little trimming.

Once you know exactly where your money goes, take a look at a well-designed budget that takes into account your own income level. You can read several articles on other people's budget makeovers, but the whole concept makes more sense if you look at your own dollars and cents.

Look at the Potential

To see what your numbers would look like in an actual budget, use an online budget guide. Financial counselor Larry Burkett's Christian Financial Concepts site offers a basic budget guide. The guide takes your income (as long as it's less than $130,001 per year — hey, no problem there!) and breaks it into preferred percentages for various items such as housing, clothing, and insurance, so you know what the numbers look like.

To use the online Budget Guide, follow these steps:

1. Use www.cfcministry.org to open the Christian Financial Concepts site.

7

Setting Up a Financial Budget

Tip

This site also includes a Mortgage Prepayment Calculator and a 15 vs 30 Year Mortgage Calculator that show you what effect paying a few extra dollars a month can have in the long run.

2. Click the Budget Guide link to open the online budget maker. Look for it in the Online Tools section.

3. Enter your gross income (all the money you make each year before any taxes are removed) and yearly taxes into the text fields. If you give a regular amount to a church, pay temple dues, or schedule any other regular giving into your expenditures each year, enter that yearly total in the Tithe text box.

4. Click Calculate Budget to see how your numbers add up. The Online Budget Guide shows you how much money you have to work with each year, how that translates into monthly totals, and what percentage of the total the amounts reflect, as shown in Figure 7-3.

5. Each category appears as linked text, so if you want more information on topics such as Ent/Rec (Entertainment and Recreation) or Investments, click the link for an explanation of the category. The linked information also explains what items the category typically includes, plus suggestions for minimum budgeting amounts for categories such as Clothing and Savings.

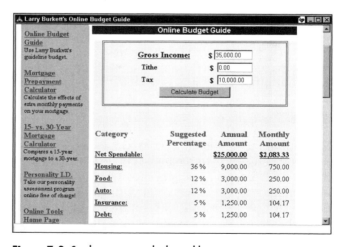

Figure 7-3. See how your new budget adds up.

Now the goal is to make your current spending fall more in line with the recommended percentages. When you do that, you have money for everything — saving, transportation, new clothes, and eating out.

When You Really Need a Hand

Several organizations exist to help you get a handle on spending and budgeting. Unfortunately, some are less than reputable and actually focus on your pocketbook rather than your welfare. If the day comes that you feel like you're swamped with bills, you need some impartial advice, or you could use some personal budgeting assistance, avoid the temptation to hook up with the first company that calls. Instead, contact a company that will truly help you get back on your feet.

The Consumer Credit Counseling Service (see Figure 7-4) is a national nonprofit organization that counsels families in financial crisis, helps them set up budgets, and keeps them accountable for debt repayment. Their services are free, confidential, and available in person or online. Their Web site, at `cccsintl.org`, contains articles about consumer scams, successful budgeting, and common purchasing mistakes. Access these articles by clicking the Consumer Info button on the left.

Figure 7-4. The Consumer Credit Counseling Service helps you get back on your financial feet.

Set up an online budgeting program by following these steps:

1. Click the Online Consumer Counseling link in the main Consumer Credit Counseling Service window. This link opens the MoneyManagement International site, which provides free financial counseling over the Internet.

2. Click the Money Management Online link in the main MoneyManagement International window to see the registration form. An Information Statement appears.

3. Fill in your personal information, income information, monthly expenses, and creditor names and balances into the form.

4. Click the Submit Now button to send the information. However, before you click Submit Now, be sure to read the fine print at the bottom of the screen. It says that you authorize MoneyManagement International to contact your creditors and reach a repayment agreement, which is what credit counselors do.

5. When Money Management gets your information, a credit counselor contacts you to set up a budget that helps you pay off the debt.

For more information on the whole process, click the How It Works button at the top of the Web page. Learn more by clicking the Counseling Session link once you've read the How It Works details. These two pages give you a pretty good overview of the service.

Creating a Special Fund

Saving for specific expenses helps take the jolt out of upcoming costs. And if you saved for them, you can enjoy them all the more, knowing that you aren't spending money you don't have. Two large expenses, college tuition and weddings, can both be saved for in advance.

What if you save for these events well in advance and they don't take place in the time frame you thought they would? Think of it as free money — you now have some extra cash to start a business, pay for unexpected expenses, or set aside for an unexpected vacation.

College

The sooner you begin squirreling away money for college expenses, the easier you'll meet the costs when they arrive. Money for college might mean the difference between one school and another — private colleges are expensive, but even out of state tuition to another state's Big Ten school can be pricey.

Learn the ins and outs of college accounts in the Saving for School forum (Keyword: **Saving for School**), shown in Figure 7-5. This window contains links to information about college budgeting, an online estimator that helps you determine how much money you actually need, and several strategies for getting you there.

Tip

Find some solid information in First Union Bank's College Guidebook. This Web site talks about planning, saving, and financial aid options. To get there, use www.firstunion.com to go to the site. Click the College button to open the College Guidebook, and browse from there.

Figure 7-5. Get some great financial tips for school.

Read through The Motley Fool's Saving for College forum, which you can find inside the Foolish College Tips folder in the Saving for School item list. This section talks about saving for college, financial aid, loans, and scholarships. The Fools also talk about online education and returning to school when you're older as two ways to achieve the goal in nontraditional ways.

One of the best links in the Saving for College window takes you to a Money.com tutorial. Either click the Details link in the Right Way To Save featured article paragraph in the window, or go there directly via www.pathfinder.com/money/101/lessons/11/intro.html. This tutorial walks you through the college savings process, from when to save and how to save all the way through tips on paying loans back after you've left college. Work through the tutorial, and, if you like, try the quiz at the end so you can see how much you learned. (See? It's not only the kids who get an education here.)

Wedding

Whether you want to tie the knot or you look to future weddings in your family, planning for the Big Day ensures that you experience no morning-after financial remorse. It's easy to get caught up in plans for receptions, photographers, videographers, and rented clothing, but jumping headlong into a project like wedding planning, with your VISA card in hand, might not be the best way to begin a lifelong relationship.

The Marriage & Money forum online (Keyword: **Marriage & Money**) leads you to online areas and Web sites that discuss combining premarriage debt, ways to spend within your budget, and other wise pointers. Take a look at Ric Edelman's Wedding Tips, which include tips for newlyweds, second marriages, and looking beyond The Day to The Life. The Wedding Day Dollars article alone is well worth reading, as it puts outlandish wedding bills into perspective (see Figure 7-6).

Figure 7-6. Marriage & Money helps you take a hard look at those wedding bills.

Also drop into The Motley Fool Wedding Tips for a few out-of-the ordinary money saving tips that will bring a smile. The 10 Foolish Money Savers, while not your ordinary wedding advice, certainly make financial sense. The first tip, for example, is to elope. Although that definitely saves on the refreshment bill, it might not be everything the bride-to-be envisioned.

Get some great advice at TheWhiz.com. Use Keyword: **TheWhiz** to open the window, and then click The Cost of Life button. Several wedding cost articles head the list. Read about wedding photographers, wedding cakes, wedding and reception sites, and more. In addition to average costs, these articles give you ideas on where to cut and still experience a great wedding.

Coming Up Next . . .

Once you get those numbers under control, it's a whole lot easier to pay Uncle Sam what you owe him every year. The next chapter covers your favorite subject and mine, the inescapable taxes. Find out how to get the information online that you need to file your taxes. If you like, you can even use an online tax preparer to streamline the whole affair.

CHAPTER

8

PAYING THE TAX MAN

Chapter 8

Paying the Tax Man

IN THIS CHAPTER

How to get online tax advice

Downloading the forms

E-filing your returns

At 11:30 p.m. on April 14, where are you? In a line of cars, inching your way to the friendly postal employee who holds the cardboard box in his hands. You said last year that this wouldn't happen again. Next year, it can all be a blurry memory.

No, next year won't bring a respite from tax filing. However, your online connection gives you downloadable tax forms, advice from professionals, and the option of filing your taxes over the Internet. Forget that trip to the local library, only to find that they don't have the one form you need — save it to check out the books you *really* want to read after your tax forms are filed.

Locating Tax Advice

Find answers to your tax questions before you file the forms, and save yourself a big headache. Several financial forums, on both America Online and the Web, tell you about new tax law changes, what you can and can't deduct, and resources for simplifying the whole paperwork process.

If you're looking for tax information in plain English, TheWhiz.com and The Motley Fool provide a good starting point. Find them both in the Tax Planning forum window, at Keyword: **Tax Planning**. Opening TheWhiz.com Tax Planning folder leads to a site with articles on filing options, deductions, and more. Turn to TheWhiz.com for good advice when you need an accountant, IRA talk has you befuddled, or some other special circumstance — maybe even a divorce — brings tax quandaries with it.

The Motley Fool Tax Strategies area talks about changes in the tax law, possible penalties, and exemptions. You'll also find a calculator to help you determine whether to convert that IRA into a Roth IRA. It also shows you how taxes and inflation can affect your savings nest egg.

Walk through the basics of taxes and tax planning at Money.com's Taxes tutorial. The online course covers the 1040 form, where to download forms, tax audits, and a test at the end to check your retention. To get there, use Keyword: **Money.com** and click the link under Money 101 to the left. Look in the list for Money 101, #19, Taxes, as shown in Figure 8-1.

For more pointed advice, as compared to Money.com's general information, visit financial advisor Ric Edelman's online forum. Located at Keyword: **Edelman**, the forum sports a folder called The New Tax Rules. Inside, you'll find articles on investing in municipal funds, the pros and cons of quarterly tax payments, and tax code changes.

Find It Online

A multitude of tax links await you at Zipee.com's tax channel (www.tax-tip.com). Whether you're looking for general tax information, payroll tips, a tax planning guide, or a tax advocacy group, you can link to it through this site.

Figure 8-1. Brush up on tax basics at Money.com.

While you're checking out the pundits, be sure to drop by The Tax Prophet's Web site, at www.taxprophet.com. In addition to current news and top topics, you can find archived San Francisco Examiner tax columns written by the prophet himself, Robert L. Sommers. These columns discuss a variety of tax topics, from mortgage interest to filing online. About four years' worth of the question-and-answer format columns reside at this site, so it's definitely worth a peek if you want to increase your tax quotient.

Another site that acts as a tax site clearinghouse, the Tax and Accounting Sites Directory at www.taxsites.com, links you to discussion areas, accounting sites, and tax updates. This is definitely a good site to bookmark; you can use this online directory as a jumping-off point for further tax-related research.

Downloading Tax Forms

Instead of running to the library or searching frantically through last month's junk mail stack for the proper tax form, you can now download exactly what you need from online sources, including the necessary instructions to complete the forms if you need those too.

Drop into the Tax Planning forum (Keyword: **Tax**) to access
state and federal tax forms. Click the Need a Tax Form
graphic, which opens the Tax Forms window (see Figure 8-2).

Tip

Figure 8-2. Get forms and general tax advice from Tax Planning.

Once the Tax Forms window opens, you're well on your way:

- ▶ Double-click the federal form you need to open its
  download window, and then click the Download
  Now button to download it into your computer.

- ▶ Click on your state name to visit the state's Department
  of Revenue (or Tax Commission) site. Once there, click
  the linked text that leads you to the forms you need.

- ▶ Click the Get Acrobat Reader button to open the Tax
  Form Viewers window so you can download the appropriate version of the reader for your computer (if
  you don't already have it installed).

Filing Online

If you have the appropriate tax preparation software at home,
you can file your federal tax return electronically through the
IRS e-file option. However, you can also file taxes online without the software by using one of the direct filing sites. These
sites take care of the software; you just fill in your numbers
to submit the online paperwork.

You can find a plethora of
forms online at the official
Internal Revenue Service
site. Known as the Digital
Daily, this site offers
up-to-date tax tips, plus
forms and instructions for
current years as well as past
years dating back to 1992.
Find it at www.irs.gov.
If you want to read the
instructions online rather
than downloading them, a
link allows you to do that,
too. Click the Forms & Pubs
link at the bottom of the
main IRS Digital Daily
window.

Note

All the downloadable forms
require Adobe Acrobat
Reader if you want to actually open the file. Either
download it from the Tax
Form Viewers window
listed earlier, or hop
directly to the Adobe site
at www.adobe.com and
download the Reader from
there. Click the Get Acrobat
Reader button to access the
free document reader.

You might want to begin with an online estimator that can tell you how much of a refund you might receive, or the general amount of taxes you'll owe. Links to estimators by SecureTax, Intuit, and H&R Block all reside at the MoneyCafe (www.moneycafe.com). Click the Tax (special) link to see the estimator links in the Great Resources section.

Once there, you enter your income, number of dependents, amount of withheld tax, and any miscellaneous credits into the estimators. Then the calculator tells you what your refund or amount due should be. If your taxes are relatively simple, this tool helps you know in advance what the scenario looks like.

When you're ready to actually file your taxes online, use one of these sites to do it:

> ▶ **Web TurboTax:** Brought to you by Intuit, the company that produces TurboTax software, Web TurboTax allows you to fill in your information and file your return in one smooth operation. You complete the forms and click to submit your information before Web TurboTax charges you. This way, you get to try out the entire system to see if you like it before you pay for the service. Web TurboTax service costs $9.95 if you file a 1040EZ, and $19.95 to file a 1040 or 1040A return. State filing costs are the same; add $9.95 to file your state return if you use the EZ form, and $19.95 for the state return if you file a regular 1040. Look for Web TurboTax at www.turbotax.com; it's shown in Figure 8-3.

> ▶ **FileYourTaxes.com:** FileYourTaxes.com files your state and federal returns electronically. As with TurboTax, you need no extra software to use this service. Fill in the online forms with your information and send it on its way. You can download completed tax copies free, or use one of an assortment of optional ways FileYourTaxes offers to receive your personal copies. The service also offers optional extra schedules you may need to file in addition to the 1040 or state forms. Visit www.fileyourtaxes.com for further information.

Figure 8-3. Web TurboTax files your forms for you.

▶ **TaxDirect:** If you file your taxes with TaxDirect, at www.taxdirect.com, they charge you nothing to set up an account and nothing to enter all your data into the forms. If you want to send the forms electronically or print them, however, you incur a fee. To process a refund for you, they charge $10.00.

▶ **TaxLogic:** Combine the assistance of a paid tax preparer with online filing and you get TaxLogic, at www.taxlogic.com. You give TaxLogic your information, and a human calls you to verify the numbers and discuss ways to reduce your liability.

▶ **SecureTax:** SecureTax allows you to enter your information free, and charges you only if you decide to use their service. In line with the other online tax filers, they charge $14.95 to file a state and federal 1040EZ form. Find them at www.securetax.com.

With all these options, you should be able to find an online tax service that meets your needs, files your taxes online, and reduces your headaches come tax time.

Coming Up Next . . .

Now that you've filed the yearly taxes, how do you want to spend the refund? If you want to use it as the down payment for a new home or a snazzy apartment, march right on to the next chapter. It helps you determine whether renting or buying is the right decision for you, and then leads you to sites that provide mortgages online. What could be easier?

Chapter 9

Affording Your Dream Dwelling

Whether you should rent or purchase a home depends on two things: lifestyle and the numbers. If your lifestyle is mobile or you don't want home-owner hassles, you're probably better off renting an apartment or a house. On the other hand, if you want a home of your own (after all, it's the American Dream), you need to be sure you can afford the payments over the long term.

This section leads you to online resources that help you determine whether to rent or buy. If a house purchase is on your list of to-dos, also look here for online financing options.

Renting or Financing?

How do you decide whether to rent or spring for house financing? From a strictly financial perspective, owning a home is generally a better move over the long term due to the value of the equity you build up, the general stability of house payments versus fluctuating rents, and your ability to deduct various costs from your income (for specifics, see your accountant) when you calculate your taxes.

To see how you qualify on the renting vs. buying scale, complete the Am I better off renting financial calculator. Use Keyword: **Looking** to open the Real Estate — Looking window, and select Am I better off renting from the Calculators drop-down list. The Am I better off renting page appears, as shown in Figure 9-1.

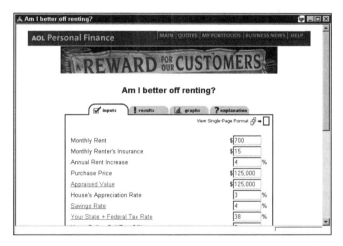

Figure 9-1. The renting vs. buying calculator tells you if renting is a better option.

This calculator takes the numbers that you know, such as your current rent and the purchase price of the house you want, and tells you whether you'll save money over a specific length of time. Here's how to use it:

1. Enter your amounts into the Input page. The Input tab should be the live tab as the page loads (if not, click that tab to bring the page to the front). The more information you can provide, the more accurate (and therefore more meaningful) the calculation will be.

2. Click the Results tab to see how the numbers compute. If the calculator tells you that you'll save a large amount of money over the next few years if you purchase a home, that's something to take into account. If, however, it tells you that, based on your numbers, you'll actually save money by renting, you should take note of that, too.

3. Click the graphs tab to see a pictorial comparison of renting versus buying over a period of years.

4. Click the explanation tab for a brief explanation of what information goes into the Am I better off renting totals.

If you'd rather read words than look at figures, iOwn.com offers an excellent renting vs. buying calculator. It takes you screen by screen, discussing the difference between renting and buying, including those little details you don't usually think about until the papers are signed. To use the calculator, follow these steps:

1. Open the Digital City window with Keyword: **DCN**.

2. Click the Real Estate button in the Digital City window.

3. Click any city (perhaps your own?) to open that city's real estate area.

4. Click the Mortgages & Loans link in the Digital City window. Look for it in the Categories list.

5. At the bottom of the Mortgages & Loans page, click the Apply Today link.

6. The iOwn Loan Center appears in the browser window. Click the Should you rent or buy link under Tools and Advice. The Rent vs. Buy screen appears.

7. Use the Quick Analysis in the Rent vs. Buy window to get a basic idea of where the banks would say you stand financially. Enter your current rent, home purchase price, yearly salary, down payment, and expected time spent in the house into the text boxes, and click the Submit button.

8. Based on the information you provide, iOwn suggests whether it looks like you should stick with renting for a while or take the plunge, as shown in Figure 9-2.

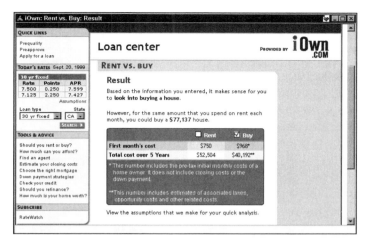

Figure 9-2. According to these figures, it might be time to buy a home.

9. To read an account of the ups and downs of homebuying, click the rewards and tradeoffs link directly above the Quick Analysis portion of the Rent vs. Buy window. To get back to the Quick Analysis page after you've already entered the numbers and seen the results, use the back arrow on the browser bar.

10. In the Rewards and tradeoffs of buying section of the iOwn site, read the paragraphs and click the More button to continue. Choose either Lifestyle needs (to learn about the lifestyle changes associated with home purchasing, along with its benefits) or Financial needs (to see the pros and cons of pouring your money into a house).

11. Continue clicking the More buttons as you read through the statements. To return to where you were, click the Back buttons.

Refinancing to Save $$

When interest rates are low, homeowners rush to the nearest mortgage company to refinance. Will refinancing actually save you money, once you take all the refinancing fees into account? Perhaps it will. Then again, maybe it won't save you enough to make it worth the hassle.

Find out how much equity you have in your home by subtracting your balance (the Remaining Amount Owed column) from your home's current value. If you don't know the current value, using the original purchase price gives you a pretty good estimate.

Get a general idea about where you stand by using a refinancing calculator. You enter the pertinent numbers and let the computer do the rest. To use the calculator, do the following:

1. Use Keyword: **Looking** to open the Real Estate — Looking window.

2. Click the drop-down calculator list, and select the Refinancing Calculator. The calculator opens in the browser window.

3. Enter the purchase price, the loan amount, the term, and the interest rate into the top four text boxes in the calculator's Input form.

4. Scan the rest of the items. If you know any of the numbers, change them. Otherwise, leaving them with the original calculator estimates should give you a pretty accurate result.

5. Click the Results tab to view the total refinancing costs and the new monthly payment.

6. Click the Tables tab to see how the loan amounts fall, month by month, through the length of the loan. The Tables section shows you at a glance the amount you pay each month in principal and interest, as well as the loan's remaining balance charted month by month.

7. For a very brief explanation of the calculator and what it does, click the Explanations tab.

Finding a Lender

Once you look at all the financial numbers, where do you find a lender? These days, the entire process can be completed online. Live the dream of a paperless mortgage application — you fill out the application online, submit it the same way, and receive approval without ever walking into anyone's office. Many mortgage companies now do business online; most of them work within only a few states. Several companies, however, process loans nationwide.

iOwn

With iOwn you can move from online loan application to closing in as few as ten days. The iOwn site allows you to check the progress of your loan 24 hours a day, charges no application fee, and includes no "hidden" costs in the loan process. You can get to the iOwn site, as shown in Figure 9-3, through any Digital City site. Here's how:

1. Use Keyword: **DCN** to open the Digital City National window.

2. Click the Real Estate button.

3. Click any city name to open that city's Digital City area.

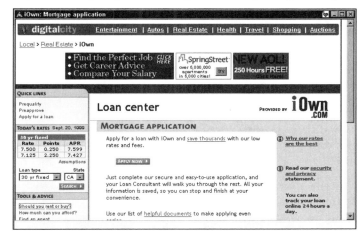

Figure 9-3. iOwn makes online loan applications easy.

4. Click the Mortgages & Loans link. The bottom of the browser window shows the mortgage and loan information.

5. Click the Apply today link to open the iOwn site.

6. Once you see the iOwn site, you're ready to apply for the loan. Click the Apply Now button to begin the process.

7. Before you submit an application, you need to register with the site. Enter your e-mail address and a password, and click the New User button.

8. Reenter your password as instructed and click the Submit button.

9. Voilá! The online application appears. Fill in the text boxes with the required information: name, number of dependants, current address, and contact information. Click the Next button.

10. Enter your employment information and income amounts, and click the Next button.

11. Enter your financial assets and auto information, and click Next.

12. Answer the legal questions, such as "Are there any outstanding legal judgments against you?" Then click Next.

From here on, follow the prompts and work your way through each screen until you complete the entire application.

Other Lenders

Although other lenders might ask for different information on various screens, the online process is much the same from application to application. Every lender needs to know who wants the home, how much it costs, and how you want to pay for it. They need your social security number to run a credit check, and they want to know how to reach you during the day. Once you've given the prospective lender all that information, the loan application is pretty well finished. Following are a couple of other online lenders you might want to visit:

▶ The Lending Tree (www.lendingtree.com) sends your loan application to several different lenders, then you pick the one you like best. Click the mortgage button in the Lending Tree site to begin the loan process.

▶ Quicken Mortgage (www.quickenmortgage.com) lets you fill out an application, select an online lender, and then submit the application. The Quicken mortgage interview makes some educated guesses as you proceed through it, which might save you time. Or, you might find yourself changing quite a few answers along the way.

Coming Up Next . . .

Socking a few dollars away here and there helps you to afford that new home or cool vacation even sooner. The next chapter covers the ins and outs of investments, including several places to start if your perception of "putting money away" involves a well-designed pillow case. Learn about the basics of investing — if you like, you can even complete your investment transactions online.

Chapter 10

Investing for the Future

Dreaming of financial independence? Perhaps you simply want to build a nest egg for tomorrow. Unless you expect to wake up one morning and find a million dollars under your pillow, wise investments provide the surest way to financial success.

Learning about investing, however, can be a bit of a stretch. Those "in the know" wink slyly and mutter about some magical formula. Don't buy it. As with economists, if all the financial gurus in the world were laid out end-to-end, they wouldn't reach a conclusion; in fact, most of them seem to make more money selling their advice than they do following it. The secret to sound investing is balancing growth potential against risk, having the courage to invest

$50, $100, or more over and over again, and having the discipline to admit it when you're wrong and cut your losses.

Finance School 101

If *growth* and *risk* sound like Greek to you, then you need some introductory investment lessons. Money.com offers an online Basics of Investing tutorial that gives you the broad brush strokes: bonds, stock, funds, and inflation. When you're finished, you can even take a simple test that shows you how well you know the terms and concepts. Find the lesson at `www.pathfinder.com/money/101/4/intro.html`.

Once you've finished the Money.com investing lesson, move on to other lessons in the Money 101 Lessons list. Investing in Stocks, Investing in Bonds, Investing in Mutual Funds, and Employee Stock Options all provide good information in a lesson format. Somewhere down the line, you might also want to read through the Investing in IPOs (Initial Pubic Offerings) and the Hiring Financial Help lessons. Find them all in the Money 101 Lessons listing in any lesson window.

Learn the Basics

For a more in-depth investing introduction, turn to the America Online Investing Basics forum, at Keyword: **Investing Basics** (see Figure 10-1). Before you dump a bunch of money into a stock or fund, you need to know why you do it and what the possible ramifications might be. The Becoming An Investor series of articles presents an excellent foundation, including a "slow and steady wins the race" philosophy that makes you more money, in the long run, than investing in fits and starts.

The Investing Basics information, although well written, is virtually giggle-free. If you learn best with a smile on your face, click The Motley Fool button in the Investing Basics window to attend the Fool's School. Fool's School attendees learn 13 Steps to Investing Foolishly, which includes learning to track investment performance, opening a brokerage account, and embracing small company stocks. Reading through the 13 Steps will add to your investment knowledge, even if you've already worked through the Money.com lessons and the Investing Basics How-tos.

Figure 10-1. Investing Basics introduces you to the world of . . . um . . . investing.

TheWhiz.com (or MoneyWhiz, depending on which screen you happen to be viewing) offers several articles on their Web site that deal with basic (and not so basic) investing. Learn about fantasy investing games (think about fantasy football, but using the stock market and Monopoly money instead of an imaginary pigskin). Read about setting financial goals *before* you invest, and then meeting those goals through your investments. Find out about the pros and cons of mutual funds as a place to park your money. To find these juicy investment articles, follow these steps:

1. Use Keyword: **TheWhiz** to open TheWhiz.com window.

2. Click the Investing button. The Web site opens, displaying the top ten MoneyWhiz investment articles.

3. Go to the bottom of the window and click the Investing archive link. This displays all the investing articles, regardless of whether they fit into the top ten.

4. Look for article links on mutual funds, stocks, and beginning investing (although, if you have the time, all of these articles are worth reading).

Additional Resources

Once you have the basics down, visit these areas for more information, as well as tools to help you manage your wealth:

▶ **AOL Investment Snapshot:** Look up stock quotes for any company that trades on Wall Street. Once a company's stock information appears in the results window, you can select a chart that plots stock performance for the day, the month, the year, or over a three-year period. Keyword: **Snapshot** takes you there.

▶ **My Portfolios:** Keep an eye on a few of your favorite stocks, or use this area to house your investment information.

▶ **Investing Forums:** The Investing Forums window, at Keyword: **Investing Forums**, links you to several online investment areas, as well as a set of message boards devoted to stocks and the stock market.

▶ **Active Trader:** Turn to the Active Trader forum, at Keyword: **Active Trader**, for cutting edge investment topics such as Internet Stocks, Equities, and Futures (see Figure 10-2).

Figure 10-2. Join the trading world.

Online Investments

So you've read all the introductory information and now you want to invest in a few promising stocks. Where do you go? Depending on what you want to buy, your choices are varied. You might be able to purchase stock directly from the company involved. That's generally the least expensive route. Or you could look for *no-load* funds, which are mutual funds that include no built-in management fees and/or commissions to be automatically subtracted from the money you invest, before you've acquired share one. In other words, *all* your money goes into shares; those handling the funds don't skim five or six percent right off the top.

A little further up the scale, you could opt for a discount broker such as Ameritrade or E*Trade, which charges a low standard fee for each transaction and lets you invest in a variety of stocks, bonds, mutual funds, and options. Your other option is to connect with a full-scale (and full-price) broker, like the brokers attached to your local bank. Both MoneyWhiz (Keyword: **TheWhiz**) and The Motley Fool Fool's School (Keyword: **Motley Fool**) discuss the pros and cons of various brokerage options.

A rising trend in investment circles, online investing — much like online banking — takes the hassle out of investments. Using an online account with an online brokerage like E*Trade, you complete your transactions online 24 hours a day. You spend no time on hold (waiting for your broker to finish another call), you leave no messages (hoping that the brokerage house will complete your transactions before the stock price changes radically), and you save money with each transaction (since most online brokerages are discounters).

Online Brokers

Here are a few online brokers that you might want to preview, especially if you're thinking about jumping on the online brokerage wagon:

- ▶ **Ameritrade:** Sign up for a free copy of Darwin: Survival of the Fittest (an options trading simulation) when you first visit this site to check out the Ameritrade Internet demo. Complete transactions, view your portfolio, and get quotes online. Keyword: **Ameritrade** takes you to their AOL window. Also access the site through www.ameritrade.com.

- ▶ **DLJ Direct:** DLJ offers a demo of their brokerage service. Spend some time playing with the windows before you sign up, so you know what you're getting into. With DLJ you can trade stocks, bonds, options, and mutual funds. Use Keyword: **DLJ** to see for yourself.

- ▶ **E*Trade:** Play the E*Trade Game and learn about the stock market and online investing. Or walk through the E*Trade demo to see what E*Trade offers. With E*Trade you can manage your portfolio, trade in stocks and bonds, and even qualify for a Power E*Trade account, which offers extra services to the active trader. Visit E*Trade with Keyword: **ETrade** (see Figure 10-3).

▶ **Waterhouse:** Check out the Waterhouse webBroker system and learn how their system works. A series of drop-down lists lets you choose between stocks, bonds, other types of investments, various orders to execute for each investment, and real-time quotes. Use Keyword: **Waterhouse** to visit the main forum window, and tour the webBroker system. Or, open an account of your own.

Note

Although you generally send a check into the brokerage company after you register, you might be able to transfer funds online from a bank or Certificate of Deposit to your new account.

Tip

Because it takes a few days to send in your application and check, wait for the check to clear, and activate your account, your best bet is to activate an online account *before* that golden company releases its Initial Public Offering.

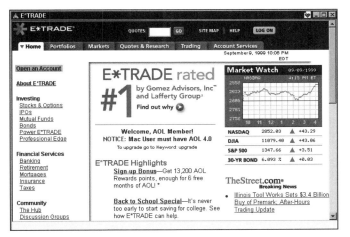

Figure 10-3. Open a brokerage account via the Web.

MoneyWhiz, at Keyword: **TheWhiz**, offers several articles about online investing in their MoneyWhiz Investing section. Click the Investing button to open the Web site, and then look for articles about online brokerage and online investing. One article even compares several online brokerages in a table that includes fees, information turnaround time, and minimum deposit.

Open an Account

To open an online account, you need to register with the site and provide between $1,000 and $3,000 to fund the account. You then trade with the amount you have in your account, adding to it as necessary.

Brokerage registrations request your name, address, e-mail address, and social security number. The broker might also ask questions, such as how experienced you are at investing, to get a better profile of his or her customer base and to ensure that he or she recommends the correct type of investment for your current situation.

When you finish filling in the online forms to register with the broker, you need to print the application you completed, sign it, and send it to the broker with a signed check. The broker needs to have your signature (and money) in hand before he or she activates your account.

Coming Up Next . . .

Once you have a handle on the basics of investing, the next step is keeping up-to-date with the rise and fall of the market. Checking your own online portfolio each day allows you to track trends with relative ease. The next chapter shows you how.

Chapter 11

Keeping Up with Stocks

Looking at the stock market with macro vision, it's definitely a full-time job to track the myriad of stock opportunities that flash by day in and day out. Without special real-time access to the markets, you can't hope to have up-to-the-second investing information each and every day.

That said, what about the casual investor? For the person who makes a living as something other than a day trader, checking the stocks once or twice a day probably provides enough information to settle the mind. If you take the long-term view of investing, which is that you're going to make money in the market if you invest in solid companies and leave your money there long enough, you aren't going to pull out at every threatened downturn anyway.

This chapter tells you how to research a company you're thinking of investing in, and how to create a portfolio to track its progress in the marketplace.

Researching a Company

Company research — especially when it becomes *investment* research — goes beyond simple stock performance. As you read through current and recent news articles about a particular company, you get a feel for their goals. Combine that with a daily check on the stock numbers and you can almost guess how the investing public will react to any changes the company makes.

Stock Quotes and More

Use the AOL Investment Snapshot area to research a company's stock performance. Here you can look up quotes, access recent news releases and stories that pertain to the company, and even add the company to your online portfolio. It's a handy window to have around; you can open AOL Investment Snapshot with Keyword: **Snapshot** or by clicking the Quotes button on the toolbar (see Figure 11-1).

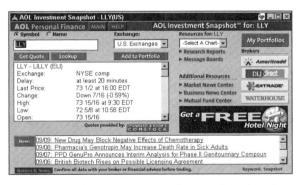

Figure 11-1. Take a company's snapshot to see how it's performing.

To see a picture of your favorite company's performance, follow these steps:

1. Use Keyword: **Snapshot** to open the AOL Investment Snapshot window.

Tip

If you do know the company's trading symbol, type it into the text box at the top of the AOL Investment Snapshot window and click the Get Quote button. The company's information appears in the Quotes window, saving you the extra steps above.

Note

The company information you get through the AOL investment areas, although considered current, is not what you'd call *real time*. By the time you see the numbers, about 25 minutes have passed — an eternity in trading terms. The AOL information is best used as a guide, unless you're checking highs and lows after a market day close. During the day, if you see numbers that look too good to be true, they probably are. Be sure to check with your broker before placing any change orders.

2. If you don't know the trading symbol, type the company's name in the text box, make sure the Name button is checked, and then click the Lookup button. A Lookup Results dialog box appears, showing the possible companies with that name that trade on Wall Street.

   For example, typing **Johnson** into the text box and clicking the Lookup button returns seven possible matches, including Johnson & Johnson and Johnson Controls.

3. Double-click the company that you had in mind, if the Lookup Results dialog box lists more than one. That company's information jumps into the Investment Snapshot Quotes window.

You can get much more information through this window than current U.S. stock quotes:

► Read the company's past few days' news by clicking the article links in the News box.

► Find quotes and news for international companies when you enter the company's name in the text box, click the Name button, set the Exchange city in the drop-down list, and click the Lookup button. The company quote appears in the native country's currency.

► Add any company to your online portfolio by showing its information in the Quote window and then clicking the Add to Portfolio button.

► When you research a company on the U.S. Exchange (which probably covers most searches), you can look at various financial reports for that company by clicking the Research Reports button.

► Chart the company's stock performance by selecting a daily chart, or chart one month, one year, or three years.

General Market Information

Keep your finger on the daily stock pulse with a look at the Market News Center. The Stocks & Mutuals section (at Keyword: **MNC Stocks**) charts the daily performance of the Dow Jones Industrials, the Nasdaq composite, S&P 500, and the Russell 2000. Click the appropriate tab in the Stocks & Mutuals window to view the day's graph (see Figure 11-2).

Figure 11-2. Check the daily stock averages in the MNC Stocks & Mutuals window.

For a written overview of the day's performance, open the AOL MarketDay article in the item list. Look in the item list for various industries from aerospace to utilities. Clicking the name of any industry shows the day's news articles and press releases for that particular industry.

Future and Past

Keeping your eyes open for new stock opportunities is just as important as reading the historical data. Do both online and within a few minutes you see the entire picture.

Check the quotes of yesterday with the Historical Quotes window at Keyword: **Historical Quotes**, as shown in Figure 11-3. Find out how that stock did over the past three years, last year, or every day last month. Either select one of the standard time periods (daily, weekly, or monthly) or create your own graph by checking Custom. Click the Quotes button to show the results table, or click the Graph button to show the results as a chart. If you click Custom, and then one of the other buttons, you get a small dialog box that allows you to specify a date range or a particular number of days to show. Set the parameters and then click Continue to see the results.

Read past company news and see where the corporation's been in the last month or so. The Company News search engine collates articles from Reuters and the AP Newswire within the past 14 days, and stories from the PR Newswire and Business Wire news within the past 30 days. Use Keyword: **Company News** to open the window. Then type the company's ticker symbol into the Enter ticker symbol text box, and click the Search button to see the headlines in the results window.

Find It Online

Hoover's Online gives you a glimpse of the future with IPO Central, at www.ipocentral.com. Glean information about upcoming Initial Public Offerings, read the IPO news stories, and check the scheduled stock price ranges. For a fee, you subscribe to Hoover's and get even more up-to-date information.

11

Keeping Up with Stocks

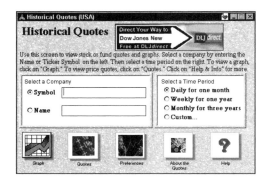

Figure 11-3. Graph last year's stock quotes here.

Creating a Portfolio

After all this work locating stock information, what do you do with it? You could post it on sticky notes all over your monitor, but eventually some would fall to the ground and become trampled. Creating an online portfolio places the information in one accessible place, out of the way of dogs and small children.

In fact, you can create a whole collection of portfolios. Use one to track potential investments, another to follow companies whose stock you currently hold, and a third to keep an eye on your investments' competitors. Create one for each industry that interests you. Use My Portfolios to track any trading company for any reason you like.

To create a portfolio of your own, do the following:

1. Use Keyword: **My Portfolios** to open the My Portfolios window, as shown in Figure 11-4.
2. Click the Create button in the My Portfolios window to launch a new portfolio.
3. Once the portfolio takes its place in your portfolio list, you need to fill it with financial data. Click the Add button and the Add to Portfolio window hops to life.

Figure 11-4. Create individual portfolios to track your own stock groups.

4. Fill in the company's trading symbol (such as LLY for Eli Lilly & Co.), the number of shares you purchased, the purchase price per share, the date, and any commissions or fees you paid.

5. Click OK to add that information to your newly named portfolio.

6. To determine the trading symbol for a company, click the Lookup button and enter the company's name into the text field. Then click the Name button. Click the Lookup button to display the company's trading symbol and relatively current information.

7. To view a portfolio's statistics once you create it, double-click the portfolio name to open it.

The portfolio window gives you several options for viewing the statistics. When the individual portfolio opens, you see the Basic configuration. Use the Portfolio Column Views drop-down list to customize the information your portfolio shows. Options include Trading Day, High/Low, Fundamentals, and My View. With My View, you select the columns you want to see in the portfolio's window. Select Customize My View to set up the My View option.

When you decide a portfolio has outlived its usefulness, highlight its name and click the Delete button. A Delete Portfolio dialog box appears to ask if you're sure. Click OK to make it disappear forever.

Tip

If you create a portfolio to track potential stocks rather than actual purchases, leave the Number of Shares, Purchase Price per Share, and Commission/Fees spaces blank. Simply fill in the company's symbol and click the OK button to include that company in your portfolio.

Tip

You also create an online portfolio whenever you invest via an online brokerage. That portfolio, however, generally represents companies whose stock you actually trade. You can also create one or more AOL *non-trading* portfolios to track potential companies, industries, competitors to the companies you invest in, or practically anything else you might think of.

11

Keeping Up with Stocks

Coming Up Next . . .

If you envision your stock portfolio providing for your later years, continue to the next chapter and read about retirement savings. Whether you're just getting started or you're about to begin the withdrawals, you'll find plenty of online help to answer your questions and point you in the right direction.

CHAPTER

12

SAVING FOR RETIREMENT

Chapter 12

Saving for Retirement

T he nest egg years are coming. You can look forward to retirement for yourself or someone you love if you've taken the steps to ensure that you'll have money to live on. Designing a retirement plan, putting money away regularly, and living within your budget now lays the foundation for carefree years later on.

Many workers looking toward the retirement years plan to continue working beyond age 65. Even if this is your idea too, putting away enough money now to live on later gives you an extra cushion down the road, should your circumstances be different than what you envisioned.

How Much Is Enough?

Retirement savings that begin with a goal, receive regular contributions, and grow at a steady pace over time provides the most return with the least amount of worry. Waiting until you receive a large windfall or two before you begin saving provides less than sure footing for the future.

Several online sites provide excellent retirement advice. They discuss trends, plans, and covering your bases when it comes to retirement investing. Begin with AOL's Retire in Style forum, at Keyword: **Retire**. With this one keyword you can link to most of the retirement areas on AOL, as well as several on the Internet (see Figure 12-1).

Figure 12-1. Delve into retirement resources via the Retire in Style forum.

Find out how much you need to put away by using online retirement calculators. Open the calculator site by double-clicking the Retirement Calculators item in the Retire in Style window item list. The Retirement Calculators site jumps to life, displaying these options:

- ▶ What will my expenses be after I retire?
- ▶ Am I saving enough? What can I change?
- ▶ What if I underestimate my expenses?
- ▶ What if I overestimate my return?
- ▶ How much effect can inflation have?
- ▶ What happens if tax laws change?
- ▶ What if Social Security no longer exists?
- ▶ How much will Social Security provide?

12

Saving for Retirement

> ▶ What will my income be after I retire?

> ▶ Which savings or income sources will be the largest?

> ▶ How much can I invest before taxes each year?

> ▶ How advantageous is increasing my savings?

> ▶ Which savings should be used first?

> ▶ How will each of my accounts grow?

> ▶ How will each of my accounts be used after retirement?

Click any of the hyperlinked questions to open that calculator and begin plugging in your numbers to find the answers.

If you plan to work through *all* these calculators, be sure you have a couple free hours and a rough idea of what monies you have stashed where. Each calculator asks for various investment information, age of retirement, and proposed monthly living expenses. It then takes that information and crunches the numbers to give you the answer to the question. Some calculators provide you with amounts set into a table, whereas others present the results in an explanatory paragraph or two.

You can also learn how much you need to put away with the retirement calculator at Money.com. Nestled into the middle of one of their well-designed Money 101 lessons, this calculator takes the amount of money you make now, the amount you think you'll need to live on (or a percentage of the money you make now), and any investments you currently maintain. It then calculates when you'll retire, when your spouse (if you have one) will retire, the amount of your savings, and your retirement income. You can even enter a dollar amount that you want to leave your heirs, and the calculator takes that into account as well.

While you're in the area, take a moment to work through the entire Money 101: Planning for Retirement lesson (see Figure 12-2). Located at www.pathfinder.com/money/101/lessons/13/intro.html, the Retirement lesson takes you through creating a retirement plan, beginning to save, the celebrated calculator, and tips for boosting that retirement stipend.

Figure 12-2. Planning for Retirement takes you through the basics.

Note

Remember, all investment involves some risk. The more risk you're willing to take, the higher your returns might be. If the idea of risking your money in the market terrifies you, several relatively low-risk investments exist. However, "safe" investments generally equate with lower returns.

Planning to Meet Your Goals

Now that you have a picture of your current situation, and an idea of the final numbers you need, you can create a plan that takes you from today through retirement. Several areas provide solid planning advice, from the Sage Company's suggestions on how to divide your investments between funds depending on your current age, to The Motley Fool's observations on the efficacy of retiring at 50.

To read through the retirement planning sections, first open the Funding Your Retirement window with Keyword: **Funding & Retirement**. The Funding Your Retirement window offers articles about tax implications, funding options, and other tasty tidbits. Work through the Plan Well Now, Live Well Later articles for some information on planning. Then click the Nest Egg Options button to open a window whose articles discuss what percentage to save, how to alter investments as you age, the ins and outs of tax-free investing, and potential risks with investments.

If You Could Retire Tomorrow

Visit the site designed for Internet denizens age 45 and over.
ThirdAge covers issues relating to the third segment of your
life. Since a big concern of ThirdAgers is retirement, the area
offers a retirement section devoted to instruction and information.

Keyword: **ThirdAge** opens the main ThirdAge window. From
there, click the Retirement Center link to open the ThirdAge
Retirement window. Divided into three areas, the Retirement
Center offers an inspirational story or two that tells how other
ThirdAgers reached their dreams in retirement. Also in this
area, the Know-How section stresses your control over retirement funds, including mortgage management. Finally, the
Assessment Tools help you establish the worth of your home,
offer you a savings and expenses calculator, and provide a
down-to-earth assessment of whether you're really ready to
retire (see Figure 12-3).

Figure 12-3. Use these retirement links to solidify your plans.

Family Money magazine offers several articles on retirement
planning. Find out how many retirement myths you might
currently believe, and learn six strategies that help you solidify
and reach your retirement goals. Use Keyword: **Family Money**
to open the Web site, and then click the Retirement/Estate
Planning link to reach the retirement articles. If you like what
you see, you can subscribe to *Better Homes and Gardens'
Family Money* magazine directly from the site.

While you're planning a retirement strategy, be sure to read a few online chapters of Ric Edelman's *The Truth About Money*. Keyword: **Edelman** opens the Ric Edelman window. Open The Truth About Money Online folder, and click the Part 9 button to read about Retirement Planning. The window contains excerpts from six chapters, detailing Ric Edelman's explanations of (and suggestions for) retirement plans, social security benefits, IRAs, and more.

Coming Up Next . . .

When you look at your current career, do you find yourself where you want to be? Take a look at your skills, your long-term goals, and determine what you really want to do. You might find that your skills match your career choice perfectly already — and that you're exactly where you should be!

Chapter 13

Dancing the Career Choice Tango

IN THIS CHAPTER

Finding your best career

Checking your sales potential

Comparing careers one to another

So many career choices — and so little time to fulfill each one. Perhaps you always dreamed of joining one of the public service branches, and the postal service, police department, or fire brigade calls your name. Maybe you enjoy working with numbers, and bookkeeping, computers, or actuarial science interests you. With all the career options available, determining what to do with your days can be a difficult decision.

Whatever career you choose, you tend to experience more career satisfaction if you jump into a career that includes tasks you enjoy. A landscaper who hates to be outside is in for a pretty miserable working life. The same can be said for a truck driver who hates spending hours behind the wheel. On the other hand, people who love the outdoors or really enjoy driving excel at these positions. Finding your niche in the work world requires a balance of skills and interests.

Matching Skills to Career

Generally, people show more interest in the things they do well. Tasks that come easy indicate an innate talent, a natural interest, or both. When you determine what career you want to follow, taking both these aspects into consideration can save many headaches later. Doing something for 40 to 60 hours a week is difficult enough without waking up each morning hating what you'll have to do that day.

If you find a position that matches your skills and interests, it tends to satisfy that internal need to do something meaningful. And if you enjoy your days at work, your position doesn't have to rank as one of the world's ten most glamorous jobs. When you tell a new acquaintance what you do for a living, your enthusiasm speaks volumes.

In fact, if enthusiasm itself permeates everything you do, you might think about a career in sales. The Online Psych area offers a Sales Personality Inventory that gives a pretty good indication of whether you're fit for the commission sales arena. To find out whether you have what it takes to add selling to your skills set, use Keyword: **OLP Games** to open the Online Psych Mind Games window, as shown in Figure 13-1. From there, double-click Do you have a sales personality in the item list to open the inventory. Answer the questions and then click the Score button. The quiz results tell you how closely your answers match the personalities of people whose careers revolve around sales, such as insurance agents or corporate account reps.

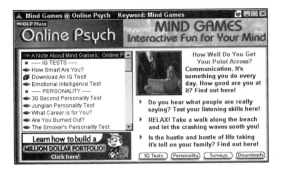

Figure 13-1. Take a quiz that evaluates your sales potential.

So What Do You Like to Do?

Select a career that allows you to spend time doing one of the things you like to do best. Perhaps you enjoy many different tasks and topics, and you'd find fulfillment in many varied occupations. Or maybe you aren't sure what you do best (sometimes you're the last to know). If you want a little guidance to point you in the right direction, take the Career Finder survey.

AOL's Career Finder assigns a personality type that depends on your answers to 20 preliminary questions. Based on the Myers-Briggs Personality Type Inventory, this quick overview tells whether you're more

> ▶ Introverted or extroverted
>
> ▶ Intuitive (ruled by your emotions) or Sensing (interested in facts)
>
> ▶ Thinking (someone who analyzes) or Feeling (going with the flow)
>
> ▶ Judgment (decision) oriented or Perception (experience) oriented

Follow these steps to complete the Career Finder:

1. Use Keyword: **Career Finder** to open the Career Finder in your browser window.
2. Click the Q&A button to begin a list of questions that help determine which careers fit you best.

3. The first screen takes you through a 20-question Personality Type Questionnaire, as shown in Figure 13-2. Each question offers two possible answers. Neither answer is right or wrong; just click whichever answer applies to you.

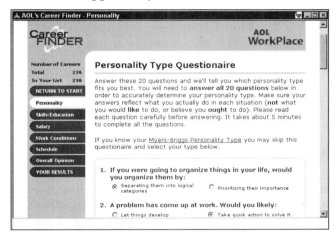

Figure 13-2. Begin by identifying your personality type.

4. When you finish answering the questions, click the Calculate button underneath Question 20. The next screen shows your results. Click Next to continue.

   If you've taken a full Myers-Briggs Personality Type Inventory test in the past, and you remember your type, go to the bottom of the screen and select the correct type, and click the Next button to move to the next section of the survey. On the other hand, if you don't want your potential personality type to influence the Career Finder results in any way, make sure the I don't want personality types considered button is checked, and then click the Next button.

5. The next screen asks you to rank various skills. Would you say you're artistic? Good at math? Have better-than-average mechanical ability? Click to set your skill levels, from Poor to Good. Then check the items that tell how much education you already possess or are willing to pursue. Check as many items as apply — for instance, you may already have an Associate degree but you're also willing to pursue on-the-job training. In that case, check both and click the Next button when you're ready to move on.

6. Select your minimum salary and click the Next button. Because salary ranges vary depending on the type of job you do and where you happen to live in the country, you might want to set a minimum salary at less than you would prefer, to see what possibilities the Career Finder turns up. The scale begins at $10,000 and tops out at $60,000.

7. How do you cope with stress? Do you like to work indoors? Would you find a hazardous job exciting? Answer these questions by clicking a radio button to set your level of comfort, and click the Next button.

8. The next screen asks your opinions about traveling for work, whether you want to work full time, and how many hours you want to spend on the job each week. Click the button that corresponds to your preferences, and then click the Next button.

9. This next-to-final screen asks you to rank the importance of a job that matches your skills, one that fits your personality, work that provides your preferred working conditions, and a job in a field for which the experts expect a greater number of openings. Set the radio buttons to match your preferences, and click the Next button.

10. Your results fill the screen, as Figure 13-3 shows. Depending on your answers to the previous questions, you may see only a few potential careers. On the other hand, your results might qualify you for more than 100 careers. The careers that most closely match your requirements-and-skills set head the list, and less likely careers trail at the end. Journalism ranked very high on my list, for example, whereas Vending Machine Repairer, a job for which I have absolutely no skills, fell very close to the bottom.

11. Click any job title in the results list for a detailed description of that career. The description sheet lists salary, education, skills necessary, probable work conditions, and several paragraphs describing the career's general job duties.

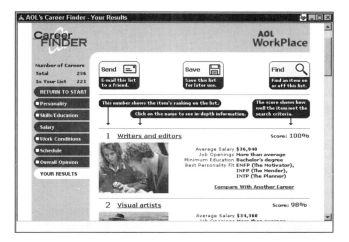

Figure 13-3. Browse through the results list to find your perfect career.

12. Click the Compare with another career link to compare any career in the list with another career. In this portion of the Career Finder, the software limits you to comparing a career with other job descriptions within that results page. So you can compare any job on results page 14 with any other job on page 14, but you can't compare it with a job on page 1.

13. Check any of the ten listed careers that you want to compare against one another, and click the Compare button. The General Information, Skills Needed, and Working Conditions results for each career appear side by side so you can see how they differ.

14. To add another career to your comparison list, click the Add another career link and select a career category, and then a career from the lists that appear. This is where you can select a job from page 1 to compare with that listing on page 14. The career description takes its place in the lineup.

You can also use the Career Finder to compare several careers that interest you, whether they fall within the same general field or not. If you know you want to work somewhere in the medical field, for example, you can use this feature to compare life as a nursing aide, an emergency medical technician, or a medical assistant. On the other hand, if you're torn between a career as an emergency medical technician or a law enforcement special agent, you can look at how those careers compare, too.

To use the Career Finder to compare specific jobs, follow these steps:

1. Use Keyword: **Career Finder** to open the Career Finder in a browser window.

2. Click the Compare button. A list of general career categories appears, such as Administrative Support and Clerical or Transportation (see Figure 13-4).

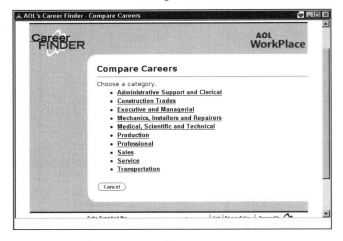

Figure 13-4. Select a category to begin your career comparison.

3. Select a category to see a list of careers that fall under that category.

4. Select a career from the list that appears. Information about that career appears in a column, with a Choose Another Career link next to it.

5. Click the Choose Another Career link. The software takes you back to the career category list, where you begin the selection process all over again.

6. Continue selecting careers; the screen can hold several side by side.

7. When you're finished reviewing the various careers you've chosen, click the Cancel button to return to the main Career Finder screen.

Coming Up Next . . .

Finding a career to pursue is your first step. Now that you
have a couple of options, move on to the next chapter, which
gives you options for locating prime places for pursuing
your dreams.

CHAPTER

14

SEARCHING FOR
THE PERFECT JOB

Chapter 14

Searching for the Perfect Job

IN THIS CHAPTER

Using the online job banks

Finding a local position

Touring the online job fair

Y ou're bored with work. Regardless of the day of the week, the work routine never varies. Or you feel like you're underpaid for the hours you spend and the productive piles you create. Perhaps you've reached the top of the ladder in your current job, and you want employment that promises more challenge.

Regardless of your reasons for searching, actually finding a job that you enjoy makes the difference between daily drudgery and delight. But this time, instead of scouring the Sunday newspapers, do a little online searching. Maybe you'll unearth a job you never knew existed but seems to be made for you.

Browsing Through the Listings

If your career plans include moving across the country, services such as Monster.com allow you to search outside the parameters of your local paper. On the other hand, if you know you don't want to move when you make your next job change, Digital City offers local opportunities.

Begin your search with Keyword: **Find a Job**, which takes you to the AOL WorkPlace Find a Job window, as seen in Figure 14-1. The Find a Job window contains several links and job listing sites for you to explore.

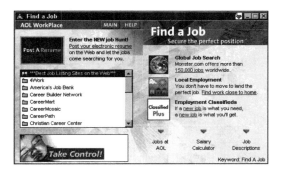

Figure 14-1. Begin your job search with Find a Job.

A Monster of a Job Site

One of the largest online job banks on the Internet, Monster.com lists somewhere between 150,000 and 250,000 job opportunities on a regular basis. Tap into this massive resource by clicking the icon next to the Global Job Search.

To conduct a job search on Monster.com, follow these steps:

1. Open the Find a Job window with Keyword: **Find a Job**.
2. Click the Monster.com link in the Find a Job window. Monster.com opens in the browser window, as shown in Figure 14-2.

Tip

If you want a job in a specific part of the country, use a city in that area as your search term. If, on the other hand, you know you need a nursing job and you don't care where you go, type your job title—in this case, **nurse**—into the text field.

Figure 14-2. Monster.com lists job openings from all over the world.

1. Type a search term into the QuickSearch text field, and click the Go button. This word (or words) can be a city name, an occupation, or even a computer package like FoxPro or Visual Basic.

2. The search term returns national and international job listings for a particular career, if you entered a job title, or it returns every job in the city or state you entered (plus a few miscellaneous extras here and there). Narrow the search with a Subsearch term, either by refining your job title or specifying a location.

3. Click the link for any job that looks interesting, and a short description of the job and its required duties appears.

4. To apply for any particular position, scroll to the bottom of the description page and click the Apply Online link.

5. To apply for any Monster.com opening online, you first need to register with the site. Click the Create a new account and apply for this job link to continue.

6. The New Account screen appears and asks for your e-mail address. Fill in the text field and click the Make me a new account button to continue.

7. A screen appears, announcing that your user name and password are on their way to your e-mail box.

8. Retrieve the message (clicking the Read button on the tool bar opens your new mail window on top of the browser window).

9. Click the back arrow on the browser bar twice (or until you see the Apply Online window again). This time, click log in and apply for the job.

10. Type in your new user name and password and click the Log me in button.

11. The site announces that you have no resume on file. Click the link to submit an online resume with Monster.com and continue the application process.

12. The Submit Resume screen appears, with space for your name, address, potential job title, and resume information. Fill it out and click the Submit this resume now button.

13. The name of the position (the one you began to apply for way back in Step 6) appears, along with an Apply for this position now button. Click it to submit your online resume.

14. A screen appears, telling you that your online resume is submitted to that particular opening.

15. You're done! To continue searching for another position, click the link in Click here.

Tip

When you're finished, be sure to click the Logout link to end your session on Monster.com.

Additional Online Job Banks

The employment sites listed in the item list of the Find a Job window, although they each have their own strengths, basically work the same as Monster.com. You enter the area, search for a job, post your resume, and then apply for any good openings you find at that site. A few of the items in the list offer specific services:

▶ If you prefer to cull newspaper ads from around the country, CareerPath.com posts the ads from around 90 newspapers online. Most of them request a faxed resume. Look for CareerPath in the Find a Job window item list.

▶ Career Builder searches through several online job posting sites, including Monster.com and CareerPath, to offer a large number of potential job openings. It also searches one state at a time, or all states at once, depending on how you set the search criteria.

▶ Government Job Openings lists employment opportunities with the federal government. From clerical position to trades and beyond, this site tells salary ranges, performance expectations, and a copy of the vacancy announcement. Although these positions usually include an e-mail address for the department with the vacancy, most of the openings require a resume sent by regular mail.

Work with a Local Flair

Most of the online ads make it easy to search for a tailor-made job in your own city or state. When you begin your search, either specify your own area as the location or search for positions solely within your city. The majority of the results you get will then be within your city, state, or region.

Another option for finding local work is to use the Digital City Employment department. Digital City divides the information city by city, so finding local information becomes a breeze. To open the Digital City Employment section, use Keyword: **DCN** to open the Digital City (Local channel) window, and then click the Employment department button. The Employment area opens, looking a lot like Figure 14-3.

Figure 14-3. Locate a new job in your home city.

Click your city's name to enter the Jobs & Careers screen for that city, and then click the Job Listings category link to open the Job Listings search screen. Select a job category from the drop-down list, and click the Search button to see the results.

The search engine returns all the selections for that category, regardless of area. To search for a specific city or state, scroll to the bottom of the ClassifiedPlus screen that displays the results and select the city and state from the Location drop-down list. Then click the Find Job Offers button at the bottom of the window to locate the local listings for your chosen category.

Finding What You Want to Do

If you find the volume of online job listings overwhelming, and you don't know exactly what you want to do, take a stroll through the Career Fair and see if anything catches your eye. The Online Career Fair, at Keyword: **Career Fair**, offers live chats with companies who are actively recruiting new employees. Sit in on a few and listen to the discussions. You might learn quite a bit simply from the questions asked. What types of workers do various companies need? What prior training, if any, do they deem necessary for new hires?

Another option is to browse the articles in the Gonyea Career Center (Keyword: **Gonyea**). The Career Center posts suggestions for alternative careers, assessing job offers, and when to change careers. Reading through a few of these articles may help you determine what you *want* to do, so that you know the right job listing when you see it.

Coming Up Next . . .

When you apply for the perfect job, the process goes much smoother if you already have a resume created. The next chapter takes you through the steps and shows you where to post your resume online.

Chapter 15

Building a Resume

Whether you want to change careers completely, move up a rung or two in your industry, or make a lateral move, a resume is essential. Acting like a snapshot of who you are at that moment, your resume conveys your background, training, and accomplishments to an audience that probably doesn't know you personally. Thanks to the online world, you can use the Internet to announce your existence with a resume, search for a job, and even meet others in the same occupation.

Getting Your Name Out

Your first step before landing that new job is updating your resume. Perhaps you need to create one from scratch. Every online job bank requests some type of resume. The easiest way to search for a new position is to create the resume first, and then upload it to a few job banks so it's there and waiting when you find an opening that calls your name.

Creating an Online Resume

To craft an online resume, use Keyword: **Resume** to open the Post a Resume window, as shown in Figure 15-1. From this window you can link to the online job banks, sample resumes, and sample cover letters. Most important, through this window you can create an online resume and post it to Career Mosaic, an online job search site. You can also create a resume Web page at AOL Hometown, America Online's Web page area.

Figure 15-1. The Post a Resume area contains lots of useful resume links.

To create an online resume, follow these steps:

1. Open the Post a Resume window with Keyword: **Resume**.

2. Click the Build your electronic resume link. The Career Mosaic resume site opens. Several of the articles listed on this page provide good information for anyone who wants to create an online resume. In particular, you might want to take a look at How to Build and Submit Your Resume in ASCII Text, and 25 Tips for a Better Electronic Resume.

A Very Important Link . . .

One link in particular, however, may be of special interest: the Click Here link at the end of the Career Moisaic Resume CM page's introductory paragraph.

Posting a resume online generally means that anyone can see it — including your present employer, if he happens to be online searching for employees to fill positions. If your online resume needs to remain confidential for any reason at all, click the link after If you would like to be considered for job opportunities but are not in a position to openly post your resume. That link leads to the Recruitment Enhancement Services employment search service, a company that keeps your online resume on file but sends it out only with your permission.

3. To go straight to the creation stage, click the ResumeCM link. The Career Mosaic Resume CM page loads. Most of the page contains several text boxes that you complete as you create your resume.

4. Enter your name and city into the text fields, and then select your state from the drop-down list. Next, if you don't live in the United States, select your country from the next item list. Otherwise, leave that box alone; it already shows the United States as the default country.

5. Type your phone number and e-mail address into the next two text boxes, and then fill in the Current Job Title text box.

6. Use the next drop-down list to select the job category that fits you.

7. Paste an ASCII version of your resume into the large text box.

8. To see your creation before you send it, click the Preview button.

9. Finally, click the I Agree, Submit My Resume button to send your resume winging on its way (assuming you agree to the terms and conditions written in the paragraph above the button).

Now that you've created an online resume, it's stored with one job search site. However, Career Mosaic is one of many such sites available. Most of them store your resume free; others may require some type of fee. To see the range of job banks, click the Pick the best database for you link in the Post a Resume window. The Online Resume Databases window opens, listing more than 50 free employment sites, some of which are shown in Figure 15-2. At the bottom of the list, the window also shows several databases that charge a fee to post your resume; generally, these services cater to specialized segments of the work world, such as chefs and cooks, agriculture workers, or the airline industry.

Tip

Since the online resume sites want you to paste a copy of your resume into their form, it saves time if you create the resume as a word processed document (in a word processing program familiar to most other computer users, such as Microsoft Word), and save it. Then save it again under another name, such as Resume2, but save it as ASCII text or Rich Text Format, whichever option your word processor gives you. Now you have a pastable version for the online job sites.

Online Resume Databases: The Riley Guide

Free Resume Databases

You are not charged for the basic service of placing your resume here.

Site Name	Particular Focus	Public or Private	Retained for...	Presented in...	Notes
name of the service	*any particular industry or occupational group served here?*	*"public" means anyone can search the database*	*how long will your resume be listed?*	*how is your resume displayed?*	*any unusual or special services offered?*
AccountingJobs from AccountingNet	Accounting / Finance	Public	90 days	HTML	Brief bios only. Confidentiality available
America's Talent Bank	None	Private (free registration)	Unlimited	Not stated	Sponsored by the US Dept of Labor. System is operated by individual states.
					Affiliated with Employment

Figure 15-2. Find a job site to house your online resume.

Crafting a Resume Web Page

Put your name in lights — or at least, post your resume on the Web so potential employers can find it. Different from sending your online resume to a specific job listing site (or two, or three), creating a resume Web page allows you to send anyone interested in your credentials to one place that houses most of the information they need.

America Online provides a screen much like the online resume sites. You fill in the information and click a button to send it to AOL Hometown, where potential employers can access it. However, the AOL Resume Web page design software is much more friendly than most of the online job sites — the system doesn't demand that you submit your resume in ASCII format, it allows you to place a decorative border on your page, and it asks for items in plain English.

Here's how to create your own resume for AOL Hometown:

1. Use Keyword: **Resume** to open the Post a Resume window.

2. Click the Create your resume web page link. The Build a Page For Your Resume window opens.

3. Click the CLICK HERE link to open the 1-2-3 Publish screen, which should look like what you see Figure 15-3.

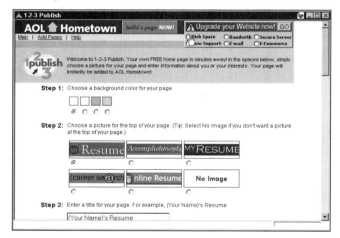

Figure 15-3. Place your resume on the Web for all to see.

4. Click to select a background color for your resume page and a banner for the top of the page, if you want one.

5. Type a title for your resume page into the text box in Step 3. This section also gives you the option to include a photo; however, though their advice will depend on the position you're seeking, resume analysts often advise against placing a photo on your resume page.

6. Next, select a divider to appear between the various sections of your resume. If you don't want a divider, click the No Divider button.

7. In Step 5 of the form, you enter all your information. The first text box contains your name. Put your address and phone number into the second text box.

8. The third text box already has Career Objective filled in. Below it, in the large text box, type a few sentences telling what you want to do. This part describes your career objective and explains your goals for your new job.

9. The fifth text box in Step 5 has been filled in for you; it says Work Experience. If you like that title, leave it. In the large text box below Work Experience, enter the experience that would make you a valuable addition to a company.

10. If you want to link to any other Web pages as part of your resume, enter those links and their Web addresses into the text boxes in Step 6.

11. If you want visitors to your page to contact you via Instant Messenger, check the box in Step 7. If you prefer that your Web page viewers *not* contact you from your Web page, uncheck the box.

12. To see an example of your Web page, click the Preview My Page button. Your resume loads on screen. See Figure 15-4 for an example.

13. When you're ready to add your page to AOL Hometown, click the Save button.

Tip

Concentrate on your career objective as you complete the Work Experience portion of the resume form. Stick to what's relevant; if you happen to have a bachelor's degree in engineering, that's great, but it probably won't help you land a cosmetology position.

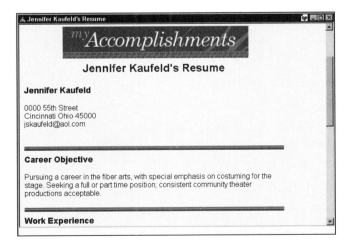

Figure 15-4. Create your own Web page resume, complete with links to other pages.

Networking: Your Key to Advancement

Although it's not necessarily true that who you know makes all the difference, knowing a large number of people in your industry certainly can't hurt. Word of many openings filters through the grapevine, both before and after the jobs go through official corporate "postings." No matter what the industry, people usually prefer to work with others they've built relationships with.

With that in mind, broaden your horizons by meeting others online who share your profession. Visit the WorkPlace channel's Professional Forums, where workers from every industry exchange messages, swap work tips, and even point out an occasional opening. To reach the Professional Forums, follow these steps:

1. Open the Professional Forums window, shown in Figure 15-5, with Keyword: **Professional Forums**.

Figure 15-5. Find your profession's forum and join the discussion.

2. Scroll through the professions in the item list. Double-click any item to open that forum window.

3. Depending on the profession, the forum window might contain a library with downloadable files, a message board, articles on how to become part of the forum's industry, links to related Web sites, or links to industry job listings. Scroll through the list for interesting items, and click a button or two to open various online windows pertaining to your profession.

You can also form professional relationships through attending a trade show or a training course. At an industry trade show, everyone speaks your language and participants automatically share some of the same interests. From vendors to other participants, trade shows and similar industry gatherings provide a good platform for meeting other people in your segment of the world.

Visit TS Central at Keyword: **TS Central** to unearth the latest in trade shows, training courses, and recent trade show Webcasts. Search for events by the event name or keyword (such as the industry name) or browse for events by industry. TS Central lists international shows as well as those closer to home, in case you yearn for colleagues around the globe.

Coming Up Next . . .

With your resume created and online, take a look at what you can do to enhance those work skills. The next chapter offers sites, tips, and suggestions for locating training courses and collecting continuing education credits.

Also look in the item list for a chat link. These scheduled chats generally occur once a week, although in the case of a forum for a big industry (like the Hotels & Motels forum), the area may schedule a different chat every night of the week. The scheduled forum chats give members a chance to actually connect with others in their industries. Some forums even send weekly chat reminders via e-mail if you request them.

15

Building a Resume

Chapter 16

Bulking Up Your Skills

Most positions these days require some kind of continuing education. Between radical shifts in technology, new scientific research, and changes in "the way we do things here," a worker who consistently takes training courses and adds continuing education credits to his or her portfolio stays one or two steps ahead of the game. Use the information in this chapter to track down the training and continuing education that will help you keep your edge in the marketplace.

Locating the Training You Need

Even if you don't need actual continuing education units (known widely as CEUs or — for continuing professional units — CPUs) to keep your professional license current, your job performance probably improves a bit when you take the time to cut another training class notch in your belt.

In addition to getting you out of the office for a couple of days, which tends to clear both your head and your perspective, a training class lets you concentrate wholly on one topic for an extended time, a luxury most corporate workers don't have unless they happen to program computers. Instead of trying to assimilate new information bits and bytes at a time, you take the course, have a couple of good lunches out, and return to the office refreshed, enlightened, and ready to go.

Rather than trying to intercept the training flyers that trickle in through the interoffice mail system, do a little online research on your own and come up with a few training classes that would benefit you specifically. TS Central, for example, lists training opportunities for many different occupations. Whether you need a class in project management, statistics, emergency response, or retail accounting, TS Central offers a link to the class in its training database.

Find a course through TS Central using these steps:

1. Use Keyword: **TSCentral** to open the TS Central area in the browser window, as shown in Figure 16-1.

2. Click the Training Center text along the left side of the window to open the Search Training Events screen.

3. To search for all available seminars with one search term, such as *statistics* or *computing*, enter the term into the Event Name or Keyword box and click the Do Search button.

4. The Search engine returns a list of available classes. Click any linked text to see details for a particular seminar.

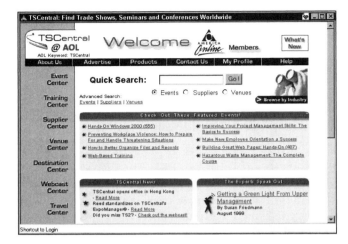

Figure 16-1. Search for a training seminar through TS Central.

5. For a more controlled search, click the Advanced Search link in the Search Training Events screen. A slightly more complicated form appears, which allows you to specify industries and training dates (see Figure 16-2).

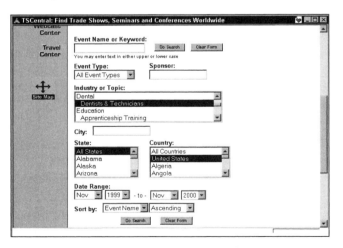

Figure 16-2. Advanced searches allow you to specify industries and seminar dates.

6. Select your industry or work-related topic from the Industry or Topic list. Then type the desired city into the City text box.

7. If you're not tied to a specific city and have a selection of states you're willing to visit to take the class (or if anywhere in the United States will do), select All States in the States list.

8. Select United States, any particular country, or All Countries in the Country list.

9. If you have particular dates in mind, select them from the Date Range drop-down list.

10. Click the Do Search button to see the Advanced Search results; the search uses all the information you entered or selected. Any fields you leave blank will be skipped, and box contents that you don't specify will search through all available entries.

11. The Results screen appears, listing the seminars that it found. Click an event name for more information about that particular seminar.

Cross-Reference

Also look to the next chapter for information on online courses. Many times, a company will apply a specific college course to your continuing education portfolio.

Continuing Education Credits, Available Online

Continuing education credits keep the world current. Designed to increase a professional's knowledge in some area, these credits are available to workers who successfully complete some course or workshop that pertains to what they do for a living. To keep a license, pay scale, or other benchmark current, many professionals need to collect a certain number of credits, or units, every so many years.

Educators, health care professionals, lawyers, accountants, and many others need continuing education credits to keep their jobs. If your profession (or your employer) requires that you amass a specific number of continuing education credits (or CEUs), take a look online to see if you can collect them there.

Collect CEUs from ZDU, the Ziff-Davis University continuing education Web site. Here you can take courses in computer programming, graphics, networking, Web design, contact software and other applications, business topics, and more. For $7.95 a month or $69.95 per year, you can take as many classes in a month as you like. Visit www.zdu.com to learn more. Click the Course Catalog link to see what courses ZDU currently offers, and click the ZDU Handbook link to learn about getting CEU credit. See Figure 16-3 for a look at the ZDU Course Catalog selection.

Note

To get CEU credit for a ZDU course, you need to apply for the credit when you register for the course. ZDU charges an extra $15 CEU processing fee for each course you take for continuing education unit credit, and they have a few rules for CEU participants — such as having to show up to the classroom at least once a week while the course is in session. If the classes Ziff-Davis offers here interest you and you don't need the CEUs for work, then the extra fee doesn't apply.

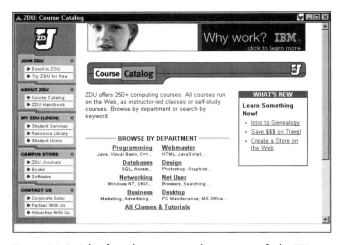

Figure 16-3. Select from these computer departments to find a CEU course.

EdCredits (located at `www.edcredits.com`), one of the more innovative ideas in continuing education credits, offers classes in document and outline form on the Web. You read the course outline, take the test, and print out your certificate. Reading the course material is free — however, you need to register with the site to take the test. One year's subscription to the site is $55, and it includes all the courses you wish to take within that year's time.

Currently, EdCredits offers medical courses such as O.S.H.A. Bloodborne Pathogen, Alzheimer's Disease, and Hypertension Review. The company is currently working on courses for professionals, realtors, and educators.

Following the Path Toward Growth

Although continuing education and training seminars both increase your skill set and your competency at what you do, neither one grows your career on its own. In order for your career to change as you change, and continue to offer new challenges, you need to spend some time charting your career course.

As you determine what you want to be doing next year, in the next five years, or even in the next ten years, the courses you take and the lateral moves you might make need to continually point toward your final goals. Some goals, such as taking one course or becoming an expert at one aspect of your job, may be short-term achievements, whereas other goals — becoming a mid- or upper-level manager or moving from one industry to another — might be considered long-term goals. These achievements might take more than a year or two to make your own.

For online assistance in establishing your goals as a professional, take a look at the Career Strategies forum. This forum, located at Keyword: **BKH Careers**, contains folders full of articles about Launching Your Career, Career Advancement, and Career Planning. Any one of these folders provides a good jumpstart for your thoughts about your evolving career (see Figure 16-4).

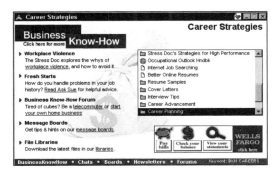

Figure 16-4. Plan your career with a little help from Career Strategies.

For a glimpse into how others in your industry view their jobs, drop by the Professional Forums (Keyword: **Professional Forums**) and visit your industry's forum. Here you'll find scheduled chats that discuss your work, message boards for industry fellows to use for sharing tips and advice, a snapshot of the industry, and some of the best Web sites that focus on what you do.

Find It Online

Use the online search systems, beginning with AOL Search but also including Yahoo (www.yahoo.com) and AltaVista (www.altavista.com), to find links to many continuing education programs.

Tip

If you decide that your best plan for career growth is actually to step out of corporate America and build a business on your own, the Start-Up Businesses forum (at Keyword: **Start Up**) provides links to several online areas devoted to entrepreneurs and business owners. In addition, you might also want to take a look at the Work From Home forum, found in the department list at Keyword: **iVillage**.

16

Bulking Up Your Skills

Coming Up Next . . .

There's more to education than CEUs. You can take a course that pertains to an interest in your life. Or begin that degree program you always wanted to pursue. With online education, you take the courses over the Internet and you don't even have to leave the computer to do it. Find out more in the next chapter.

Chapter 17

Taking a Course Online

No longer do students need to leave the comfort of home to pursue a degree or attend a class. With the advent of online courses, teachers now present material in online classrooms over the Web, in live interactive chat rooms, or via e-mail. Online courses make education viable for today's busy students, whether they're 12 or 72.

Brushing Up with Distance Learning

Distance learning over the Internet is a relatively new concept in education. Instead of students having to physically appear in a classroom across town or across the country, they now log into virtual classrooms on the Web. Here they listen to lectures, ask questions, post assignments, and chat with classmates. Students also choose whether to take one or two courses to fill a gap in knowledge or to pursue a collection of courses to become proficient and perhaps even earn a degree in a given subject.

Partially because students no longer need to physically walk into a class to attend it, distance learning appeals to a wide variety of ages. Some schools provide courses specifically for high-school-age and younger students, whereas others concentrate on the classes required for Bachelor's and Master's degrees. In addition, students taking distance classes are free to take courses from a wide variety of institutions.

To see a list of distance courses use Keyword: **Courses** to open the Online Courses window, shown in Figure 17-1. Click the University of California Extension button (UC) to see classes in arts and humanities, business and management, computer science, hazardous materials, natural science, and social sciences. Through America Online, UC Online students can also take courses and complete a certificate in either computer information systems or hazardous materials management.

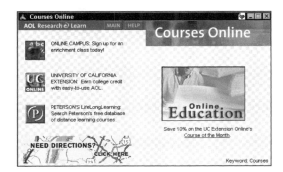

Figure 17-1. Find distance courses from colleges and universities all over the U.S.

The University of California also offers courses through the Internet; click the Course Catalog button and then the More Online Courses button to see the expanded list. Through the Internet, students can earn certificates in business administration, marketing, or program management. The university also offers professional sequences in direct marketing methods

Tip

The term *distance learning*, although often applied to Web-based courses, also includes courses delivered via video, postal mail, e-mail, cable television, and CD or CD-ROM. The courses in the Peterson's list incorporate many of these methods; to find online courses only, use the Search for courses option and highlight World Wide Web as the Delivery Medium.

and integrated marketing communications. Using Keyword: **UCAOL** takes you directly to the University of California area online.

Clicking the Peterson's LifeLongLearning button in the Courses window takes you to a searchable database of distance courses from many different universities and colleges. To find a course in LifeLongLearning, follow these steps:

1. Use Keyword: **Courses** to open the Online Courses window.
2. Click the Peterson's LifeLongLearning button to open LifeLongLearning.com in the browser window, as shown in Figure 17-2.

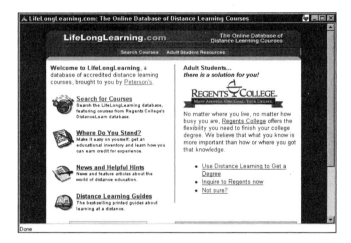

Figure 17-2. Begin a search for an online college course with LifeLongLearning.com.

3. Click the Search for Courses link. This opens the Search Page.
4. When the Search Page opens, you can search for specific institutions by name, browse for courses by subject, or search for specific courses.

Continuing Education on a Budget

Members who want information but don't particularly care whether a course offers official credit can find an enormous number of opportunities online. From computing basics to an updated look at *The Scarlet Letter*, these courses provide a specific amount of information in one to six online sessions, or via e-mail in a self-study mode. Costs range from free to about $50 per course.

Visit the Computing channel's Online Classrooms to see many different computing classes, at Keyword: **Online Classrooms**, shown in Figure 17-3. Browse through the folders in the Class Catalogue section of the window to see the various courses of-fered. Classes that fall under the AOL Basics, Beginners, HTML & Web, Music & Sound, Operating Systems, and Writing and Publishing categories, as well as most hardware classes and some Office application classes, are free. The others in these areas, including all programming classes, charge a small fee for attendance.

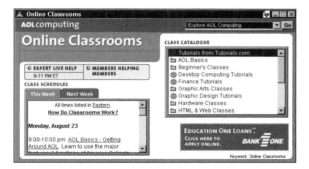

Figure 17-3. Check the Online Classroom for community education courses in computing.

You might find a class that lists no upcoming class dates, espe-cially in the Computing Online Classrooms area. Most unsched-uled classes provide a link to the class transcript, which you can read online or print with the browser print button. Keyword: **Class Transcripts** opens the Class Transcripts window, where you can browse through any of the posted transcripts from the Computing Online Classroom courses.

No matter what your interests, you can probably find online courses that match. For community courses on the arts, educa-tion, computing, history, and science, plus many other topics, use Keyword: **Online Campus** to open the course listing. The vast majority of these courses utilize live chats, Web tours, and e-mail course assignments to teach the various topics, and

Find It Online

Ziff Davis University (at www.zdu.com) offers classes in business, computer applications, programming, graphics, and home productivity. For $7.95 per month or $69.95 per year, registered students may take as many courses as they like in one month's time; courses include both live instruction and self study. Professionals may even gain continuing education unit credit for these classes, if they register with a small additional fee and attend all the sessions of a course (see Figure 17-4).

Cross-Reference

See Chapter 34 for some links to free online language tutorials.

they typically cost between $25 and $50 per course. Some of the courses are delivered via e-mail only, and a few of the classes cost nothing if you enroll.

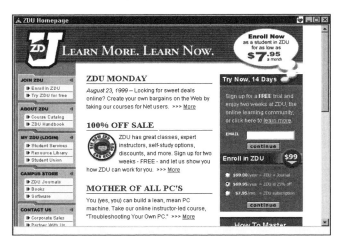

Figure 17-4. ZDU.com offers noncredit continuing education for a small fee.

Pursuing a Distance Degree

Many colleges and universities have jumped on the distance learning bandwagon. One reason is that it makes their offerings available to students who live too far away to physically attend a campus. The number of complete online degrees, however, is low compared to the entire collection of distance courses available on and off the Internet. Most colleges offer many courses online but still require you to spend a significant amount of time on campus to complete your degree.

Some schools, on the other hand, require only a short on-campus stay to complete a degree, whereas a few allow students to submit all work online with no campus visits. Indiana Wesleyan University, for example, offers a Masters of Business Administration degree, and they require only two three-day campus visits, practically a gift for busy professionals trying to attain another degree while holding down a full-time job.

Although online degrees in business far outnumber the degrees in other subjects, you can also locate degrees in computer science, education, humanities, and health care, in addition to several other options. Many schools offer Master's and certificate programs, whereas relatively few offer a full Bachelor's degree via the Web. However, such degrees are out there. The best way to find them is through search engines; since the offering schools cater to a savvy Web audience, they tend to make sure their listings are included in the online search systems.

Full degree programs via the Web will probably cost as much as physical attendance in the classroom. In fact, out-of-state fees may apply for some colleges, in addition to the tuition cost. For students wanting to pinch their pennies, Web-based instruction might not be the most cost-effective solution. But those already in the work force, students who don't want to leave home, or wildly nontraditional students (the 14-year-old Master's candidate or the 50+ degree seeker) will find distance education a viable, useful alternative to classroom instruction.

 **Find It Online**

To locate a school that offers online degrees, type **www.yahoo.com** (or **aol.com,** or another search engine address) into the browser bar and click the Go button. When the site appears, type **online degree** into the search text field and click the Search button. The site should return links to many different schools that offer online degree programs in a variety of subjects.

Coming Up Next . . .

Now that you know how to advance your education online, look at the next chapter if you find yourself on the other side of the business coin. It explains how you, as a business owner or corporate manager, can find help if you're on the hiring side of the online job search system.

CHAPTER

18

LOOKING FOR EMPLOYEES

Chapter 18

Looking for Employees

You need a new employee or two and the ad in your local paper hasn't pulled any response. Or perhaps you have an opening for something a little esoteric — know of any microcode chip programmers? Short of putting an ad in every paper in the country, or contracting with a headhunter, where do you find help?

Scour the online resume banks to fill that position. Potential employees place their resumes online hoping to find a match with that perfect job. Take advantage of their proactivity by placing your job opening in one of the online databases.

Placing an Online Ad

Find the best applicant for your job opening when you list an ad on the Web. Applicants find your listing when they click a banner ad or go to a job bank and search for positions by title or by keyword. Possible keywords include the industry term for the position, such as analyst, statistician, or electroplater, or the name of equipment used in the job, such as AS400, Excel, or FoxPro 2.6.

As an employer, you have three options available if you want to find workers online:

▶ Place a Come Join Us button on the front page of your Web site. Although this works if you cater to a dedicated clientele or you run a well-known corporation, the downside of this type of advertising is that job applicants need to search you out on the Web to click the button.

▶ Place a job listing with one of the online job banks. For a fee, you can post your job opening, and it will pop up as potential applicants search through the job database for positions in their fields. Job listings remain online for a certain number of days.

▶ Search online resumes for an addition to your staff. You can purchase access to online resumes and search for a qualified applicant yourself. This way, you don't have to wait to see if someone finds your ad.

Tip

If hiring an employee is a new process to you, check out the information at the CCH Business Owner's Toolkit site, at Keyword: **CCH Toolkit**. Here you'll find information that will help you decide whether you really need to hire someone, show how to write ads, and tell you what your legal responsibilities might be. Click the People Who Work for You link to get started (see Figure 18-1).

18

Looking for Employees

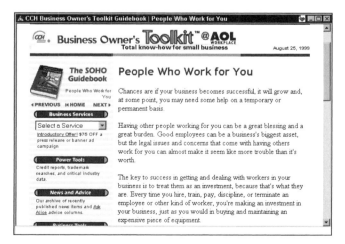

Figure 18-1. Pick up tips for incorporating an employee into your work space.

The online job sites all offer their services to employers differently. Your best bet is to find a site or two you like, which you think will provide a good return, and work with that site. For a list of many online job banks, use Keyword: **Post a Resume** to open the Post a Resume window, and then click the Pick the best database for you link.

Fraternizing with the Monster

Monster.com, one of the Internet's largest online job banks, offers employers a couple of ad placement options. Companies either purchase a one-time ad or they become employer members of the Monster.com site, which allows them to post multiple openings with Monster.com.

To place an ad for a single job opening with Monster.com, follow these steps:

1. Type **www.monster.com** into the browser bar and click the Go button. Monster.com blazes to life in the browser window.

2. Click the For Employers text at the top of the screen to enter the Monster.com Recruiting Office. The page asks for your user name and password — ignore those dialog boxes for now.

3. Instead, click the post single ads link above the text boxes to open the Monster Direct Web page. If a small Security Alert dialog box appears to announce that you're entering a secure Web connection, click Yes to make it go away and proceed to Monster Direct.

4. Read the price and posting information, and then click the link behind If you are an employer to open the Employer Ad Posting form.

5. Fill in the text boxes with your company information, billing address, and payment information. At the bottom of the form you see text boxes under a Job Information heading. Here's where you type the information about the opening: the job's title, location, and industry. Then type the specifics for the job into the large text box, or cut and paste the ad information (see Figure 18-2).

6. When you're finished, click the Submit Ad button at the bottom of the page to send your ad winging on its way to Monster.com.

Your one-time posting fee places the ad with Monster. com for 60 days. If you want to post more than one ad, Monster.com offers companies a membership program that lowers the advertising costs. Find out more by clicking the membership benefits link in the Monster.com's Recruiting Office page.

18

Looking for Employees

Figure 18-2. Post your job opening with the Monster.

Becoming a Tile in the Mosaic

Another online job site, Career Mosaic, uses a slightly different strategy. Job applicants search the Career Mosaic JOBS Database for possible job openings, then have the option to set up a Job Agent that uses their search criteria to continually look for promising positions. When the Job Agent finds a match, it drops the listing into the applicant's e-mail box.

Career Mosaic offers several services designed to help an employer get the word out. Employers can participate in an online job fair and become a featured company. They then get a corporate profile screen in addition to having their openings included in the JOBS Database. The company profiles introduce the applicant to your company. This page might include your company's history, its place in the industry, and a word or two about your corporate culture.

See for yourself what Career Mosaic has to offer by following these steps:

1. Type **www.careermosaic.com** into the browser bar and click the Go button. Career Mosaic appears in the browser window.

If you want to place more than one ad at a time on the Career Mosaic site, you save money by setting up an account rather than posting each job separately by yourself. Each posting stays online for 30 days.

2. Scroll down the page and click on the Post a Job link.

3. The JOBS Direct Placement page appears. This page details the cost and duration of the ad you place with Career Mosaic.

4. Click the New Advertiser Form link to open the JOBS Direct Placement: New Advertiser screen. Scroll down to about the middle of the page and enter your information into the text boxes. The form asks for company information first, such as name, e-mail address, and any comments you might have. Below that section, fill in the job information, specify how you want to pay for the submission, and click the Submit Information button to send it on its way.

5. Career Mosaic then sends you an e-mail with your ID number.

If you want to find out about the online job fairs and corporate profiles, in addition to the other Career Mosaic options, you need to fill out a request for additional information so that Career Mosaic will get in touch with you. Here's how to make it happen:

1. Open the Career Mosaic Web site, if it isn't already showing in your browser window, by typing **www. careermosaic.com**.

2. Click the Post a Job link. You'll see it under Employers Only, as shown in Figure 18-3.

3. When the JOBS Direct Placement page loads, click the additional information link at the bottom of the introductory paragraph.

4. The request form appears. Check the boxes showing which information you want to receive: Profiling My Company, Placing Multiple Jobs, Participating in Online Job Fair, and so on.

5. Fill in your contact information, and click the Submit button. A Career Mosaic representative takes your information and calls you to discuss options.

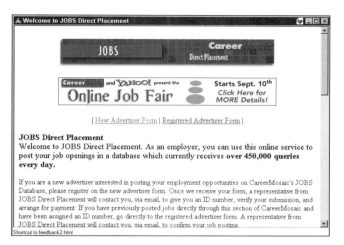

Figure 18-3. Look in JOBS Direct for Career Mosaic job listing information.

Searching the Resume Banks

Rather than posting your jobs online, you might want to search the online resume banks for likely candidates. Although this takes more time on your part, you know what kind of applicant you want and which strengths you need for a particular position, so you might save effort in the long run by doing the searching yourself for someone to fill your position.

Both Monster.com and Career Mosaic allow you access to the applicant database, for a fee. Of the two, working with Monster.com's information is a much more intuitive process. To find out about the Monster.com resume base, do the following:

1. Open the Monster.com Web site by typing **www. monster.com** into the browser text field.

2. Click the For Employers link in the main Monster.com window.

3. Click the Monster.com products link in the Welcome to Monster.com's Recruiting Office window. It opens the Monster.com Solutions Product Description screen.

4. You'll find the search information under the Resume Database heading.

5. Give Monster.com a phone call and they'll help you gain access to the database. The phone number is listed at the bottom of the Monster.com Solutions Product Descriptions screen.

To search the Career Mosaic resume database, you need to call them and set up a resume search account. For assistance with doing that, click the Help button and then scroll down to the Recruiter Questions at the bottom of the page. There you'll see How can I sign up to search Resume CM? Clicking the question link opens a small window with several links to rates and subscriptions details.

Coming Up Next . . .

Where you live can reveal a lot about who you are. Introducing friends into your ultra-modern loft apartment says a much different thing about you than throwing a housewarming party in your new, small-town Cape Cod. The next chapter takes you on the search for that perfect nest, whether you call it a house, an apartment, or something else entirely.

PART

IV

HOME IS WHERE THE ART IS

Chapter 19

Looking for the Perfect Place

IN THIS CHAPTER

Finding the online listings

Locating the perfect realtor

What to do if you need a new apartment

Y ou're growing out of your present apartment, condo, or house, and you need to search for a new hangout. Will that next step be a rental or a purchase? Would you like to move across the country?

No matter where you're headed (or even if you're staying put), AOL offers house-hunting resources designed to save you loads of time. Forget driving around the city on Sunday afternoons, searching for your next abode. Instead, spend a little time online refining your search and narrowing your choices.

Accessing the Listings

Begin your search with AOL's Real Estate — Looking area (Keyword: **Looking**). Clicking the Search over 1.3 million homes link loads the Realtor.com Homes for Sale Web site, as seen in Figure 19-1. From this site, you can search through over 1 million house listings. Look at listings near home or far away.

Tip

The abbreviation MLS refers to the Multiple Listing Service. It's a computer system that realtors use to keep track of houses for sale; each property has a unique code number.

Figure 19-1. Begin your real estate search at Realtor.com.

To use the Realtor.com site, follow these steps:

1. Click the Realtor.com graphic in the Real Estate Looking window. The Realtor.com Web site loads into your browser.

2. Click the Find a Home button. A page appears, asking how you want to search — by clicking the map image, by entering the target city and state, by typing the ZIP code, or by using an MLS number.

3. Click the link for your search method of choice.

4. If you choose any method except the map image, a page loads and you can select the target price range, amenities, and other features you want your home to have.

   If you use the map exclusively to select homes, the site asks you to narrow your search to cities within a state, and then to counties and individual townships before you list your home criteria.

You can also use your Personal Planner to keep track of neighborhoods you discover, and home search criteria in addition to individual listings.

5. Click the Find Homes button when you finish entering your home criteria. The site returns available listings that match your price range and amenities choices.

6. Along the bottom of each listing, several buttons allow you to glean more information about a particular listing. Click More Information to gain access to a Printable Flyer button. The Neighborhood Information button leads to school and neighborhood rankings for individual properties. With the Personal Planner button, you can save any listing to a private portfolio.

Finding a Realtor

Most homebuyers purchase a home with the help of a realtor. Often realtors come your way via personal recommendations from friends and family members. If no one you know has sold or purchased a home recently and you need to locate a realtor of your own, you can do that online too.

Realtors on the Web

Realtor.com (www.realtor.com) contains a complete Find a Realtor section on their site. To locate a realtor through Realtor.com, follow these steps:

1. Click the Find a Realtor button in the open Realtor.com main page.

2. After the Find a Realtor page loads, click the state on the map that appears or enter your city and state into the text boxes under the map.

3. Click the Continue button.

4. You now have two choices: Search for a realtor online through either the Yellow Pages or the White Pages. Choose one and click the appropriate button.

   If you want a realtor in, say, Churubusco, Indiana, use the White Pages to search for one. On the other hand, if you want a real estate agent with a particular affiliation or training, use the Yellow Pages form.

5. Enter enough information to begin the search, and click the Find button. It might say Find Realtors or Find Offices, depending on which area you choose to use.

6. The next page shows your search results. Hyperlinked agent names lead to their personal Web pages, which contain more information. Each listing also includes an e-mail link so you can send the realtor e-mail.

Diving into Digital City

Digital City, in AOL's Local channel, also offers real estate services. Offering a different list of realtors from Realtor.com, Digital City specializes in local resources. Find a realtor through Digital City using these steps:

1. Use Keyword: **DCN** to open the national Digital City window.
2. Click the Real Estate button along the left side of the Digital City window. A Web page opens, listing Digital Cities all over the nation as shown in Figure 19-2.

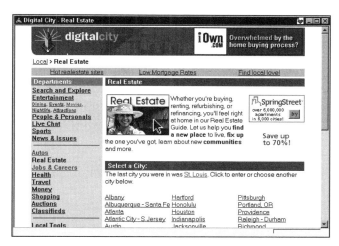

Figure 19-2. Find a partner for your real estate transaction in Digital City.

3. Find your city, or your closest city, and click its hyperlink.
4. Scroll down near the bottom of the page and click the Real Estate Services link.
5. When the browser displays the Real Estate Services Providers page, click the Agencies/Agents link for a list of real estate agents.

Searching Through Century 21

You might want to mark the Real Estate Services Providers page as a favorite place. It lists links for home inspection, builders, real estate attorneys, and other helpful people in the property biz.

If you want a real estate agent affiliated with a well-known organization, Century 21 makes it easy to find a local office through AOL. Use Keyword: **Century 21** to open the Century 21 Communities window. To find individual Century 21 offices, click the Find a Century 21 Office button in the main Century 21 Communities window.

When the small browser window appears, enter the pertinent information (such as state) into the text boxes and click Find Offices. One of the most useful portions of this window allows you to select languages other than English that your agent must be able to speak, including American Sign Language. Available offices that match your criteria appear in the browser window.

To obtain information about a specific area of the country, select the state from the drop-down list and then select a city from the state window that opens up. Each city's window contains a city profile and information on local government, attractions, colleges or universities, and available transportation. The city profile offers information on median income, housing, schools, and other pertinent facts for potential homeowners. Overall, the Century 21 area is well worth a visit. It's easy to use and provides a wealth of details, especially for homeowners planning to move from one city to another.

Locating an Apartment

For many people, renting an apartment makes sense. People who live a mobile lifestyle, who don't have the down payment for a house, or who prefer not to deal with the hassles of home ownership benefit most from apartment dwelling.

When the time comes for you to pack your belongings and head to a new apartment, AOL's Real Estate Renting department is there to help. Keyword: **REC Renting** opens the Renting window. From here you can navigate to various rental resources online.

Click the SpringStreet graphic to open SpringStreet, an apartment search site that also offers some nifty articles for movers, like the Mover's Checklist and tips for truck rental (see Figure 19-3). If you enjoy the college atmosphere, or you're headed for the ivy-covered halls, you can search for apartments by college or university. If you have a city or even a street intersection in mind, you can search that way, too. To search for an apartment with SpringStreet, do the following:

1. Click the SpringStreet icon in the Renting window, if it's open, or use Keyword: **SpringStreet** to open the SpringStreet Web site.

Figure 19-3. Search SpringStreet for that new apartment.

2. Click the Apartment Search link in the orange Find Your Place section on the SpringStreet page.

3. Scroll down the page until you find a search method that appeals to you: search by college or university, search by city and state, or search by intersection.

4. Once you select an option, add the required information in the text fields. You must enter your current ZIP code and then include the other information requested: city, state, or college.

5. Click Search to begin the process. If you selected the college search, the page presents a list of possible colleges (or your college). Click the appropriate link to continue.

6. Next the software asks your intended moving date. Fill it in, and then click to check any additional cities that you might want to search. Click Search Checked Cities to continue.

If no link appears near the bottom of the individual apartment listing, click the apartment name, which appears as a hyperlink, to see any additional information available on that apartment.

To save apartment information to My Places, you need to register with the site. When you attempt to save the first apartment to My Places, a screen prompts you to enter. Scroll down to the text fields and enter your name, e-mail address, and a password.

7. The next screen asks for your preferences: price range, number of bedrooms, and required features. Fill in your requirements and click the Continue Search button.

8. The search results window appears, showing your apartment choices. Each apartment listing includes the apartment's lowest price next to its name; click the Photos, Floorplans, and More Info link to see more details.

9. Once you view the additional information, if you like what you see you can save that listing to a personal apartment portfolio. Click the Save to My Places link near the bottom of the individual apartment's page.

10. Click the Continue button. A Tell Us About Yourself screen appears.

11. Fill in as little or as much information as you like. Only the fields with the orange stars are required by SpringStreet for registration. Click the Join SpringStreet button.

12. Congratulations! SpringStreet creates your account and drops the selected apartment information into it.

Rent Net provides another alternative to apartment locating online (Keyword: **Rent Net**). In addition to apartments, Rent Net offers information on temporary suites, senior housing, and vacation rentals. To begin a search for a Rent Net apartment, click the state you want to live in. Then scroll down the city list, checking those that interest you. Click Search Selected Cities to return a list of apartments in the section you check; click the hyperlinks for each apartment community to see additional information.

Going Your Own Way

House purchasing no longer exists solely as an agented activity. It's also possible to buy a house entirely on your own. If you want to purchase a home without the assistance of a realtor, you'll find plenty of online assistance. This section provides a few links to get you started:

▶ ClassifiedPlus, AOL's classifieds system, lists private homes for sale. Use Keyword: **ClassifiedPlus** to open the main window, and then click the Real Estate link.

▶ For Sale By Owner, or FSBO.com, lists a variety of properties for sale; use www.fsbo.com to open the site (see Figure 19-4). Click the Search for Property button to find a property; select the state, property type, and price range from the drop-down lists. Some properties appear with photos and a few contain links to Web sites that describe the home further.

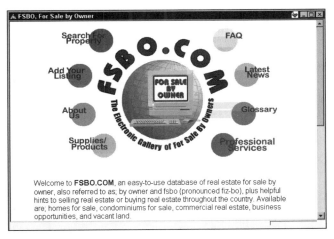

Figure 19-4. Do the work yourself and save a lot with FSBO.com.

Coming Up Next . . .

The kitchen sink drips, the linoleum needs some attention, and your basement is dark and cold. Jump online and get some tips as you join the ranks of do-it-yourselfers. The next chapter leads you to some online areas that you can use as reference points. If you like, you can even find step-by-step tutorials that lead you through more complicated projects, such as replacing windows all by yourself.

CHAPTER

20

DOING THE
DO-IT-YOURSELF THING

Chapter 20

Doing the Do-It-Yourself Thing

Your kitchen faucet leaks, the door to the bathroom squeaks, and your carpet looks like a refugee from the last local flood. Which of these projects should a beginner tackle? Is any home repair job too big for a serious amateur?

Before giving up in despair and picking up the phone, take a deep breath and look at your project list. Some big projects save you time and money in the long run if you hire them out, but using a professional carpenter or plumber for the small stuff ends up costing you more. In addition, calling a professional to complete a job you could do yourself makes the pro unavailable for complicated jobs more suitable to his expertise.

So hop online to find home improvement tips that help you complete the jobs with the least amount of mess and stress. Many people begin with one or two smaller projects, and before they know it, they consider home repair one of their major hobbies. Grab your hammer and join in the fun.

Picking a Doable Project

For a first couple of projects, you'll save frustration and time if you pick a relatively simple job. Although the house may *really* need a new roof job, it's a process that takes several days of sunshine, and it requires that you have the time and the stamina to work day after day on one repair project.

On the other hand, fixing a leaking faucet promises to be a much quicker project. Although you can find yourself more involved than you thought when you first decided to tackle the project, many repair jobs allow you to get in, fix the problem, and get out.

America Online's Home Improvement department leads you to several online resources. Use the links in the main window to visit Learn2.com, where you can read about fixing faucets, replacing windows, and removing wallpaper. Keyword: **Home** opens the main Home & Garden window; click the Home Improvement button to open the Home Improvement window (see Figure 20-1).

Figure 20-1. Check Home Improvement for tips on finishing that repair job.

Caution

One of the options, however, needs to be undertaken with heavy gloves and a lot of caution. Although Repairing a Window isn't impossible, it does require working with broken glass, which can be dangerous.

Tip

Learn2.com offers a lot more than these featured tutorials. In addition to the Home & Garden channel, which also includes information on hiring a contractor, patching wall holes, and weatherizing your home, Learn2.com presents information on a host of other topics. Visit them directly at www.learn2. com and browse through the Automotive, Health & Fitness, or Technology channels, to name a few.

Members could probably complete most of the Learn How To projects in the Home Improvement window after following the links and reading the instructions. These projects include

▶ Lighting a Pilot Light

▶ Painting a Room

▶ Hanging a Picture

▶ Fixing a Running Toilet

▶ Fixing a Leaky Faucet

You can also use the Home Improvement window to estimate the amount of materials you need for that next project. Click the links across the top of the window to estimate the amount of paint, wallpaper, drywall, or tile you'll need to finish that room in style. The links lead to an estimator that helps you determine the correct amount; too much wallpaper and you have enough to make matching origami projects for the next twenty years, while too little requires some *really* creative decorating solutions.

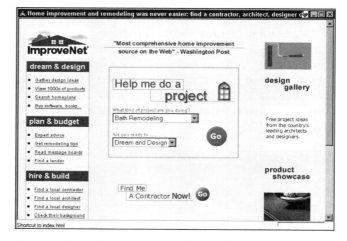

Figure 20-2. Find a contractor with a little help from ImproveNet.

Tips from the Pros

Before you jump headlong into a project, gather a few tips from the people who do whatever kind of work is involved all the time. They often publish time-saving hints, cost-saving measures, and other advice meant to save you a load of time and money. An hour or so spent browsing the Internet prior to beginning a project will streamline your efforts.

If you read the Home Doctor's syndicated column, you'll enjoy the Home Doctor Web site at `http://homedoctor.net/main.html`. This site archives past articles by topic, so look under the department buttons for article links. In addition to the usual home repair topics, this site also discusses allergies, lead hazards, and security.

Bob Vila and Friends to the Rescue

Open the HomeArts window with Keyword: **HomeArts Home**, as shown in Figure 20-3. Then click the Handy Home Advisor button to open the HomeArts Web site and read repair and decorating tips from many different home and lifestyle magazines. Clicking the Shelter button opens a window that includes links to several instructional articles, such as a how-to on stenciling, as well as a link to Make It Easy, Do It Right articles that offer repair advice.

Figure 20-3. Go to the HomeArts Web site for decorating tips.

Use this window to visit the HomeArts Web site. Also look in the Shelter window for tips and tricks from *Bob Vila's American Home* and *Popular Mechanics Homeowners Clinic*. Clicking the Popular Mechanics link opens the Homeowners Clinic, full of instructions for common (and not so common) household repairs. In addition to a searchable home improvement database, the Homeowners Clinic also offers instructions and advice divided into categories:

Find It Online

When you find a project that you don't feel comfortable tackling yourself, check the Net. ImproveNet, a site listing contractors, architects, and designers, can help you find the person to help with that fence installation, electrical repair, or roof checkup (see Figure 20-2). Find them at `www.improvenet.com`.

Find It Online

A few well-chosen Web sites might show you exactly the instructions you need. *Hometime How To*, the TV show, offers a Web site with help for painting, basement redos, home maintenance, and much more. Find them at `www.hometime.com` and browse through the topics for yourself. Visit HomeIdeas (at `www.homeideas.com`), the Web site of *Today's Homeowner Magazine*, to find project articles, free product brochures, and online estimators for fencing length and carpeting cost.

20

Doing the Do-It-Yourself Thing

You can also open the HomeArts.com Web site directly by using www.homearts.com. If you do that, you'll find the Shelter button under the HomeArts Exclusives link along the right side of the screen.

▶ **Solving Problems:** Struggling with rusty water, a rocking toilet, or a cracked house foundation? Turn to this section to help you fix these problems and many more.

▶ **Sweat Equity:** Find out how your own labor can lower costs and still achieve the look you want. From an article on hammer basics to turning that extra bedroom into a home office, this section focuses on projects you can do.

▶ **Appliance Care Tips:** Tune your lawnmower, ensure that your electric furnace is safe, and replace a refrigerator door gasket. This section on appliances covers all this and more.

▶ **Woodworking:** If you love to work with wood, this section offers tool reviews and project ideas. Create a desk for the home office, a Shaker step stool for the kitchen, or a woodworking bench for future projects.

▶ **Bookshelf:** Read reviews of home and garden books. The reviews all contain contact information and e-mail links so you can order the book. You can also order the books directly from Amazon at www.amazon.com and have them shipped to you.

▶ **PM Zone:** Drop into the Zone for current features on home improvement, technology, and cool stuff on the market

Dig into the Encyclopedia

Better Homes & Gardens Online, in addition to the decorating help you'd expect from Better Homes & Gardens, also contains the Home Improvement Encyclopedia, a reference full of repair tips. To get there, use Keyword: **BHG** to visit the Web site, and then click the House & Home department button.

The House & Home department features several articles on home building and decorating in addition to the Home Improvement Encyclopedia. Clicking the Home Improvement Encyclopedia link takes you to that section of the site. There you can select a major topic such as plumbing, wiring, or masonry, and browse the encyclopedia for the instructions you need (see Figure 20-4).

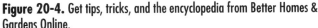

Find It Online

You can also go to the HomeArts main page at www.homearts.com.

Figure 20-4. Get tips, tricks, and the encyclopedia from Better Homes & Gardens Online.

Instructions in the Home Improvement Encyclopedia go beyond general introductions: These projects include step-by-step instructions as well as an occasional video sequence showing you how it's done. Topics tend to be more in-depth than not; turn to the encyclopedia when you need to know how to drill the holes for a door lock or installing showers rather than instructions on the latest painted wall treatment.

Coming Up Next . . .

When your aspirations reach beyond home repair to actual room design and home building, turn to the next chapter for online assistance with floor plans, space utilization, and finding a contractor.

20

Doing the Do-It-Yourself Thing

CHAPTER

21

ALTERING YOUR SPACE

Chapter 21

Altering Your Space

The faucet leaks, but your dreams soar past such mundane things. You'd really like to rip out the entire bathroom, make it twice the original size, and replace that old tub with a garden Jacuzzi creation. Short of a Saturday morning trip to the library and a detailed phone call to your favorite contractor, how do you even start a project like that?

Begin by browsing. You can find floor plans, instruction sets, product reviews, and even contractors online. With the help of one or two really good home improvement Web sites, you're well on your way to some great renovation ideas.

Finding the Perfect Floor Plan

Before you begin a large renovation project, you need to know
what it's supposed to look like when it's done. Start your renovation by finding a floor plan that meets your needs; if you
intend to rip out a set of kitchen cabinets and replace them
with a different configuration, that kind of plan can be created
on graph paper. On the other hand, if you plan to move windows, doors, or walls, your needs become much more detailed.
At the same time, you then need a specific plan to ensure that
studs and window framing appear in the appropriate places.

Other Renovators' Efforts

Sometimes you get the best ideas from looking at what other
changes homeowners have made. If you spend some time looking at completed projects and reading about the processes
involved, you might find an idea that would work great in your
own home. At the very least, a few finished renovations can
put your creative mind in gear and help you see the promise
in your personal space.

For a remodeling project, begin with the ImproveNet Help Me
Do a Project selection boxes, at www.improvenet.com. Select
Remodel/Addition and Dream & Design from the drop-down
lists, and click the Go button to see the Remodeling & Additions
page, shown in Figure 21-1. The section that appears explains
how to open your personal project folder online, and then how
to select ideas and products and save them in the folder for later.

To go directly to the designs, click the Design Gallery text.
ImproveNet categorizes designs by kitchens, bedrooms, living
rooms, baths, and exteriors. For some intriguing renovation
ideas, look in the Living Spaces and Other Spaces sections.
These offer ideas for home theater systems, space-saving
hallways, and more.

ImproveNet designs don't include floor plans to purchase. Instead, they give you the name and address of the original architect. If you like what you see and want to modify the look to fit your own home, you can engage a local architect through ImproveNet.

Figure 21-1. See ImproveNet's renovation photos for ideas.

Home Magazine Online contains photos and articles on kitchens and baths, general remodeling, and show homes. Read about universal design (which makes rooms accessible to everyone), successful renovations, and ergonomics. Keyword: **Homemag** takes you there.

Remodeling Online, at `www.remodeling.hw.net`, focuses on remodeling and renovation. From design ideas to locating a contractor, this site covers it all. Take special notice of the Design section (click the Design button on the navigation bar to open it). Here you can browse through articles detailing major remodeling efforts, before and after transformations, and design ideas for specific rooms, windows, lights, and accessibility. Look in the Design Library (in the Design section) for articles arranged by topic.

Full Home Plans

More Web sites offer home plans than renovation plans. You can browse the available plans, and when you find one you love, purchase it over the Internet. Most of the sites work basically the same: when searching for home plans, you check options that tell what kind of structure you have in mind (Colonial, French, vacation), number of bedrooms, number of bathrooms, and preferred square footage. Then click the Search or Go button and the site returns one or more available home plans.

▶ At eplans.com, click the links that lead to further information on one of the featured plans on the site. Or, search for plans by type, number of bedrooms, and building cost. Use `www.eplans.com` to get there (see Figure 21-2).

▶ ImproveNet offers predrawn home plans, in addition to architects' services. Go to `www.improvenet.com` and click the Search homeplans link to get to the plans. ImproveNet asks you to define the square footage and number of floors in addition to the normal bed and bath count.

▶ Browse through the Better Homes & Gardens Online Home Plans to find that perfect layout. Whether you want a traditional two-story or a compact vacation home, the Online Home Plans search system lets you specify everything but construction cost, including a minimum and maximum width for the house. If you need to place a house on a narrow lot, try looking through the Better Homes & Gardens Online collection of house plans. Keyword: **BHG** opens the Web site.

Figure 21-2. Find that perfect house plan at eplans.com.

Maximizing Your Space

Find It Online

The Closet Lady excels at closet design. Her Web site, at www.closetlady.com, offers a worksheet to help you determine how much stuff you need to pack into one closet. Once you determine that, you can print an order form, and for a fee the Closet Lady designs the space for you. You then find a contractor to install the storage pieces, or you can do it yourself with a trip to a good hardware store.

The Closet Factory Web site, another online resource, offers services in several areas of the country. The Closet Factory designs and installs closet organizers, home offices, pantries, and garage organizers. Find them at www.closet-factory. com, as shown in Figure 21-3.

More stuff fits into space that's organized well. Rather than a huge overhaul, perhaps your best bet is to design a closet organization system, finish part of a basement, or build some shelves. Turn that closet into a compact home office, build storage into under-the-stairs space, or convert the attic into living space. Taking advantage of the space you already have can be a lot less expensive, in the long run, than trying to add more.

Visit Better Homes & Gardens online for a host of space-saving and renovation articles. Keyword: **BHG** opens the site; from there click the House & Home link. Then use the search engine to locate articles on storage, attic and closet design, and more. Better Homes & Gardens Online also offers a good article on closet redesign in their Carpentry section:

1. Use Keyword: **BHG** to open the Better Homes & Gardens Online site.
2. Click the House & Home link to open the home improvement and renovation section.
3. Click the Home Improvement Encyclopedia link. The Encyclopedia page loads.
4. Click the Carpentry button. The carpentry links appear.
5. Click the Cabinets, Countertops, and Shelves link and browse for the Organizing a Bedroom Closet article.

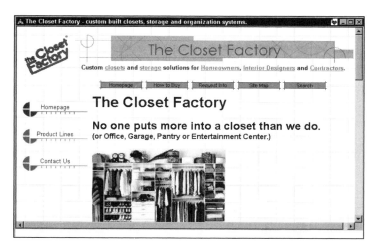

Figure 21-3. The Closet Factory offers custom designed storage solutions.

Locating a Contractor

If you decide that fundamentally altering your living space is too big a job to do by yourself, look for a local contractor. A good contractor will be happy to take the remodel from beginning to end. If you want someone who will install the new framing, or do the framing and drywall while leaving the finish work to you, it should be relatively easy to find a contractor willing to do part of the work as well.

Beginning your hunt for a contractor in the phone book generally proves to be an exercise in frustration. Instead, hop online to ImproveNet and find a contractor in your area who specializes in what you want to do. Each contractor recommended by ImproveNet passes the ImproveNet certification process, which means that the contractor is properly licensed where necessary, carries insurance, has a clear legal record, a clear financial history, and is recommended by his peers and customers.

Open the ImproveNet Web site (at www.improvenet.com), and look in the Hire & Build section to track down a contractor. The site leads you through steps designed to find a contractor who has experience in your particular type of job:

1. Open ImproveNet by typing **www.improvenet.com** into the browser bar, and click the Go button.

2. When the page loads, click the Find a local contractor link. The Find a contractor section loads, as shown in Figure 21-4.

3. At that point, select your upcoming project from the drop-down list and click the Next button.

4. Enter your zip code into the text box that appears, and click the Next button.

5. Check the boxes that provide the contractor with more information: How large is your project? How much work needs to be done? When you've made your best estimates, click the Next button.

6. Next, tell the site what progress (if any) you've made on your own, and when you want the project completed. Click the Next button.

Figure 21-4. ImproveNet helps you locate a contractor in your area.

7. Select your target price range for the project, and click the Next button.

8. Use the Project Details text box to include specifics about your project. If you want a deck constructed from redwood only, you have a basement overhaul in mind, or the new room addition must have a slate roof, these points should be included in your job description for the contractor. When you're satisfied with the description, click the Next button.

9. Fill your name, phone number, and e-mail address into the Registration text boxes, and click Next to continue.

10. Select a time for an initial call from the contractor, and provide your street name and nearest cross street so the contractor can find you. Click Next.

11. The next screen presents the project information you specified, and then asks if the details are complete. If you have no alterations, click the Next button. To change any of the specifications, use the back button on the browser bar.

12. Finally, the site asks if this is what you really want to do. If so, check the boxes that tell what you're willing to do (actually start the project, return contractor phone calls, and answer surveys when the project is done) and then click the Find a Pro to Do My Project Now button.

When ImproveNet receives your request, they fax a copy of your job to several area contractors, who then notify ImproveNet if they want a chance to bid on the job. ImproveNet then e-mails you the names of up to four possible contractors. You talk to them on the phone, meet with them to determine which one you like the best, and hire your contractor. ImproveNet does *not* require that you hire a contractor they send you; however, along with each contractor's information, ImproveNet does let you know how they rank each contractor on quality issues.

Tip

The system is designed to help you find a contractor within two months of your start date. If you specify that your project is two or more months out, ImproveNet offers to take your name and e-mail address and contact you within the two month range.

Coming Up Next . . .

Once you've designed and renovated your personal nest, turn to the next chapter for hints on how to make it glimmer with decorating tips you glean online. From finding decorating trends to where to locate actual project ideas, you'll have plenty of inspiration for how to redecorate your home in no time.

DECORATING YOUR PERSONAL RETREAT

Chapter 22

Decorating Your Personal Retreat

Pillows, pictures, and paint. A little decorating flair and a few well-placed accents go a long way toward making a house or apartment a home. Whether you prefer white walls or warmly painted rooms, the online decorating sites offer hot trends, great tips, and detailed how to's. Many sites even link you to an online store where you can buy the items you need to finish that room right now.

Tracking the Trends

Find the latest decorating trends online — from next season's colors to the furnishings that finish the look. Online sources gives you the decorating insights you need. For decorating forecasts and current styles, take a look at several Web sites that tell you what's coming:

▶ Start with HomeArts.com's Eye on Design section for the latest in furnishings and collectibles. Eye on Design's StyleWatch department contains articles on the latest in furniture and floor coverings, and The Collector highlights a few choice objects that should maintain their value. Drop into Viewpoints to see how some of today's top designers see the world. Keyword: **Homearts Home** opens the HomeArts window; from there click the Eye on Design button to go to the Web site.

▶ Glean ideas from House Beautiful, one of the magazines featured at the HomeArts site. Use `www.homearts.com` to open the main HomeArts window, and then use the Pick a magazine drop-down list at the very bottom of the page to select House Beautiful from the list (see Figure 22-1).

▶ Drop into the Home and Garden TV Web site and print instructions for that trendy painting treatment, or check the upcoming week's schedule. If you missed a show, or want the story from a specific show that aired on HGTV, drop into the HGTV Library and search by topic, episode number, or week of release. Look for the Library in the Designer's Point Town Square village graphic; visit HGTV at `www.hgtv.com`.

Figure 22-1. House Beautiful helps you decorate yours.

Even though magazines still tout the new, the hip, and the unusual, designers also place a lot of emphasis on your personal style. The current hot designer decorating look is useless if you decide you hate it. Knowing what you like and where you feel comfortable is the key to picking the current hot decorating tips that fit your lifestyle as well as your personal style. Take the Better Homes & Gardens Online Decorating Attitude quiz to see where you fall on the contemporary/casual/traditional scale.

To get there, use Keyword: **BGH** to open the Better Homes & Gardens Online site. Then click the House & Home department button and look in the Special Features list for the What's Your Decorating Attitude link, as shown in Figure 22-2.

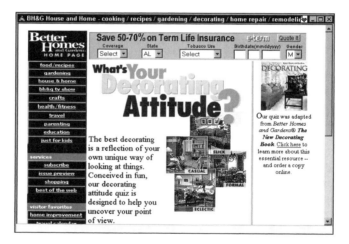

Figure 22-2. So what's your style? Find out by taking this online quiz.

Spiffing Up Your Surroundings

Paint the walls. Rearrange the furniture. Purchase a new accent item or two. Create a desktop water fountain for that bare tabletop. No matter what direction you go, you can decorate a room without breaking your back or destroying your bank account.

Whether you decide to begin from scratch and completely redo the decorating scheme, or you want to add only a touch here and there to finish a look, use online resources to design the furniture layout, order the wallpaper, and answer all your questions. Then sit back, refine your ideas, drink an espresso or two, and wait for the components to arrive.

Start with the Design-A-Room Web site (at `www.designaroom.com`). This unique resource lets you "try things on" by helping you arrange the furniture you already have (or want to purchase). First create the room size, and then select furniture to place into the room. Move the pieces around, rotate them, try different combinations — in short, play with the arrangement until you figure out what might work best for you, without straining your back. Here's how to design your own room:

1. Open the Design-A-Room site (`www.designaroom.com`).

2. In the Room dialog box, give your room a name and enter its dimensions. If you measure a room in any units but feet (such as meters), select the measuring unit from the drop-down list in the Room dialog box.

3. Click the Create Room button. A grid showing your dimensions appears in the browser window.

4. Use the Furniture dialog box to show the dimensions of the furniture you need to fit into the room. If you own somewhat normal furniture, as in bookcases, standard-size beds, coffee table, or chairs, you can use the drop-down list to select the pieces that go into your new room.

   Each piece you select appears in the Furniture Storage box. From there, you click and drag each piece onto the grid and place it where you want.

5. If you own unusual furniture pieces, such as a grand piano or a specially sized couch, use the text boxes in the Furniture dialog box to "design" your furniture piece and then place it onto the room grid.

To create and assemble a few decorative accessories for your décor, visit Christine Dimmick's Home How-To in the Electra forum. Keyword: **Electra** opens the main window; click the Style button to access the Style department, and then click the Home button in the Style window. Home How-To features a wide variety of decorating projects (see Figure 22-3), from lavender pillows to flower boxes to a desktop water fountain. You'll find the decorating projects in the How To Projects section.

Locate various decorating sites by searching the Web. To find sites where you can order wallpaper, for example, type **wallpaper decorating** into the browser bar and click the Search button. Likewise, **paint decorating** gets you paint and decorating sites, and **window decorating** reveals sites on window treatment.

Figure 22-3. Pick up a few decorating ideas in Home How-To.

To get you started, here are a couple of decorator merchant sites:

▶ Leland's offers blinds, wallpaper, stencils, draperies, fabric, and more. If you've been looking for window coverings that resemble etched glass, Luminette sheers, or Nascar borders, you'll find them at Leland's, located at www.lelandswallpaper.com.

▶ Wallpaper Plus sells wallpapers and borders at a discount. They don't stock discontinued patterns, but their online catalog covers everything from traditional to novelty papers. See for yourself at www.wallpaperplus.com.

While you're at it, learn how to complete these projects on-line, too. Hometime, at www.hometime.com, offers instructions for faux finishes, wallpapering, and stenciling. For more in-depth instruction you can order instructional videos and books directly from the site. Also use this area to get names, addresses, and phone numbers for various paint, wallpaper, furniture, and window treatment companies. To reach the instructions, first open the site. Then click the Paint & Decorating button to see the list of article and product links, as shown in Figure 22-4.

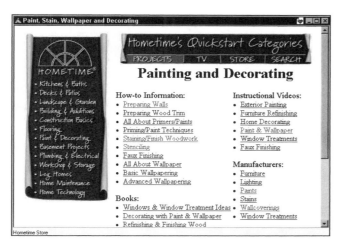

Figure 22-4. Brush up on those painting techniques at Hometime.

To learn how to paint a room, visit Learn2.com at `www.learn2.com`. Click the Home & Garden channel link, and then click the 2torial Index link to see the list of available online tutorials. Paint a Room, Remove Wallpaper, and Varnish a Wood Surface are three tutorials that might interest you here.

Coming Up Next . . .

Turn your attention to the outside, where the trees move in the breeze and flowers grace the walkway. If you have changes in mind for your world's exterior, the next chapter tells you where you can find landscaping help, ideas, and tips. Decide what to plant, get it in the ground, and then keep it green.

22

Decorating Your Personal Retreat

Chapter 23

Landscaping Your World

Your grass looks scraggly, the one lone bush is growing through your back door's screen, and the maple tree sprouted only half its leaves this year. Even the rock garden looks wilted. If this describes your exterior, take heart. Armed with a trowel or two, some pruning shears, and information from the Internet, you'll be an ace gardener in no time.

Whether you want to plant a killer garden, enjoy flowers year round, or preside over a glorious set of window boxes, you'll find enough resources here to make your thumb sprout. Dig in and explore a few sites, and remember to mark the best ones as favorites so you can find them easily later on.

Beautifying Your Surroundings

With a few well-placed bushes and flowers, you can turn your back porch or front yard into a delightful personal retreat. The changes can be simple or lavish, depending on your budget and personal style.

Landscaping is very much a do-as-you-can activity. Although your dream exterior might include a new trilevel deck, an in-ground water fountain, and profusions of flowers, you can take the plan one step at a time and complete a little or a lot. Schedule improvements as you have time, energy, and money, and you'll see gradual but steady changes in your outdoor spaces.

How do you find instructions or assistance for all these changes? Dip into online resources for much of it. Learn what blooms best in various climates from online gardening sites. Pick up a few unusual garden ornaments from an online store that specializes in Japanese gardens. Take a peek at what other gardeners and landscapers have done in their spaces, to spark your imagination.

For general information about landscaping and gardening, take a look at the U.S. Department of Agriculture. Each state operates their own division of the Department of Agriculture called a Cooperative Extension Service. (Cooperative Extension, by the way, is the agency that sponsors 4-H programs in each state.) Developed to help homeowners and farmers with agriculture and homemaking problems, the Cooperative Extensions address questions about food safety, water quality — and landscaping. Visit the Landscaping and Gardening division directly at www.usda.gov/news/garden.htm, or use the main Web address (www.usda.gov) to mouse around and discover all sorts of useful tips for homeowners. From the main USDA window, click the Agencies button to locate the Cooperative Education and Extension Programs division. Figure 23-1 shows the USDA Home Gardening site.

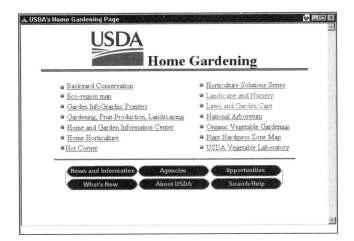

Figure 23-1. Research that landscaping topic.

Use the Home Gardening site to locate articles on creating a landscaping plan, tree and shrub management, and lawn care. These, plus a host of other landscaping topics, are covered through the articles archived in Home Gardening. The window is divided into several links: Home & Garden Information Center; Gardening, Fruit Production, and Landscaping; Landscape and Nursery; and Lawn and Garden Care, to name a few. Each of these links is maintained by a separate state's Cooperative Extension Service; if you need information for your particular area of the country, click the links to identify the service closest to you.

Gardening Sites

Broaden your landscaping search by including online gardening resources as well. Usually encompassing much more than vegetable gardens, the sites offer products such as seeds and tools, online encyclopedias for plant identification, and message boards where visitors can pick up various tips and tricks.

Browse through an online gardening magazine, design that next bed layout, or shop for gardening products at Garden.com (www.garden.com). Registering as a free member entitles you to garden planning access, answers to any landscaping questions you might have, and the opportunity to keep an online garden journal. All told, Garden.com offers home gardeners a plethora of information and services, once

they register with the site. To register with Garden.com, follow these steps:

1. Click the Join here for free button.
2. Fill in your name, address, a member name, and a password. Make sure you enter your e-mail address, too.
   Then click the Continue button.
3. Next, select a level of gardening expertise and a range
   that tells how many hours you garden per week. Check
   your top gardening interests, and then click the Next
   button.
4. Answer a couple of questions about garden plant and
   tool purchases, and click the Next button.
5. The next screen asks why you visited Garden.com and
   if you purchase items over the Internet. Answer the
   questions and click the Next button.
6. Answer a few questions about which magazines you
   read and where you live — or decline to answer them.
   Click the Finish button.
7. Finally, the software asks you how you heard about
   Garden.com and how you found Garden.com. Answer
   the questions, click Next after each one, and the site
   congratulates you on a job well done.

Find It Online

To find more gardening sites,
use the browser bar to
search for **garden** or
gardening.

Exchange seeds and plants, browse through the Garden Web
Directory, and more at Gardenweb. Located at `www.garden-
web.com`, this site reaches gardeners in North America, Europe,
and Australia. Garden Web answers your gardening questions,
provides a place for rose lovers to congregate, and offers a
Bazaar section where Garden Web aficionados can request
gardening-related catalogs from a selection of companies.

Focusing on Landscaping

Whereas gardening takes a micro view of your outside world
and focuses on plant cuttings, compost, growing season, and
similar concerns, landscaping takes a macro view. Once the
plants settle into the ground, what is the overall effect? What
does it all look like? Do the beds look healthy, well-designed,
and inviting?

Landscaping sites offer estimators for figuring out how much
of the various landscaping materials you'll need, bed design

23

Landscaping Your World

Also use the Sierra Home Gardening site to purchase LandDesigner software, which helps you lay out your landscaping projects.

help, and professional assistance to help you install it all if you want that as well.

For example, Sierra Home, the software publisher, offers a nifty site at www.sierrahome.com/sierrahome/gardening, shown in Figure 23-2. In addition to a Landscaping Calculator that helps you estimate the materials cost by area or volume, the site also offers a Home Gardener's Problem Solver and a handy Plant Encyclopedia. As you design flower bed layouts and bushy borders, the Plant Encyclopedia provides information on individual plants. You can also use it to key your choices to a particular flower color, growing zone, or level of required sunlight.

However, you might need to be a bit creative as you use the specific type of plant search. *Pansy* returned no information, but *Heartsease* gave two different matches for *Violas* — rather interesting, since all three are names for the same flower.

Figure 23-2. Sierra Home presents a collection of gardening articles, plus software, online.

About.com, a site known for Guides who develop their areas with passion, contains a Landscaping section. To get there, use www.about.com, and then type **Landscaping** into the search text box and click Search. The first item in the results list, Landscaping GuideSite, is the one you want.

The Landscaping GuideSite (also simply called Landscaping once you get there) links you to sites and articles that discuss edible landscaping, landscape design, decks and patios, and a host of other topics. Browse the NetLinks to find a huge amount of information, and click the Articles link to read past articles on landscape photography, pest control, and online garden catalogs, as shown in Figure 23-3.

Find It Online

To find a landscaping company in your area, type **landscaping** and your state into the browser bar text field, and click the Search button. AOL Search shows you the companies that have a Web page.

Figure 23-3. Use the Web links here to learn about everything from irrigation to weed control.

If you want a few unusual ornaments to lend interest to your landscaping, visit the Cherry Blossom Gardens site (at www.garden-gifts.com) for Japanese-style lawn ornaments, rain chains, benches, and bridges. They offer many other items as well, and you can order directly through the site or print an order form to fill out and mail.

Keeping It Green and Healthy

Once you've got it in the ground, how do you keep it alive? Although this might seem like a straightforward question, a trick or two might be required if you plant a strain that needs lots of tender loving care. Several online sites cover general love and care of plants; in addition to those listed in this section, nearly every site mentioned in this chapter contains some kind of gardening tip forum to help planters keep their investments alive.

23

Landscaping Your World

Bloom, a division of HomeArts, contains a Gardener's Library for reference, stories and tips taken from Rebecca's Garden T.V. show, and articles derived from Country Living Gardener magazine. Ms. Grow-It-All, the HomeArts growing guru, answers questions about wilting flowers, plant care, and proper pruning. Get there by using Keyword: **HomeArts Home**, and then click the Bloom button to open the Web site.

Next, wander through the Virtual Garden (at www.vg.com), as seen in Figure 23-4. Drop by the Gardening Basics section to learn about keeping houseplants pest free, winterizing roses so they'll bloom next year, and mixing your own potting soil. The Landscaping section talks about maintaining healthy lawns as well as general lawn care. For answers to specific questions, first register with the site and then drop into the forums to find out how other gardeners deal with pests, diseases, weeds, water gardening, orchids, and many other topics. Questions about roses, bulbs, or organics? Virtual Garden's forums likely hold the answer.

Figure 23-4. Immerse yourself in the Virtual Garden for healthy plant guidance.

If your idea of healthy landscaping includes fewer homemade concoctions like garlic spray, and more reliance on a select group of well-chosen plant sprays and fertilizers from a commercial maker, visit a site such as Ortho Online. Before telling you which products might enhance your landscaping and lawn, Ortho first discusses watering, fertilizing, disease, and other basic care issues for various types of plants, trees, and shrubs.

Use www.ortho.com to open Ortho Online, and then click the
text in the graphic to navigate through the site. Your choices
include Roses, Flowers, Trees & Shrubs, Vegetables, and Lawn.
Clicking any section heading, such as Flowers, jumps you to
that part of the site. The main part of the screen presents an
introduction to that type of plant; look along the side border
for links to specific portions of a section, such as Perennials
or Bulbs, for further information and links pertaining to
those topics.

Coming Up Next . . .

Delve into the world of shopping online with the next
chapter. When you know you want to purchase something,
whether it's a car, a computer, or a cat, America Online's
Decision Guides take your preferences and presents you with
a list of options, based on your ideas of the perfect purchase.

PART

V

BUYING THE EASY WAY

Chapter 24

Purchasing to Match Your Personality

You want to replace your car but you're not sure whether to look for a new one with a body that sparkles, or a used one with a rebuilt engine that's tried-and-true. Perhaps you need a new computer, but you don't know which features you *really* want. And vacation time is coming. Taking a cruise would be nice, but which one — out of hundreds of possible trips — would you choose?

The world is full of buying choices. Aesthetics, quality, price, and performance all play a part in making you a satisfied customer, but selecting the right addition to your lifestyle can prove to be almost more hassle than it's worth. Take the stress out of buying decisions by using online surveys that guide you to your best selection.

Looking Through the Buyer's Eyes

When you see a new widget that you want, certain things appeal to you. Perhaps you like the color — widget blue — or its streamlined shape makes it look state-of-the-art. Maybe it does its widget duty better than any widget you've ever seen. Whatever its qualities, something makes you want to take that widget home and make it yours.

Now take the same widget and put it next to a thousand others. Some are red. Others are green. A few might even be widget blue with stripes. Most contain up-to-date widget parts, but a few might be constructed of last year's parts — not quite the spiffiest performers you've ever seen, but they carry last year's lower price tags.

Peering at the expanded widget selection, which one do you choose? Add attributes such as size and suitability to the color, shape, and performance/components you noted before and making your choice quickly becomes much more complicated. Enter your online decision helper, the Decision Guides, shown in Figure 24-1. Designed to help you sift through available products, the Guides take what you know you want (or what you know you want to do) and translates your preferences into a list of possible choices. Instead of turning you loose in a bike shop with 400 different bicycles (which actually all look pretty much the same to somebody who knows nothing about bikes), a Decision Guide shows you several bikes that most closely resemble what you think a bicycle should be.

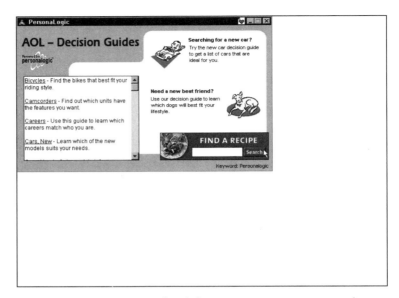

Figure 24-1. Use a Decision Guide to help pinpoint your next important purchase.

Guiding You to the Right Decision

Whether you're in the market for a Porsche or a pooch, AOL offers a Decision Guide to help you with the purchase. Many of the guides show you a list of possible products, and then they allow you to purchase any of the items online. Decision Guides encompass transportation, electronics, vacations, and more.

All the Decision Guides provide information in one of two ways: They work through a series of questions that narrow your expectations for the new product, or they compare one specific model with another to help you decide which one you prefer.

Cars

Car-buying decisions take a lot of time and energy. Selecting a new vehicle versus a used one, or deciding between a car, sport utility van, minivan, van, or truck provides enough brain stimulation without throwing in available options and color choices.

Streamline the selection with New Car Guide or the Used Cars Decision Guides. The New Car Guide, designed to track down the best new vehicle for you, looks at current models only. The Used Car guide finds models from the previous decade.

To search for a new car based on your preferences, follow these steps:

1. Open the Decision Guides window with Keyword: **Personalogic**. The PersonaLogic window opens and presents the main Decision Guides window.
2. Click the Cars, New link in the Decision Guides screen.
3. Click the Q & A button to begin a step-by-step selection process.
4. Check whether you want the current year's cars, next year's models, or both. The guide also asks your preferences on car type, such as sedan, convertible, or wagon. Check those that interest you and click the Next button (see Figure 24-2).

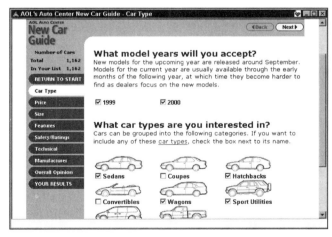

Figure 24-2. Begin your car search by selecting your favorite types of cars.

Tip

Don't know how much you can afford to pay for a car? This screen contains a cost calculator, which is one of the handiest features in the Decision Guides. Fill in the monthly payment you're able to make, add a reasonable percentage rate (after making sure it's currently available!), enter your down payment, then specify the length of the loan. Then click the Calculate button and the system sets the slide marker for you. Although this feature isn't included in the Used Car section, you can always use the calculator first to figure out how much you can afford to pay for a used car, too.

Note

If you use the calculator to determine how much you can afford when buying a used car, keep in mind that loans on used cars sometimes carry higher interest rates than loans on new ones.

24

Purchasing to Match Your Personality

Note

The New Car Guide screen offers a More Detail tab near the bottom of the page. If you know the minimum space in inches that you need for heads, legs, and cargo, click the tab and the site presents sliders you can use to set the vehicle's interior and exterior dimensions.

5. Decide how much you want to pay for the car, and set the cost slider somewhere between $9,000 and $135,000. Click the Next button.

6. Set this screen's slider to show the number of passengers your new car needs to carry, from two to fifteen. If you regularly tote visitors around town, carry the family dog and parakeet everywhere you go, or play chauffeur to your child's three favorite friends, you might want to adjust the passenger number accordingly. By car standards, if you select an auto that carries four people it will carry four people comfortably. No more.

7. Check the number of doors you want your vehicle to have, and then set radio buttons that correspond with your need for more or less head room, leg space, and cargo space. When you're all finished with that, click the Next button.

8. This screen gives you a list of possible features, and then asks you to rate them on a scale from No Opinion to Must Have. Depending on prior selections and preferences, you may find many of the choices marked with black text that reads "All remaining cars offer this," or red text which informs you that "No remaining cars offer this" (see Figure 24-3). Set your preferences for each remaining feature and click the Next button to continue.

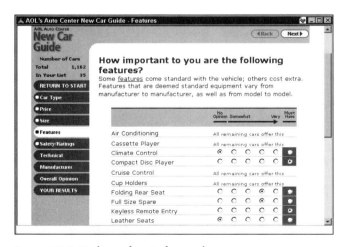

Figure 24-3. Rank your favorite features here.

9. Tell the software your opinion on safety features, such as anti-lock brakes and child safety locks. Then decide which ratings are most important to you — for example, reliability vs. vehicle theft ratings — and set your preferences. Then click the Next button.

10. This screen asks you which technical features you want, such as fuel (diesel or gasoline) and transmission types (automatic or manual). Check any features which appeal to you and click the Next button.

11. Now the guide asks you which car manufacturers interest you. If you will not purchase a car from certain manufacturers, click the Won't Accept radio button and indicate which ones to eliminate.

    As with the features list, your prior answers determine which manufacturers now appear in this list. (Some options may already be marked with No remaining cars are this.)

12. The final opinion screen asks you to rank various features against one another. Set your preferences and click the Next button.

13. Voilà! The Decision Guide offers several choices in this final section. Click the vehicle's hyperlinked name to find out more about it. To compare a car in the results list with another auto, click the Compare With Another Car link. To purchase the car, click the Buy this car button and fill out the purchase information.

14. If you decide to compare one car with another, a screen asks you to select the cars from your results list for comparison. Check any autos to compare them, and click the Next button.

15. The information appears on screen in columns, so you can see how the cars resemble and differ from each other.

If, in your own decision process, you've already narrowed the choice to two or three cars, you can then hop onto AOL and see how they stack against each other. The Compare Cars feature of the New Car Guide allows you to see the cars side by

24

Purchasing to Match Your Personality

Any grave differences, such as comparing completely different car types (minivan versus convertible) or other "red flag" information, as in passenger-seat airbags, appears highlighted so you notice it as you look down the list of features. Look for text underneath the highlighted numbers that explain the differences. In the figure, for example, the text notes that the cost of these two vans differs significantly.

side and compare various features, prices, strengths, and weaknesses. To compare two cars, do the following:

1. Use Keyword: **Personalogic** to open the Decision Guides window.

2. Click the Cars, New link. The New Car Guide introduction screen appears.

3. Click the Compare button to open the Compare Cars section.

4. Select a manufacturer from the list. A list of that manufacturer's vehicles appears.

5. Select a model from the list. That model's information and photo appear in the comparison screen, along with a Choose Another Car link.

6. Click the Choose Another Car link.

7. Select a manufacturer from the list.

8. Select a model from the list. That model's information and photo appear in the comparison screen, along with a Choose Another Car link. To add more cars to the list, click the Choose Another Car link and continue as before. To stop with a two-car comparison, ignore the link (see Figure 24-4).

9. Clicking the car's name link brings up that model's complete write-up — price, features, warranties, and performance.

10. Finally, to remove a car from the comparison list, click the Remove link above the vehicle's photo.

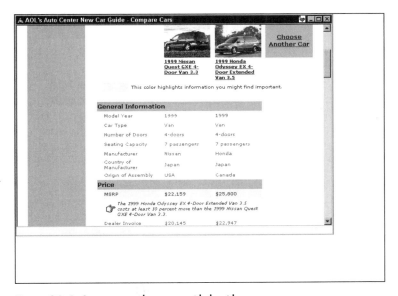

Figure 24-4. Compare two dream cars side by side.

The Decision Guides excel at pinpointing that perfect used car, too. Use the Used Cars Decision Guide to find a car for yourself, compare two or more cars side by side, or browse available used car ads online. You can even offer your own car for sale from this area.

To find a car with the Used Car Decision Guide, follow these steps:

1. Use Keyword: **Personalogic** to open the Decision Guides main window.
2. Click the Used Cars link. The Used Cars section opens.
3. Click the Find the best car for you link. A screen opens, showing car types and a year range.
4. Select the model years in the From and To drop-down lists, and then check any categories that interest you: sedans, convertibles, or hatchbacks, for example. Then select maximum price from a drop-down list. Click the Next button.
5. Select the number of people you want to fit into the car, check the number of doors the car needs to have, and select your preferences for head room, leg room, and exterior size. Click the Next button.

6. Click the radio buttons in the Features list to tell the software how important accessories such as air conditioning, cruise control, and cassette players are to your life (and your car). Click the Next button.

7. Select any technical must-haves, such as front-wheel drive and manual transmission. Then select the minimum and maximum number of cylinders you want (if you care), minimum gas mileage figures, and click the Next button.

8. Click the radio buttons to show your preferences for various manufacturers, and click the Next button.

9. Set your preferences for various features. If driving a car from your favorite manufacturer is more important to you than price or features, this is where you make that known. Click the Next button when you're done.

10. The Decision Guide presents you with a list of possibilities. Depending on your earlier selections, the list may be quite extensive. As with new cars, for more in-depth information on any car in the results list, click the vehicle's name link. To compare it with another car in the list, click the Compare With Another Car link.

Bicycles

Whether you want a mountain bike or a touring work of art, turn to the Bicycles Decision Guide to help you narrow your choices. The Guide also presents you with specific model information when you finish entering all your preferences.

The Bicycles Decision Guide operates much like the car guides, with one distinction. The Guide begins with a section to help you determine which type of bike you want. As with the car guide, you can check one or more of the bike types if you know those styles interest you. Otherwise, the area contains a set of questions about riding surface, length of trip, and riding discomfort. Your answers to these questions automatically select your bike types.

Cruises

Much like the Car Guides Q & A section, the Cruise Decision Guide Q & A section begins by asking where you want to go. Then it asks about your lifestyle — whether you're single, a senior, or would prefer to travel with the kids, for example. As you select your list of preferred cruises, you tell the software how much you're willing to pay for each day of the cruise, which amenities appeal to you the most (such as an indoor pool or a beauty salon), and which cruise lines you prefer.

When you're finished, the Guide presents you with a list of possible cruises, keyed to the names of the ships. Clicking one of the ship's names opens a page with more extensive information about the cruise, as well as a link to the cruise line's Web site.

Pets

Although the Cat and Dog Decision Guides won't link you to a specific breeder at the end of your search, you'll probably feel more prepared to seek the puppy or kitten of your choice. Interested in a more exotic pet? The Pets Decision Guide ranks your appreciation of critters such as ants, ferrets, hermit crabs, and fish.

Each animal's in-depth breed information sheet includes the breed's background, general health, personality traits, height, and average food costs per month. As far as food costs go, ants and hermit crabs are real bargains.

Camcorders

Start your search through the Camcorder Match by selecting the recording format you want, or complete a quick set of questions about resolution and recording time. Once you (or the site) determine which format you want, you continue by selecting features and a target price. After you work through the Decision Guide, it shows you a list of possible camcorders.

Click the model name link to see detailed specifications on any camcorder. The specs page also provides a link to the manufacturer's Web site, where you can research further.

Computers

What kind of computer do you want? What do you want it to do? The Desktops Decision Guide and Laptops Decision Guide steer you to a computer that meets your needs.

24

Purchasing to Match Your Personality

As with the Car Decision Guides, you can work through a step-by-step selection process to discover computers that meet your criteria, or you can directly compare two or more computers with each other. When you find one you like, click the Buy Now button to purchase the computer online.

Coming Up Next . . .

When it comes to the big-ticket items, such as cars and computers, it pays to compare prices and features to ensure that you get the best deal. The next chapter tells how to find on-line reviews, select a vendor, and even specify the features you want for your new purchase.

Chapter 25

Saving Money on Large Purchases

When it comes time to replace that car, computer, or electronics gear — or you want to add to your current collection — use online resources to cut your search time and save money. With your online connection, you can see the variety available, read current reviews, and even purchase the item online.

Looking over the Lineup

DVD. MP3. Digital camera. Convertible. Where do you begin the search to add cool new gizmos to your life? A good place to begin is Shop@AOL, AOL's own shopping channel. Click the Shopping button on the left side of your Welcome screen or use Keyword: Shopping.

Shop@AOL connects you directly to more than 200 retailers, with offerings in more than 16 categories, including some of America's oldest household names. Categories also include the latest Deals & Steals, seasonal displays, and other exclusive deals and specials.

Shop@AOL is essentially a big shopping mall, which includes familiar retailers such as J.C. Penney and Macy's, plus such specialty shops as the Gap, Victoria's Secret, and Eddie Bauer. Mail-order favorites such as Lands' End, Spiegel, and Chef's Catalog are also here.

Here's how to make a purchase at Shop@AOL:

1. Pick a store you'd like to visit — for example, AOL's very own AOL Shop Direct. You'll find it in the A–Z Listing of Stores link in the Shop@AOL window, or by using Keyword: Shop Direct.

2. In the AOL Shop Direct window, click the Books button on the left side. Most stores organize their products into categories like this.

3. Now click the Details button below the featured item displayed on the right side of the window.

4. Read the information carefully in the product detail window, using the scrollbar to move down the document. Price, shipping, tax, and delivery details are usually given at the bottom.

5. If you decide to order the product, click the Order Now button at the bottom of the product detail window.

6. Use the Review Your Shopping Cart/Checkout button if you've already ordered something and you'd like to review it, or when you're ready to complete your order. Use Cancel if you're not interested in this product and want to return to the store.

Tip

Experience the showroom feeling when you visit any of the car makers' Web sites. These corporate sites show you all the new models, features, and colors — complete with compelling ad copy.

Find It Online

Go directly to a manufacturer's Web site by using the company name as a Web address, such as www.astonmartin.com or www.gateway.com.

Even if you click Order Now, you won't actually be purchasing the item until you "checkout." So feel free to order items while you're learning to use the shopping system — just don't checkout unless you're really prepared to buy.

From beginning to end, you're free to check the contents of your shopping cart, add or remove items, or quit shopping altogether without spending a cent or divulging your personal information.

Stores in this area maintain an electronic shopping cart to hold all the items you select. Many stores (including AOL Shop Direct) will retain the contents of your shopping cart even if you leave the store, though this isn't true of all.

7. When you're sure you're ready, click the Checkout button. Now you'll be asked to enter your credit card information (the AOL Store accepts Visa, MasterCard, American Express, and Discover/Novus) and then your delivery information. That's all there is to it! On the other hand, if you have a particular manufacturer in mind, start with the company's Web site to find specifics, including pricing information.

On the other hand, if you want a specific item (a digital camera, for example), try using the item's name as a keyword to open that area online. For example, Keyword: **Digital Camera** opens the Digital Camera window, complete with reviews, articles, and links to online stores.

For computers and computer-related electronics, stop by the C|Net Web site, Keyword: **CNET,** shown in Figure 25-1. Use this site to find a new computer, look into MP3 recording devices, check out the newest in DVD players, and more.

Figure 25-1. Unearth the newest technology at C|Net.com.

To see the latest four-wheel wonders, use Keyword: **Auto Center**, which opens a window with links to online statistics for cars, vans, wagons, sport utility vehicles, and trucks. Selecting a particular model shows you price, sizing, features, and technical information such as number of cylinders and brake configuration.

Selecting from Online Reviews

When choosing between Product A and Product B, it's sometimes nice to find out what somebody else thinks before you plunk down your hard-earned credit card. Reading an online review or two helps clarify the product pros and cons so that you can make the best possible choice for your needs. After all, buyer's remorse is a bad thing, especially with larger purchases. A little research before you buy could allow you to enjoy your purchase to the fullest.

Computers and electronics

Turn to the C|Net Web site for reviews on computers, electronics, printers, software, and more:

1. Keyword: **Computing** opens the AOL Computing channel.

2. Click the button next to any of the C|Net Consumer's Guide Reviews to open the C|Net Buying Guide site. Hardware reviews include desktop PCs, notebooks, printers, cameras, and more. The More button takes you to the full list, including modems, memory, and monitors.

3. When the site opens on screen, select a product category. For a new desktop PC, the listed categories include processor or price. On the other hand, if you're looking for a digital camera or a Webcam, you can browse by either manufacturer or price.

4. Click the link for your desired category. A product list appears, as seen in Figure 25-2.

5. Click any Review link to read a product's review; even here you have several choices. You can read the basic review and glance at the overall rating out of a possible ten, read a full review that covers the product details, or read the opinions of people who actually bought the technology.

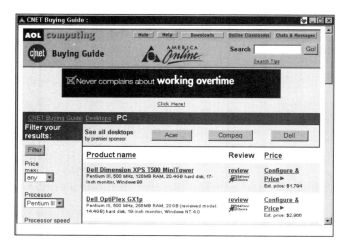

Figure 25-2. C|Net reviews hundreds of products on its Web site.

Cars and trucks

Whether you have your eyes on a new truck, an almost-new Mercedes, or a used convertible, several Web sites feature used car reviews. Gathering their material from various sources, and offering much more comprehensive service to the Web surfer than reviews, these sites deserve a spot on your Favorite Places list if you're in the market for new wheels.

▶ **Autoweb.com:** AutoWeb.com, at www.autoweb.com, gives you a site where you can research that new or used car, visit a virtual showroom, and submit a purchase request, all in one place. For reviews from New Car Test Drive and actual owners and drivers, click the Research tab and then the Car reviews link.

▶ **Cars.com:** Open the site at www.cars.com, click the Reviews button, and select the make, model, and year. From this site you can read a review of the 1998 Ford Explorer or the 1994 Alfa Romeo 164. Click one of the links under Latest Reviews to read about the latest cars on the lot.

▶ **AutoTrader.com:** Read vehicle reviews from Car and Driver, Road and Track, and Consumer Digest. Open the site with www.autotrader.com, and then click the Reviews & Information link to dig into this review gold mine.

▶ **Edmund's:** Drop into the Edmund's Web site, at www.edmunds.com, to identify the best and the worst — and potentially save yourself several thousand dollars on that new car, van, or truck at the same time. This site offers candid reviews of new and used cars, plus an actual cost analysis for each vehicle so you know exactly what you're paying for.

Tip

If you want, you can purchase computers and electronic equipment directly from manufacturers and resellers through the CI Net site.

Finding a Vendor

Especially with electronics and computers, when you find what you want you can generally purchase it directly from the manufacturer. However, you get the same warranty, and sometimes a better price, if you go through a discount dealer such as PC/Mac Connection or PC/Mac Warehouse.

When it comes to new and used car purchases, the easiest way to purchase online might be to work your way through the decision and purchase steps in the New Cars or Used Cars areas online, at Keyword: **New Cars** or **Used Cars**. These areas take you step-by-step through the location, selection, vendor, and insurance process (see Figure 25-3).

Find It Online

For other computing vendors, look for PC or Mac Connection at www.pcconnection.com, or PC or Mac Warehouse at www.pcwarehouse.com.

Figure 25-3. Work through the steps and that new car is yours!

For other online options, though, try one of these Web sites:

▶ **Autobytel:** Autobytel contacts a dealer in your area, who then phones or e-mails you with the lowest price they'll offer for your vehicle. Find them at www.autobytel.com.

▶ **AutoTrader:** Specializing in the used car market, AutoTrader links you with dealers in your area or private individuals who list their car for sale. The AutoTrader new car vendors are managed by Priceline.com. You tell them what you want and the price you're willing to pay, and Priceline contacts you with a vendor.

▶ **Autoweb.com:** When you're ready to buy, use the Autoweb site (`www.autoweb.com`). You tell them what car you want, select any options, choose up to two dealers in your area, and they get back to you with a price.

Comparing Prices

When it comes to the big stuff, fifty dollars off here or a hundred dollars off there can add up to a lot. Find out if you're getting a good price when you comparison shop online.

C|Net (`www.cnet.com`) offers a huge price comparison area. The Compare Prices link leads to a page listing computers and computer components, software, graphics cards, accessories — even service agreement comparisons. To use this area, follow these steps:

1. Open the site by typing **www.cnet.com**.

2. Click the Compare Prices link.

3. Select an item to get comparisons for.

4. You may need to click a link to narrow your search. For example, clicking the Monitors link shows you an assortment of monitor sizes, and you need to select a size to continue.

5. Products are first grouped by manufacturer, and then listed in increasing price order (see Figure 25-4). Clicking any item name in the final list opens a table showing you various prices for that item from different vendors.

6. Browse through the list. To arrange the vendor list by price, click the Re-sort by Price link.

7. When you find a price and a vendor you like, click the Buy Info link. The product's specifications appear, along with some kind of Buy Now button.

8. To purchase the item, click the Buy Now button and fill in your information.

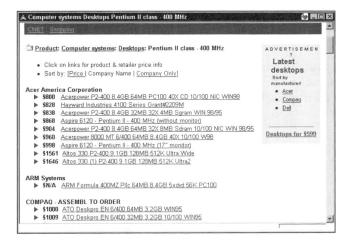

Figure 25-4. Locate the manufacturer and your preferred price.

To see how various vehicles compare in price, use the AOL Decision Guide's New Car Guide or Used Car Guide to compare auto features and prices. Open the online area with Keyword: **Decision Guide**, and then select New Car Guide or Used Car Guide from the list. When you select two or more autos to compare, the software lists them side by side, with all pertinent information on the same line. That way, you can tell at a glance which car is less expensive, offers better features, and so on.

Choosing Your Options

These days, you don't even have to take a preconfigured computer if you have a better idea. Gateway and Dell will both build computers to *your* specifications, which you can order online. (IBM and Compaq offer this option, too, but their personalized computers are available only through resellers like Office Depot or CompUSA.)

If you want a bare bones business machine, you need a computer that handles the latest games, or you have definite ideas about what you do and don't want to see on (or in) your computer, then a customized configuration might be for you. Find out how one of these companies can build the computer of your dreams by visiting Gateway at www.gateway.com or Dell Computer at www.dell.com.

Coming Up Next . . .

What do you give the person who has everything? How do you keep track of the myriad of birthdays, anniversaries, and special days in your life? Turn to the next chapter to find out where in the online world to go in search of that perfect gift.

CHAPTER

26

FINDING THE PERFECT GIFT

Chapter 26

Finding the Perfect Gift

I t's that time again. You wrote it into your planner, but when the date for gift giving arrives, it still comes as a shock. Or maybe you're one of those people who loves to plan ahead — your gifts are purchased, wrapped, and tagged a full six months before the giving date. Regardless of your approach, the giving seasons of life still come like clockwork. And because they generally include the same people, after 17 years or so you tend to run out of ideas.

Refresh your mental inventory of gift ideas with suggestions from online vendors. You can even purchase gifts online — with minimum hassle and using a fraction of the time and gasoline you would spend if you hopped into your car in search of a gift. Best of all, as detailed in this chapter, purchases from AOL Certified Merchants come with a 100 percent satisfaction guarantee. Period.

Certified Shopping

Every merchant mentioned in this chapter, save one, is an AOL Certified Merchant. This means that your shopping experience is guaranteed to be both safe and satisfactory. When you enter your credit card number into the secure shopping carts these stores use, no one else will ever find your number floating around the Web somewhere. The number goes to that merchant only. The store processes your order, bills you, and sends you the merchandise (usually in record time).

If you receive something and for some reason you don't like it, you can always send it back for replacement or refund. Always. Each AOL Certified Merchant offers a return policy. Some request returns within the first 30 days, others request products back within 90 days. A few, like Lands' End, offer a "but I thought it would be a different shade of blue" guarantee — no matter what you don't like or how long you have it before it ceases to satisfy, these vendors replace, exchange, or refund the goods.

Each store puts its own return policy in writing somewhere in its online area. To see the overall AOL shopping guarantee, use Keyword: **Guarantee** to open the AOL Certified Merchant Guarantee area, as seen in Figure 26-1. This area also contains a complete Certified Merchant list; each store's name is linked to the individual store's online area, so you can go directly there.

I've been shopping online for more than seven years and have never had a problem with a merchant or merchandise that I ordered. Of course, it's possible — that's why the guarantee is in place — but sticky situations are relatively rare. Remember, if the merchant provides less than sterling service, he or she probably won't be in business long. Retailers rely on customers for their livelihood.

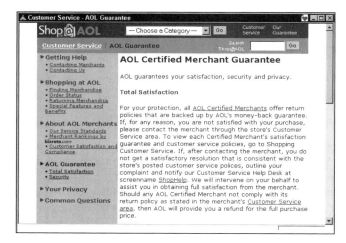

Figure 26-1. AOL certifies your satisfaction in your online shopping experiences.

Double Guarantee Means Double Value

Essentially, AOL gives you a double guarantee on your online purchases. If you shop with one of their Certified Merchants and you experience something less than total satisfaction, you first take it up with the merchant involved. If the vendor fails to satisfy you according to its own written policy, then AOL steps in and works with the vendor to satisfy you. If the merchant still fails to follow through on its own written policies, AOL then refunds your entire purchase price. That's service.

AOL's Certified Merchants include some of the best-known names in retail. FAO Schwartz, Eddie Bauer, and the Disney Store, for example, are legendary for great service, selection, and satisfaction. More than 150 other stores join them to make up the Certified Merchant list that you'll find online.

The Person Who Has Everything

Uncle Harry, the corporate executive, already owns seventeen silk ties in various shades of gray, an indoor golf putting green, and a live cactus collection that decorates his desk. What more could you add to his life?

Plenty! Give him a gift certificate to the establishment of his choice — you don't even need to know what his selection will be when you order the certificate. Browse stores who cater to people who collect gadgets, china plates, or writing instruments, among other things.

A good place to begin your hunt for Harry-esque items is the Gifts Department online, at Keyword: **Gifts**. Every merchant listed in this area is certified by AOL (see Figure 26-2). Although this area contains too many vendors for us to cover each one individually, these selections give you an idea of the breadth of items available:

▶ **Red Envelope Gifts:** Red Envelope Gifts offers bath and gourmet baskets, golf gifts, and home office items. From Grandparents Day to Mother's Day and every day in between, look to Red Envelope Gifts.com for some intriguing items. If your gift needs to get there in a hurry, check the Last Chance Gifts section. These gifts ship overnight.

▶ **Collectibles Today:** Precious Moments, Hummel figurines, and snow globes take their place beside angel collectibles, signed baseballs, and NASCAR memorabilia. From Snow Babies to teddy bears, check Collectibles Today to find a gift for your favorite collector.

▶ **GiftCertificates.com:** Order gift certificates to restaurants, clothing stores, airlines, hotels, and toy establishments — all through one site. Better yet, the GiftCertificates Super Certficate allows the recipient to choose his or her own gift certificate(s) in whatever amount you specify. All you need to send a Super Certificate is your own credit card number and the recipient's e-mail address. Fast, easy, and sure to please.

▶ **Lillian Vernon:** From housewares to personalized gifts, Lillian Vernon has long been known as a mail-order mecca. In their online store, you can select from kids' products, housewarming gifts, or small executive treasures. Search for a product or gift and you can specify the price range. How about a silver-plated certificate holder or a set of translucent envelopes? Get them both from Lillian (use Keyword: **Lillian**).

Cross-Reference

Chapter 25 contains extensive information on how to shop using AOL's own shopping channel, Shop@AOL, at Keyword: **Shopping**. You can also reach AOL's Shop Direct window via the A–Z Listing of Stores in the Shop@AOL window, or by using Keyword: **Shop Direct.**

26

Finding the Perfect Gift

▶ **Personal Creations:** Personal Creations specializes in putting your (or more accurately, the recipient's) name in brass. Or embroidery. Or even emblazoned across a ceramic coffee mug. If the name's the thing, make those of the people on your gift list shine with personalized gifts. Personal Creations offers selections for office dwellers, Irish devotees, and sports lovers in addition to many other categories.

▶ **Hammacher Schlemmer:** Step up and take a look at the extraordinary. Hammacher Schlemmer offers electronic gizmos and executive delights, such as an Electronic Pants Presser. Whether you're in the market for a pop-up playhouse for the kids or a portable DVD player for yourself, turn to Hammacher Schlemmer.

▶ **Gourmet MarketPlace:** Visit the Gourmet Marketplace for international foods, desserts, and gourmet items, as well as classics from Hickory Farms and Mission Orchards. If your taste runs toward baklava or brie, you'll find plenty to choose from.

Figure 26-2. Select your gift from an amazing array of items.

Unless you're one of those tremendously organized people who purchase and wrap all gifts well ahead of time, sooner or later a gift occasion sneaks up on you. When that time hits, browse the Quick Gifts area (Keyword: **Quick Gifts**) and select gifts that arrive within 48 hours. Some vendors, such as Red Envelope Gifts, Hickory Farms, and Beyond.com, do even better than that: Red Envelope Gifts' Quick Gifts ships overnight; Hickory Farms arrives within 24 hours when you specify Rush delivery; and, you can download selections from Beyond.com directly into your computer.

Unearthing the Esoteric

Every now and then someone on your gift list deserves something well out of the ordinary. When the urge hits, browse through the online areas listed here to see if anything fits. Also check the vendors at Keyword: **Gifts**, if you haven't — it's hard to top some of the items offered by merchants such as The Sharper Image or Art.com.

▶ Drop into the WSC Weather Mall to find gifts for the weather afficionado on your list. Whether you have emergency rations or temperature gauges in mind, the Weather Mall offers several items to match your needs. Select from weather books, instruments, videos, and more. Keyword: **WeatherMall**.

▶ The only merchant not specifically listed as an AOL Certified Merchant, 800-Trekker specializes in Star Trek and science fiction products. If you know somebody whose heart thrills at the thought of a pewter alien or Planet of the Apes trading cards, 800-Trekker is the place to visit. Use Keyword: **Trek** to open the online Star Trek Fan Club, and look for 800 Trek in the item list.

Please Remind Me

On your way home from work, you remember that it's your anniversary. Oops. You talk to your mother and recall — after you hang up — that her birthday was yesterday. Uh oh. Once you extricate yourself from these sticky relationship situations, take the steps you need to be prepared the next time. Never forget that important date again with AOL's Free Reminder Service.

The Reminder Service, at Keyword: **Reminder**, sends you an e-mail 14 days before the Big Event so you'll remember in time. If you like, it also reminds you 4 days before the date you specify. Here's how to set up your own Reminder:

Note

Many of the smaller vendors that you find in the various online forums, rather than in the general Shopping channel, do not appear on the AOL Certified Merchant list (Keyword: **Certified Merchant**). However, I purchased from a couple of them in the past and was highly satisfied with the merchandise and service I received.

Tip

If your gift recipient follows an interest or hobby passionately, look to that subject's online area (such as sports or entertainment) for gift ideas.

26

Finding the Perfect Gift

1. Use Keyword: **Reminder** to open the Free Reminder Service window, as seen in Figure 26-3.

Figure 26-3. Use the Reminder Service to jog your memory.

2. Click the Create Your Reminder button. Your personal reminder list appears in its own window. At this point, the window should be empty.

3. The Reminder Service offers two types of reminders for your list: *Personal Reminders* include any date you specify, from your dog's birthday to your great grandparent's anniversary, and *Holiday Reminders* provide a list of recurring gift occasions (such as Valentine's Day) for you to select from. Click the Holiday Reminders button to begin.

4. Enter your first name (or whatever you want the e-mail messages to call you when they appear in your mailbox). The box also asks for your gender and whether you want to receive reminders four days before your special occasion. If you want the extra reminder, click the Yes button.

5. The rest of the window contains various holidays, such as Easter, Mother's Day, Father's Day, and Chanukah. Check any holidays to add them to your Reminder list. Click the Continue button when you're finished, and the service adds those holidays to your Reminder list.

6. Now click the Add Personal Reminder button. The Add a Reminder Here window opens. Fill in the gift recipient's name, the occasion, the date, and check whether it recurs annually. If you want the Reminder Service to offer gift suggestions, check the recipient's age range (child, teen, or adult) and gender. Click the Save button when you finish.

7. When you've finished adding reminders for the main recurring events in your life, click the Quit button to save your results and close the Reminder Service button.

8. A small dialog box appears, thanking you. Click the OK button to make it go away.

To edit your selections later, use Keyword: **Reminder** to reopen the window and click the Edit button. Your Reminder list window appears. Highlight any Reminder that needs your attention and click the Edit button. Change any pertinent information and click the Continue button (for Holiday Reminders) or the Save button (for Personal Reminders).

When you want to delete a Reminder from your list, click the Edit button in the open Free Reminder Service window. Highlight the event you want to delete and click the Remove button. A dialog box appears, asking if you really want to delete the item from your Reminder list. If you have a change of heart, click Cancel. If you're still sure, click OK and that item is no more. But be warned — once you click OK and delete an item from your list, you need to recreate it from scratch to replace it.

People give gifts on many different occasions throughout the year. To be sure that you don't miss any of your important dates, click the Important dates you shouldn't forget button and take a look at that list. In addition to holidays for the current year, this list also suggests adding your anniversary or parent's anniversary, your significant other's birthday, and any upcoming weddings.

Be creative! If you want an e-mail reminder for an annual holiday party you plan (whether it includes gifts or not), include it as an event, and the service will remind you 14 days before it occurs. Maybe you have yearly gift exchanges with work friends. Even if you draw names four days before the event, create a reminder for the date so that you can think about the upcoming exchange.

Coming Up Next . . .

Leaving the subject of online gift giving, the next chapter talks about the world of online auctions, where bidding on items is just as much fun as actually winning the war.

CHAPTER

27

JOINING THE BIDDING WAR
IN ONLINE AUCTIONS

Chapter 27

Joining the Bidding War in Online Auctions

A OL members who drive by estate sales and farm auctions with a longing sigh will find a haven in the online auction world. No matter what you seek, someone offers it for sale on one of the auction sites — or they will soon. Especially in the world of collectibles, the hunt for a rare item provides more than half the fun. Online auctions enable you to hunt for as much or as little as you like.

Much like an auction you attend in person, online auctions consist of offered merchandise (both new and not-so-new) that bidders compete for. Bidders send their bids via the online auction's Web site, and the seller then notifies the winner by e-mail of his or her success.

Before Taking the Plunge

It's easy to get caught up in the whirlwind of an auction — even when you're bidding online. Let's face it: Attending an auction is *fun*, and walking away with a new possession you've won after contesting so hard for it is exhilarating! If you feel like you got a great deal, the feeling is even better.

Sometimes, though, you can "win" at an auction and still feel like you've lost. Perhaps you think you spent too much for an item, or you ended up with something you really didn't need. Online auctions were designed to be enjoyable — here are some tips to keep the spirit fun:

▶ Decide whether you really want anything. If there's nothing you really need, maybe now's a good time to browse, see what items each auction might carry, and save the information for another day.

▶ If you're looking for something unusual, an online auction is a great place to start. It could save you hours of searching and gallons of gas.

▶ Check your mental (or written) list of items to buy. You might stumble upon a fantastic price for computer equipment, electronics, housewares, or one of the other items the auctions specialize in.

▶ Establish a maximum price before you start, and stick to it. How much is the item worth *to you*? If you were to write the price yourself, what sticker would you attach to the offered item? Make that amount your top offer, and you can relax and enjoy the fun knowing that you've already set your own limits.

▶ Read the fine print. When looking for an item to bid on, be sure to read everything listed about that product. Check for warranties (if applicable), shipping costs, and whether the item is new or refurbished.

Be sure to check the Feedback Profile before bidding on a seller's goods; a high number of negative comments from buyers reflect badly on the seller's integrity.

Previewing the Merchandise

Spend some time looking through the offerings before you place a bid. Depending on what you want to buy, and the size of the selection available, browsing the lists could take an hour. On the other hand, you might drop into your favorite category and see the item you want immediately.

Check out the online auctions listed below. Each one carries a varied selection, and none of them really duplicate each other's items.

eBay

An online auction house that allows anyone to buy or sell, eBay offers screen after screen of items, from collectibles and sports memorabilia to books and toys (Keyword: **eBay**). Each seller's name carries a Feedback Profile; this is a "level of satisfaction" score assigned by buyers who deal with the seller, and rate their satisfaction with the seller's goods and performance.

Amazon Auctions

Links for everything from antiques to weddings fill the Amazon.com auction screen (www.auctions.amazon.com). Buyers and sellers meet online to offer and bid on collectibles, electronics, music, and more. Each seller receives a performance rating from the buyers he or she deals with, and the rating is reflected in the number of stars next to the seller's screen name. The more stars listed (up to five), the better the seller's performance rating in the eyes of those who have bought from him before (see Figure 27-1).

Auction Sales

Auction Sales (Keyword: **Auction Sales**) specializes in computers, computer equipment, software, and electronics. Although many bids start at $1 per item, they might require an incremental bid of $25, which means that each time someone places a bid the amount must go up by another $25.

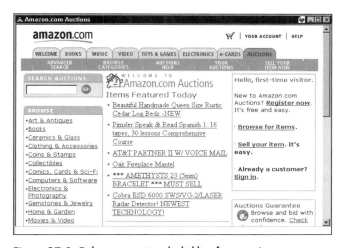

Figure 27-1. Fight your way into the bidding frenzy at Amazon.com

Bid.com

Electronics, cameras, and copiers are all available from Bid.com (Keyword: **Bid.com**), along with an assortment of T-shirts, gifts, and household items. Several of Bid.com's auctions are Dutch auctions, which means the price starts high instead of low. Then, as the minutes and hours tick away in the timed auction, the price falls a little at a time. The bidder who waits the longest gets the best price . . . if any of the items are left.

First Auction

First Auction (Keyword: **First Auction**) offers a wide range of products. From furniture and collectibles to apparel and sports equipment, First Auction covers most general categories. Unlike some of the online auctions that take days to conclude, at First Auction some auctions last 30 minutes from beginning to end, and others last for 48 hours. Quick and efficient.

uBid Online Auction

You can find a little bit of everything at uBid (Keyword: **uBid**). From computers and electronics to sports and jewelry, uBid carries a nice general selection. Many of the computers and

Use your AOL address when you register at the eBay site and you won't need to enter any credit card information to prove who you are.

electronics are refurbished, but a good number seem to be new. The refurbished computer models and add-ons generally carry a warranty, but it might not last as long as the warranty for a new machine.

Placing Your Bid

Before you place your bid, you need to register with the auction house. Registration is free, and required information ranges from name and address to personal information and how you plan to pay.

To register with an online auction as a buyer, follow these steps:

1. Click the Place a Bid or Join Now button on the Web site. Each online auction phrases theirs a bit differently, but you want the registration area. Figure 27-2 shows the eBay registration window.

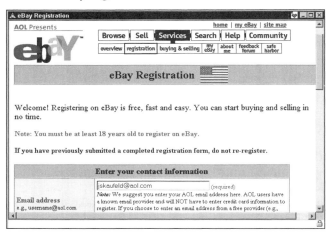

Figure 27-2. Register with eBay, and you'll be buying in no time.

2. The registration area opens, and a screen explains how to sign up for the auction so that you can place a bid. Scroll down the screen until you find the User ID (or E-mail address) text boxes.

3. Enter your e-mail address into the User ID box if the screen asks for it; otherwise, enter a nickname to use at that auction site.

4. If the next text box asks for a password, think of a password at least five characters long. Retype it into a second password text box to verify it.

5. Fill out any other information the site requires, such as full name and address, credit card information, or shopping preferences.

6. Click OK (or Submit or Join) at the bottom of the registration screen to send the registration information to the Web site and process your membership name and password. Figure 27-3 shows a completed registration form for uBid Auctions.

7. Often, the Web site will send you an e-mail with your password or a welcome message as confirmation of your registration.

Tip

As a general rule, only the text boxes with asterisks next to them contain required information. Everything else is optional.

Caution

Sending credit card information over a secure Internet connection is very safe; however, if typing your credit card number into the Web browser still makes you uncomfortable, you might want to deal with online auction houses that take personal checks.

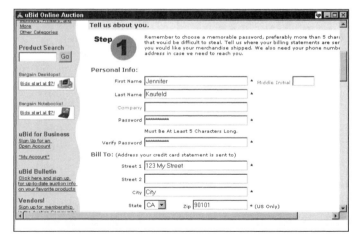

Figure 27-3. Fill in the registration form, and you're ready to shop with uBid.

Each auction Web site works a little differently. On-screen buttons have varying names, for example, and the information below might be entered in a slightly different order, depending on which auction site you're using. In general terms, to place a bid on an item, the steps are as follows:

1. Double-click the item's link. A screen opens explaining more about the item.

Caution

Bidding for an item in an online auction means that you're willing to buy it for that price. If your bid is the highest at the end of the auction, and the seller accepts your offer, you're obligated to pay for the item — including any stated shipping costs. Bid only what you're willing to pay for an item.

2. Scroll through the information until you see a button that says Bid, or something similar. Click the Bid button.

3. Type your bid amount into the Bid (or Maximum Bid) text box.

4. Enter your User ID into the text box requesting the bidder's name.

5. Enter your password. Make sure you type it correctly, or your bid will be rejected and you might have to enter it again.

6. Click the Bid Now (or Submit) button.

Your bid wings its way to the bid bin, where it's compared against other bids received for that item. Sometimes, another person may outbid you while your own bid is still in transit. If that happens, the site informs you that you are not the current high bidder, and you then need to rebid if you still want the item.

Keeping Abreast of the Race

Once you place a bid, the race truly begins. Keeping an eye on your e-mail box becomes a necessity; the Web site notifies you by electronic mail if someone outbids you. Then you race against the clock to place a higher bid via the Web site as the clock counts down the remaining hours (or minutes) left in the auction. When the auction's alloted time expires, the highest bidder wins the lot.

If another bidder tops your offer and you decide you didn't want that cranberry serving dish anyway, you do nothing, and the bidding continues without you. This is where a fixed dollar amount comes in handy; it's easy to bid "just a few dollars more" if you haven't previously decided how much you'll pay for an item.

Coming Up Next . . .

Taking some time off doesn't mean you have to spend your life savings. The next chapter talks about how to save money and time on your next vacation. From booking discount airline reservations to saving on that rental car, you'll find out how to plan a great vacation and still have some money left when you're finished.

P A R T

VI

GOING THERE FROM HERE

CHAPTER

28

SAVING ON VACATION RESERVATIONS

Chapter 28

Saving on Vacation Reservations

IN THIS CHAPTER

Planning your dream vacation

Making online reservations

Diving into adventure travel

Getting away from it all doesn't have to break the bank, and with online reservations the preparations themselves become fun. Whether your idea of a vacation includes camping in a tent, visiting a theme park, or seeing the sights of a major city, this section helps you plan it. If your ideal vacation includes adventure, such as whitewater rafting in California or traveling by elephant in Africa, you can find that in these areas, too.

Planning a Vacation Online

Before you pack your bags, taking some time up front to plan your vacation online will save you a lot of time, and maybe even some money, later on. First, decide where you want to go and what you want to do. Several online areas provide help here; for example, if you'd like to visit a major city, drop into Digital City Travel (Keyword: **Digital City Travel**) to see what the locals say about their own cities. Digital City excels at providing solid city information, from the best places to eat to the neatest things to do, and all their information comes from local residents. When Digital City Travel appears in the browser window, click any city's button on the U.S. map to open that city's area (see Figure 28-1).

Tip

If you're in the mood for an inexpensive yet interesting vacation, click the city nearest you (which might be your home city) and investigate attractions and dining. Then create an itinerary, take a few days, and explore your own city as though you were a tourist. Take the scenic walks, eat in interesting restaurants, and visit the attractions. You'll save on hotel and perhaps some meal expenses (because you return home each night), but more important you'll get a picture of your city that most residents never see.

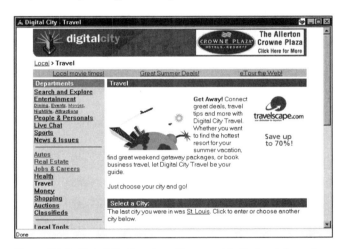

Figure 28-1. Digital City Travel provides a wealth of urban information.

Previewing Travel Destinations

Take a look at what various vacation sites throughout the country (and around the world) have to offer. The Travel channel's Destination Guides window (Keyword: **Destinations**) gives you attraction information, hotel and dining reviews, and local maps for each destination. The guide even tells you the best time to visit.

To select a city from the window, click any of the three drop-down text boxes to reveal its contents. The first text box lists

28

Saving on Vacation Reservations

U.S. cities, the second lists cities in Mexico and the Caribbean, and the third presents international destinations. If you have an idea or two for a vacation destination on your own, type it into the Know your destination text box and click Go.

You might have a grander vacation in mind than one that involves only one or two cities. In that case, click the Worldwide Tourism Info tab in the Destination Guides window and select a destination from the three drop-down lists that now appear: continents, countries, or states. The guides that appear for these areas offer more general information, and allow you to select from a group of cities within that state or country.

Pointing the Way to the Boats and Parks

Say you've narrowed your vacation to a National Park visit or a cruise, but you're not sure where to go from here. Which park? Which cruise? What amenities do you want? How much do you want to spend? AOL's Park Guide and Cruise Guide help you find the answers by asking you a few questions about your expectations. Then the guides suggest several possibilities based on your answers.

To try one of the decision guides, follow these steps:

1. Open the Destination Guides window with Keyword: **Destinations**.

2. Click either the Parks Guide button or the Cruise Guide button, depending on your preference. The guide opens in the browser window.

3. Click the Q & A button to load the decision guide. The first screen asks you about your general preferences, as seen in Figure 28-2.

4. Answer the questions or click the check boxes to mark your preferences, and then click Next for each new screen.

5. When you've answered all the questions, the decision guide presents you with a list of possibilities. Click the park or cruise line's name for more information.

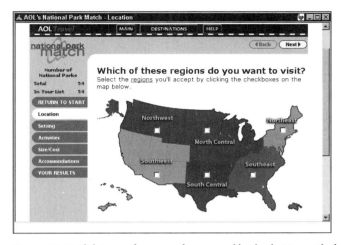

Figure 28-2. Click to specify your preferences and let the decision guide do the rest.

Reserving Air Fares, Hotels, and Autos

Save yourself the headache of phone calls and agency visits when you book your hotel and transportation online. When you make your reservations through an online agency such as Preview Travel, you set up everything from the comfort of home or your office. In addition to hotel and transportation rentals, Preview Travel also books complete vacation and cruise packages for the traveler who wants an all-in-one solution.

Here's how to set up an account with Preview:

1. Use Keyword: **Preview Travel** to open the Preview Travel window online (see Figure 28-3).

2. Click the Air, Car, & Hotel button. The Preview Travel Reservations window opens.

3. Click the Sign In button in the Preview Travel Reservations window. The browser window opens, prominently displaying the Reservations page's New User section.

28

Saving on Vacation Reservations

Figure 28-3. Begin your journeys with Preview Travel.

4. You need to register to use Preview Travel's service. First check the Enter system in the secure mode box, and then click the Join Now button to begin the registration process.

5. You see a message about the security of the information you're about to enter. Click the Continue button.

6. The Create a Preview Travel Account page appears. Enter a user ID, password, your name and e-mail address, and decide if you want a business or leisure account. Business accounts contain space for more information, such as discount codes and a business mailing address.

7. If you want to create a complete travel profile online and store frequent flyer numbers in your profile, check the box next to I would like to store a complete travel profile. Otherwise, leave that box blank.

8. When you're finished filling in the information, click the Create New Account to continue.

9. If you opted for a business account, the page asks you for business information, such as frequent flyer and frequent hotel numbers. Click Create New Account to continue.

10. An Account Confirmation page appears. Look over the personal information, as well as the terms and conditions, and click Accept Terms to finish the account setup.

11. You're done. A screen welcomes you to Preview Travel. From here, click one of the Reserve buttons to begin your reservations.

To reserve a flight, car, or hotel through Preview Travel, do the following:

1. Use Keyword: **Preview Travel** to open the Preview Travel window.

2. Click the Air, Car, & Hotel button. The browser window opens, displaying the Preview Travel Reservations page.

3. Click the Sign In button. The browser window opens with an active Returning User tab.

4. Enter your password and click the Sign In button. The Begin Planning Your Trip page loads.

5. Click the button that corresponds with the kind of reservation you want: Air, Hotel, or Car.

6. The site then asks for travel information: date of departure, date of return, preferred amenities (for hotel), name of rental company and level of car (for auto), and departure and return airport (for plane).

7. Fill in the required information and select from the choices the site gives you. If you like what you see and want to book a reservation, click the red Reserve button to make it so. On the other hand, if you decide you want to change options, click the Start Over button. Start Over takes you right back to the beginning page with the buttons marked Reserve Air, Reserve Hotel, Reserve Car.

Booking travel components individually, although a bit more demanding initially, might save you money in the long run. If you deal with only one airline, one hotel chain, and one rental agency, the process might actually save you time, too.

▶ Visit Continental Airline's online area with Keyword: **Continental.** You can book your flight on Continental directly from this area.

▶ Fly another airline? Check out Northwest Airlines at www.nwa.com, United Airlines at www.ual.com, American Airlines at www.aa.com, or U.S. Airways at www.usair.com.

▶ Reserve your Avis, Budget, or Hertz rental car directly from the rental agency. Keyword: **Car Rental** takes you to the direct rental screen, as seen in Figure 28-4. All three companies offer exclusive AOL discounts.

Tip

Budget flyers might want to check into Southwest Airlines. You can find their Web site at www.south west.com. If you book a flight on Southwest, you'll probably want to arrive at the airport earlier than usual — the airline seats flyers on a first-come, first-served basis.

28

Saving on Vacation Reservations

Tip

Simply planning far enough ahead can save you lots of money. Booking airfare 45 or more days in advance saves you the most. Short of that, reserving your flight 21 days in advance saves a fair amount. If you book less than seven days in advance, you pay premium rates.

▶ Keep your pulse on last minute travel specials with Travel Bargains (Keyword: **Travel Bargains**). From deals designed for students to last-minute airfare wars, Travel Bargains keeps you posted.

▶ Make vacation plans with the whole gang in mind. The Family Travel Network (Keyword: **FTN**) specializes in bargains, interesting destinations, and great travel ideas — all family style.

Figure 28-4. Book your car directly and save.

Stepping Off the Beaten Path

Crossing one more U.S. city off the map each vacation year isn't for everybody. Some families crave adventure. Admittedly, adventure comes in different forms. For one family, excitement might be a trip to that really cool computer museum. Another couple might prefer two weeks in the wilds of Australia.

No matter how you spell adventure, turn to these areas for vacations a little out of the ordinary. Ranging from the educational to the esoteric, the vacations here might make your heart thrill.

The Family Travel Network's Interests & Ideas section (Keyword: **Family Travel Network**) suggests trips to take with toddlers, factory tours, farm vacations, railroad vacations, fall and winter trips, and other family-oriented fun. Definitely multi-generational in scope, this area suggests ideas for trips with grandparents as well as getaways for just mom or dad.

Check into Outdoor Adventures Online, at Keyword: **OAO**, for vacations dedicated to horseback riding, hang gliding, eco tours, motor sports, and snowmobiling. If the desire for international travel runs through your veins, you can learn about traveling in the Himalayas, kayaking in the Caribbean, or hiking through the Lost World of Venezuela.

Coming Up Next . . .

Vacations are a whole lot more fun when you know how to get where you're going. The next chapter tells you how to find and print maps and directions. Whether you want a general overview of an area or you need door-to-door assistance, you can find the map you need online.

Chapter 29

Mapping Your Way Around

Most experienced travelers keep a map collection. The typical stash contains a map from every area they've ever visited, in case they travel there again. The more places they go, the bigger the map stack becomes, until they need one of those heavy-duty rubber bands to keep them all together.

If you're such a traveler, the question then becomes: If the maps aren't arranged alphabetically (which brings up a whole new discussion), how do you find the one you need as you walk out the door on another journey? And equally important, if the map is more than a year old and includes any urban areas, how do you know it's still any good? Most of our cities are changing — especially on the outskirts — as fast as developers can lay out new streets and throw up new housing.

Free yourself from all that bother by charting your course online. With online map software, you can create each map as you need it, and let your computer store all that information for you.

Charting a Trip Online

When you plan a trip to another city, visit the online Maps & Directions area to provide citywide views of your destination. Keyword: **Mapping** opens Maps & Directions in the browser window, as seen in Figure 29-1. For a glimpse of your target city, click the City & Regional Maps tab. Then type the city name into the text field, select the appropriate state from the drop-down list, and click the Create My Map button. For an even more targeted view of a large city, type the ZIP code into the ZIP code text field and click Create My Map. Once the map loads, use the Zoom radio buttons and the directional pan buttons to enlarge the map, show a specific area, or otherwise customize it to your needs (see Figure 29-2 for an example).

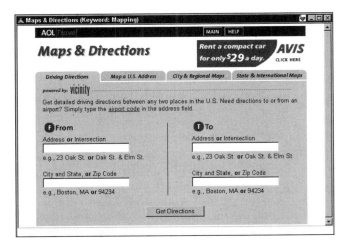

Figure 29-1. Locate that city or address through AOL's Maps & Directions area.

Use the State & International Maps tab to show a state, Canadian province, or country at a glance. In addition to good overall knowledge, such as a quick way to locate cities and towns in relation to each other within a particular state, these maps would be great for elementary school "State of the Month" or "Country of the Month" reports.

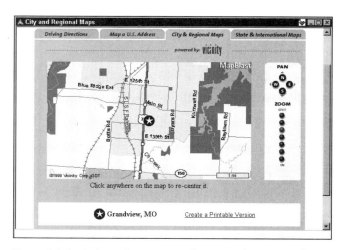

Figure 29-2. Thinking of a visit to Grandview? Use the maps you find here.

Many times, especially with hotel and event reservations, you have an address and a phone number, but no useful directions that tell how to get to that particular spot. When you find yourself with this type of dilemma, use the Maps & Directions area for a targeted address map for virtually any area in the United States.

To obtain a map to a specific destination, click the Map a U.S. Address tab. Enter the address, such as 4500 E. 16th Street, or the intersection, as in 16th St. & Grand St., into the Address or Intersection text field. Then enter the city and state or ZIP code into the City and State or Zip Code text field, and click the Create My Map button. In a matter of seconds, you'll get a detailed map of the area on screen, with a star marking the address. If you need even more (or not quite as much) detail, use the zoom buttons to enlarge or reduce the magnification.

You can find maps of popular international cities under the State & International Maps tab. Select the city from the Cities drop-down list and click the Go button. The site then presents the city map. Popular attractions and necessities, such as hospitals, airports, and universities, appear on the map as well. Note the international city maps are preset; they contain no zoom feature or navigation buttons. Each city map shows the city center and some surrounding areas.

Printing Maps to Your Destination

As with life, planning a trip becomes a lot easier if you know exactly where you're going. With the Maps & Directions area, you can plot a map from your home to your hotel across the country, or chart your final destination by printing a map from your arrival airport to your hotel. In fact, with a little help from the Driving Directions section you can create a map for virtually any trip within the U.S.

To print a map with driving directions, do the following:

1. Use Keyword: **Mapping** to open the Mapping & Directions area into your browser.
2. The Driving Directions tab should be active; if it's not, click the tab to bring the Driving Directions section alive.
3. Enter your departing address (or airport code) into the From text fields. Then type the arriving address, intersection, or airport code into the To text fields.
4. Click Get Directions and watch the area do its stuff. You get both a map and written driving directions, as seen in Figure 29-3.

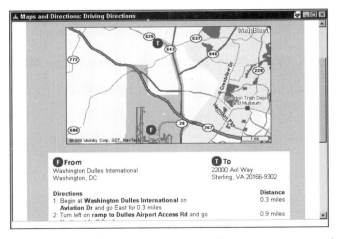

Figure 29-3. Use the Driving Directions to get from your airport to your destination.

Tip

The Driving Directions section also works great if you find yourself giving directions to your home often. Plot a trip from a generally known intersection to your door, and then print the map and carry a couple copies in your planner or purse. Then, when someone wants to know how to get to your home, hand them a preprinted map.

5. To alter the map's instructions, use the links at the bottom of the written directions: Get Turn by Turn Maps divides the map into a collection of small maps showing one turn at a time, whereas Return Route plots the information backwards to get you back to your starting point.

6. To print the map, whichever version you prefer, click the Create Printable Version link. That removes all the background color and extra graphics so the map will print more clearly.

7. Click the Print button on the tool bar to retrieve a paper copy of the map you made.

8. To e-mail the directions to someone, click the E-Mail Directions link at the bottom of the text directions. Enter the receiving person's e-mail address and your own e-mail address into the appropriate text boxes, include any message you want to send with the directions, and click the E-Mail Directions button to send it on its way.

Coming Up Next . . .

Business trips, although they get you out of the office every now and then, sometimes require extra time and effort prior to launch. The next chapter talks about the details of business trip planning, from frequent flyer miles to connecting to AOL while you're away.

Chapter 30

Packing Your Briefcase

On the job used to mean a 9-to-5 work day. Now, the term often applies to flight time, hotel time, and meetings-away-from-home time. If you happen to have a laptop computer, you can connect to AOL while you travel and keep up with online friends and colleagues while you're away. But even if you don't have access to a laptop, AOL offers a lot of business travel information that you can check before hopping on the plane. When you need to hit the road for work, use these online resources to help make the trip as smooth as possible.

Planning a Business Trip

Depending on how far you plan to travel, you might want to consult the current yen exchange rate. On the other hand, you may simply need to book a rental car. Do both online.

International Travel

To help plan international travel, check the Market News Center Currencies window. Keyword: **MNC Currencies** opens the window. This area graphs the daily rise and fall of the Japanese yen, British pound, Swiss franc, and the euro. The window also leads to a currency converter (click Currency Calculator in the item list), which tells you how various world currencies are faring against each other, as seen in Figure 30-1. Select the Home Currency and the New Currency from the drop-down lists, and click the Calculate Currency button.

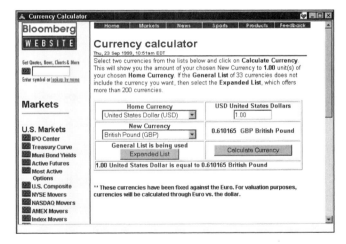

Figure 30-1. Find the exchange rate with the Currency Calculator.

Prepare for a long jaunt by dropping into the International Travel area (Keyword: **Intl Travel**). In addition to general continent-hopping travel tips, the area also contains an Etiquette Tips section for business travelers. In some business cultures, manners can make or break negotiations. Spend a few moments reading the etiquette document for your destination, and you'll be better prepared.

Booking the Trip

Streamline your efforts when planning a business trip, and book your entire trip online through the Business Travel Center, at Keyword: **Business Travel**. Reserve your hotel, keep track of frequent flyer miles, print a travel guide to the destination city, and more — all through one area.

To take advantage of many Business Travel Center resources, such as online reservations, you first need to create a free Preview Travel account. This account keeps track of frequent flyer numbers, preferred hotel chains, and other numbers necessary to the business traveler. If you're not a member, open the Business Travel Center window and then click the Join now link in the area requesting User ID and Password.

The Business Travel Center provides a couple of different reservation options. You can book your hotel, airfare, and car separately or you can book everything at one time using Trip Express. Trip Express is a one-window travel planner for people who simply want to go and return, with as few extra details to worry about as possible. To plan a trip with the Trip Express feature, do the following:

1. Use Keyword: **Business Travel** to open the Business Travel Center, as seen in Figure 30-2. The area opens in the browser window, displaying the Travel Express section.

2. Enter your User ID and Password into the text boxes.

3. Fill in the From and To text boxes with city names or airport codes, and then select travel dates and times. If you prefer a specific airline, be sure to select it from the drop-down Preferred Airline list.

4. If you want a rental car, check Add a rental car and then select any preferred car agency or car type from the drop-down list.

5. To book a hotel room at the same time, check Add a hotel room and then select any preferred hotels.

6. If you want the information to be sent over a secure connection, check Enter system in a secure mode.

7. Click the Continue button. The system leads you through a series of screens that ask you to select from an assortment of outbound and returning flights, hotel options, and auto options.

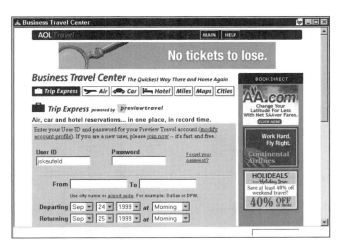

Figure 30-2. Book your business travel arrangements online.

You can also book air, hotel, and car rental reservations one step at a time. First, click the appropriate button at the top of the Business Travel Center browser window. Enter your travel information, and continue from page to page as the system offers selections and refines your reservation choices.

Look in the Business Travel Center for several features that help organize your trips and your life. From a map generator to city sights to see, the Center provides some neat travel assistance.

▶ The Business Travel Center Miles Manager service keeps track of frequent flyer miles. Especially designed for travelers who use several airlines, it automatically keeps track of frequent travel miles from an assortment of carriers. Click the Miles button in the Business Travel Center window to learn the details.

▶ Get driving directions or a city center map from the section located under the Maps button. Get an airport terminal layout, map the location of your hotel, or plot directions from the airport to the hotel.

▶ Create a Custom Mini-Guide for your destination. Click the Cities tab in the Business Travel Center, and then select your destination from one of the drop-down lists: U.S. & Hawaii, Mexico & Caribbean, or International Cities. Check off the items you want included in the Mini-Guide to get started. Depending on choices

Tip

If you prefer a certain carrier, be sure to specify it when you book your airline reservations. Otherwise, the system displays flights for the airline that maintains a hub at any particular airport. Flights arriving in Minneapolis generally offer Northwest Airlines as a carrier, whereas visitors flying to San Francisco see several United options.

30

Packing Your Briefcase

Road warriors who do pack a computer should also take along a 20-foot phone cable so they won't have to sit on top of the phone jack to use the connection. Some hotel rooms offer very little phone wire.

If you carry a Palm Pilot with you when you travel, you can now access your e-mail from your Pilot. Keyword: **Anywhere** tells you more.

available, the site may ask you to select from several subcategories before you read the fascinating features for your city (see Figure 30-3).

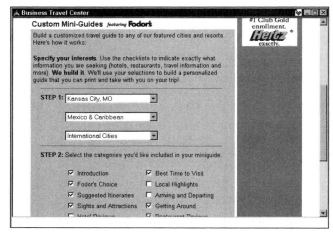

Figure 30-3. Create a Custom Mini-Guide to your next destination.

Connecting on the Road

Your travel schedule needn't hinder your online connectivity. Even if you don't travel with a computer, you can use the guest login feature to sign onto America Online, provided you have access to any computer with AOL software installed. To sign onto AOL as a guest, open the AOL software and then select Guest from the Select Screen Name list. Click Sign On, and the service does its stuff. Then, once the computer connects to America Online, you see a dialog box requesting your screen name and password. Type them in, click OK, and you're online.

If you have access to a computer connected to the Internet, but it doesn't have AOL loaded, you can still check your e-mail. Open the AOL Web site (at www.aol.com), and then click the AOL NetMail link. Once the AOL NetMail page loads, click the Read My AOL Mail Now button. An America Online dialog box appears on the next screen. Enter your screen name and password, and then click the Enter NetMail button.

The next task is to create a new location with AOL access numbers that are local wherever you are. Naming the location with the city name (instead of the very helpful Location 5 that the software recommends) helps you keep the locations straight later.

Whiling Away the Evenings

Bored with pay-per-view movies in the hotel room? If you carry a laptop with you, connect to AOL while on the road and find local amusements as well as online diversions:

▶ Use Moviefone.com (at Keyword: **Moviefone**) to locate movies in the city you're visiting. Select movies by theater, by city area, or by movie title. The system returns movie times, theater locations, and often provides previews you can view with Real Video.

▶ Eschew the local radio stations, download and install Spinner (at `www.spinner.com`) and choose from over 125 music channels, ranging from classical to Celtic. You select 18 favorite music genres to program the Spinner player, and then click the buttons to switch from one music style to another. The style you select then pours out of your computer speakers (see Figure 30-4).

▶ Use the Business Travel Center (Keyword: **Business Travel**) to search for restaurants in the area. First click the Cities button, and then the Restaurant Finder link. Then follow the on-screen instructions to select the city, types of cuisine you want, and price range. Click any hyperlinked restaurant name to read a full review in the list that appears; the site even provides a map, if you like.

▶ Pursue leisure-time interests by typing a subject into the browser bar text field and clicking Search. AOL.com searches both AOL and the Web for your topic and returns a list of possible links. Use the tabs at the top of the AOL Search window to toggle between areas on America Online, various Web sites, and other online resources.

Tip

Once you arrive at the hotel, call the main desk and verify that local access numbers you entered are, in fact, local. Just because a number shares the same area code doesn't make it a local call — especially in large cities. A quick phone call before you sign on could prevent a fight with the checkout clerk later.

30

Packing Your Briefcase

▶ Drop into the Digital City you're visiting for the local spin on entertainment, dining, and news. Keyword: **DCN** opens the Digital City National window; click the button next to the city's name to find out what's hopping in your temporary residence.

Figure 30-4. Listen to your favorite music anytime with Spinner.

Coming Up Next . . .

You don't have to leave home to experience international flavor. The international AOL services (AOL Germany, AOL Australia, AOL Sweden, and so on) deliver a taste of other cultures to your own monitor.

Chapter 31

Cruising AOL Worldwide

You want to travel the world but can't afford a month or two from your schedule to visit Europe. You've always been interested in a foreign country — maybe even learned the language to some extent — and you want to learn more. Or maybe you (or members of your family) hail from a foreign seaport and you want to taste your ancestors' culture without breaking the bank.

No matter what your reason, a romp through AOL's international services can open your eyes to the rest of the world. What currently interests residents of Germany? What are people in the U.K. reading these days? What cultural events would Parisians recommend if you were to visit their city? Find this information, and much more, as you walk the virtual halls of an international AOL service.

The Many Faces of AOL

In countries other than the United States, members know America Online as simply AOL. Thus a visit to the International channel reveals AOL Australia, AOL Austria, AOL France, AOL Germany, AOL Japan, AOL Sweden, AOL Switzerland, and AOL UK.

Although each AOL service looks and feels a little different from each of its international counterparts, they all work basically the same. Generally, the main window features several channel buttons such as News, Weather, or Interests that in turn lead members farther into the service's contents. Sound familiar? Each AOL service definitely projects its own personality, however, and the international services do a great job of capturing the essence of each country's culture. Of course, it helps that the individual services appear in the host country's home language, but it goes further than that — even the screen designs and colors chosen for the various windows mirror popular colors, designs, and trends within that culture. Figure 31-1 shows the main AOL France screen.

Figure 31-1. Click a channel, any channel, to explore AOL France.

Tip

Members can visit every AOL international service directly through America Online, except AOL Japan. Because of the differences between languages and alphabets, your computer needs to have a Japanese version of Windows and special AOL Japan software before you can actually see AOL Japan. For those who don't read and type Japanese, AOL provides translations of news and events from AOL Japan in the Japan cultural area, Keyword: **Japan**.

Visiting Vicariously

When you open one of the international AOL services, you have access to that service's chat rooms, message boards, articles, news, and other features. Simply browsing through the service will teach you a lot about that country, but if you want a concentrated view of local life, see the various areas dedicated to it.

- ▶ In AOL Australia, go to the Lifestyles channel, and then the Metro area, for links to local cities, beaches, and towns.
- ▶ Find out about the best pubs, current theatre, and local sports in AOL UK's Local Life channel.
- ▶ Check out AOL Germany's Lokales channel for city trends and tidbits.
- ▶ Follow French local life in the Pres de Chez Vous channel.
- ▶ Connect to Canadian Digital Cities with AOL Canada's Local channel; keyword **CDN Local** opens the window without going through the International channel.

To open an international AOL service, follow these steps:

1. Click the International channel button or use Keyword: **International** to open the International channel.

2. Look in the lower-left corner of the window for four featured international AOL services. Click one of the buttons to open that service's Terms of Service window, and skip to Step 5.

   To visit one of the services not listed as one of the featured areas, hover the mouse over North America, Europe, Asia, or Australia. Click one of the buttons to open that continent's window.

3. Any AOL services located in the selected continent will appear as buttons on the continent's map, as seen in Figure 31-2. Click any button to open the Terms of Service window for that international AOL service.

Figure 31-2. Click the button on the map to select any European AOL service.

4. The Terms of Service window displays the national flag of the country you're about to virtually visit. Click the flag to connect to the service.

5. Once the AOL service main window opens, you're ready to explore, as seen in Figure 31-3. Click any link or button to activate areas, windows, and Web sites.

Figure 31-3. The AOL Today UK window, ripe for exploration.

While you're visiting another AOL country, spend some time in a chat room or message board listening to the locals. Hearing (or in this case, reading) conversations generally gives you quite a bit of information about people, especially if you're watching people of a different culture interact.

Caution

The general code for behavior in the international areas can be summed up as "When in Rome, do as the Romans do." When you visit an international AOL site, that country's Terms of Service becomes your Terms of Service while you're there. If you act nice and play fair, you'll be fine no matter where you visit.

Tip

It's generally a good idea to watch the conversation awhile in a chat room before jumping in. Most online denizens consider it polite, as well. This is especially true if you communicate across international borders. First get a feel for the flow and topic of the conversation. Then join in the fun.

31

Cruising AOL Worldwide

Coming Up Next . . .

If you've always wanted to learn about one or two particular countries, yet put it off because you never thought you had the time, turn to the next chapter. There you'll find out how to study another culture in depth without ever leaving your computer.

CHAPTER

32

LEARNING ABOUT
A COUNTRY

Chapter 32

Learning About a Country

Statistics, demographics, and economic projections — oh my! Although these provide a good starting point when you research a country, the numbers don't provide a lot of meaningful information unless you're a statistician or you can pop your own country's numbers off the top of your head for comparisons. Demographic numbers look great in a report, but they don't tell you what you really want to know when you learn about a country halfway around the world: how these people resemble you and how they differ.

Thankfully, the online world promises a wealth of information about any country in the universe. By beginning your search

in AOL's International channel, you can save yourself a lot of
Web searching time and still unearth a variety of cultural
resources.

National Flavor in Print

Regardless of which country interests you, a brief foray into
statistics gives an overview of that country's position in the
world. General information tells you about the nation's type of
government, number of children born, average life expectancy,
and imports and exports. Although it won't give you a true
taste of the country, the general information helps to put
everything else you learn into perspective.

To get to any country's general information, do the following:

1. Click the International channel button to open the
   International window.

2. Click the continent's button in the International
   window's world map, as shown in Figure 32-1. The
   window opens for that continent.

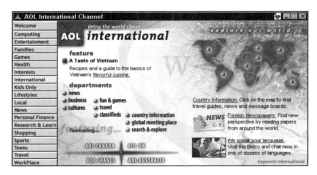

Figure 32-1. Check out a country's information from its continent window.

3. Look in the item list for the target country and double-
   click it. The country's window opens, chock-full of
   national resources.

4. The country's Stats & Info Web link appears near the
   top of the item list in the country's window. Double-
   click Stats & Info to open the Web page. Along with a

Tip

If you're in a hurry and you know exactly which country you want, use that nation's name as a keyword. For example, Keyword: **Botswana** opens the Botswana window.

general map of the country, the site presents information about the country's geography, government, people, economy, communications, transportation, and military.

Beyond the Basics

Many nations (and citizens, for that matter) post "We love our country" sites on the Web. These sites are wonderful — in addition to transmitting a genuine love for the nation, they generally talk about national customs, costume, and consulates. Other sites managed by local museums and universities also often provide interesting tidbits about the country.

Look for these gems in a country's window. The window's item list might contain a Travel & Culture folder, a History Folder, or an Additional Sites of Interest folder. Any of these might contain a link to interesting additional information.

To find cultural sites about your country, type the country name into the browser bar and click the Search button (see Figure 32-2). If you've already read the information in the AOL links that appear when the Web browser opens, click the Rest of the Web tab for Web sites.

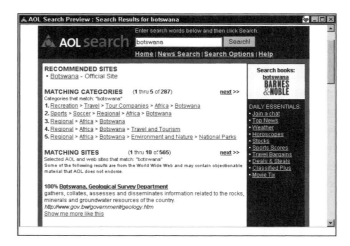

Figure 32-2. These sites put Botswana on the Web.

National News

Read a country's breaking news stories and become current on that country's national happenings. To access news around the world, use Keyword: **Intl News** to open the International News window. Then open the Wire Updates by Country folder and look for your target nation in the list.

AOL also provides links to international newspapers. Read one for yourself when you open a country's national window, either by using that country's name as a keyword or by clicking the world map in the International channel window. Click the Newspapers link to open a window listing various international newspaper Web links. Depending on the size of the country you research, the link might say Local newspapers or Area newspapers; sometimes the country itself offers only a choice or two, so AOL adds other newspaper sites to give you a taste of the area in general.

Tip

Remember that any international newspaper site you open will probably be written in that country's native language. The site might contain an English version link. Then again, it might not.

Add Spice to Your Knowledge

What helps to create the image of the best vacation? The foods you ate, the music you heard, and the people you talked to all play a part in making an experience complete. When you study a country unfamiliar to you, these little extras can help make meaningful differences between the knowledge that resides in your head and the memories that rest in your heart. Spend a little time poking through these sections, and perhaps you'll find the little tidbits that can help make your international study a more complete experience.

Recipes

You know the saying: It's taste that makes the world go round. Jump into cultural study with both feet when you create a meal or two from a different country; along the way you might find a few recipes to throw into your permanent recipe file. With a little research you can create a holiday meal, cook an everyday meal, or use one category (such as desserts) to add sparkle to your regular fare.

32

Learning About a Country

Look for international recipes with Keyword: **GG**. The Global Gourmet window opens, at which point you can double click on the index item in the list box and open other folders until you find your favorite country. Or for an alternative (and perhaps easier) route, open the country's international window. If AOL hosts any recipes from that country, you'll find a Recipes link in the country's window. Short of that, look for a Travel & Culture folder in the window's item list. This folder generally holds a Cuisine folder that links to the Global Gourmet window for that particular country, as shown in Figure 32-3.

Figure 32-3. Cook up a Brazilian storm with these national recipes.

Anthems

National music enhances any cultural occasion, which makes dining to a country's national anthem, while eating indigenous cuisine, an especially fulfilling experience. You can download the anthem from the individual country's online area. Just follow these steps:

1. Use the country's name as a keyword to open the country's window.

2. Click the Sing along link in the country's main window, or look in the item list for a National Anthem link. The National Anthem window opens.

3. Click the Download Now button to begin the anthem download. When the MIDI file finishes downloading, a small player appears on screen.

4. Click the Play button (it looks like an arrow) to begin the anthem.

Chats

Visit a chat hosted in the native language of the country you study, and you might learn a lot about the country's culture as you listen in. America Online offers several different foreign language chats that you can access, depending on what you're looking for.

> ▶ Speak in languages ranging from Arabic to Tagalog in The Bistro's foreign language chats. Keyword: **Bistro** takes you there, as seen in Figure 32-4. Click on any language name to open the window devoted to that language's chat rooms and resources.

Figure 32-4. Pick a language, any language, in The Bistro.

> ▶ Join in conversations south of the border with Hispanic Online. This area, at Keyword: **Hispanic Online**, offers scheduled chats for every country in Central and South America — and Puerto Rico and the Dominican Republic as well. These chats are primarily in Spanish or Portuguese.

> ▶ Visit any of the international AOL services to find chat rooms galore. First open the International channel window, then click the Europe, North America, or Australia button to access a map showing the AOL services for that continent. Click the AOL service button, as in AOL France or AOL Canada, for example, and that AOL service opens.

Message Boards

Each country's individual window contains a button that opens message boards for that country. Here members post questions and replies about travel, culture, politics, and language. Open any individual nation's window by using that country's name as a keyword, and click the Message Boards button to open the country's messages window. International message boards also lurk in other online areas:

▶ Hispanic Online (Keyword: **Hispanic Online**) contains message boards that discuss various Latino issues, as well as Latino countries.

▶ Each language listed on the left in The Bistro offers its own message board. Connect with other members who speak the language with Keyword: **Bistro**.

Coming Up Next . . .

Brush off that high school German and immerse yourself in online foreign languages with a little help from the next chapter. Find out where to locate online tutorials, foreign language chat rooms, and the latest online newspaper printed in your target language.

Chapter 33

Brushing Up a Foreign Language

Y ou haven't spoken a word of Italian since high school. Maybe you're in high school, and want to practice your Japanese. Or perhaps you simply want to explore a new language. Regardless of the reason for your interest, AOL offers plenty of foreign language resources for the beginning, as well as the fluent, speaker.

Building Vocabulary

When toddlers pass the 300-word vocabulary mark, suddenly they're a whole lot more fun to talk to. Granted, they don't ask questions like "Which way to the train station?" but the same could generally be said for foreign language learners. Those who have a reasonably large vocabulary simply have more to say, and can say it without groping for language, than people who are currently functioning beyond the "see Spot run" level.

Downloadable Software

Enhance your basic vocabulary with a few software packages. How about a program that emphasizes holiday words in Spanish? Or maybe an introduction to Russian? AOL contains files to help with French, Spanish, Greek, Japanese, Arabic, Chinese, Vietnamese, Hebrew — you name it, the files are ready and free for the download.

To download language software, follow these steps:

1. Use Keyword: **Download Center** to open the Download Center window. The Shareware tab should be active.

2. Double-click the Education & Reference folder to open it.

3. Double-click the Foreign Languages folder in the Education & Reference window. The Foreign Languages window opens.

4. Double-click the Foreign Language software library entry in the item list. It opens, showing a window full of downloadable software.

5. To see information for any item in the list, double-click it. To download the software into your computer, highlight it and click the Download Now button.

Language dictionaries

Every now and then you get stuck for a word. Maybe it's "windshield wiper" in French — *pare-brise essuie-glace*. Perhaps you need a specific phrase to make a thought complete. When the need for a specific noun or verb arises, turn to the foreign language dictionaries for help.

Use Keyword: **Foreign Language** to open the window, as seen in Figure 33-1. Click the book graphic to open the Dictionaries by Language window, where you can select the language you want to research. Each language lists at least one or two online dictionary resources for that language.

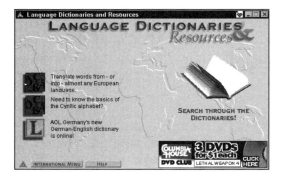

Figure 33-1. Begin here to find that elusive word.

If your target language hails from Europe, click the green button next to Translate words from — or into — almost any European language. This opens the EuroDicAutom, a site that allows you to translate a word or term into any language from Danish to Swedish.

Online Tutorials

Jump online to get a foreign language boost. Several Web sites offer free online language tutorials. You can use these sites to explore a new language, resurrect a half-forgotten language, or keep basic skills current.

> ▶ **Spanish:** Use the more than 50 online lessons at StudySpanish.com to study everything from noun genders to reflexive pronouns. Located at `www.studys spanish.com`, this company also offers a CD version of its free courses.

> ▶ **Japanese:** Over 40 free lessons await you at the Teach Yourself Japanese Web site. This course covers numbers, grammar, some vocabulary, and more (`www.sf. airnet.ne.jp/~ts/japanese/index.html`).

> ▶ **French:** Use the free French Language Course page to increase your written French skills so you can communicate via letter or e-mail. Find it at `www.jumpgate. com/languages/french`.

Reading International News

News articles from around the world can be a lot more interesting if you can read them in their original languages. AOL offers links to many international newspaper sites online, and you can count on their loading into your browser in the country's native language — from Arabic to Urdu.

To visit the international newspapers, use Keyword: **Intl News** to open the International News window, as shown in Figure 33-2. The newspapers reside in the Foreign Newspapers folder. You'll have to open several windows to get to the individual news links. Here's a brief how-to:

1. The area groups several newspaper links under in the scroll box Open any regional folder, such as Central American Newspapers, to see a list of countries within that region.

2. Select an entry, such as Mexican Newspapers, from the list that appears. Open the country's folder.

3. Web links for various newspapers within that country appear in a country's Newspapers window. Double-click any entry to open the browser and load the site.

Figure 33-2. Find foreign newspapers in International News.

Also look to the worldwide AOL services for international news in native languages. Although you can go through the International channel window to open the individual international AOL services, the International News window contains a section that saves a lot of time by providing alternative routes to many foreign sources.

The AOL Foreign News Sources window does not list AOL Sweden. So, if you want to see news from Stockholm you need to go through the International main screen.

With the International News window open, find the AOL's Foreign News Sources link in the item list. Open it, and a handy AOL's Foreign News Sources window appears, with direct links to many of the worldwide AOL news windows.

Spending Time in the Language Chats

Share your opinions on life at the same time you practice a foreign language. Many chat rooms online provide foreign-language chats to anyone who wants to visit. Select a language, drop into the room, and join in the fun.

The Bistro presents most of the international chats on AOL. Part of the International channel, The Bistro offers chat rooms for speakers of Greek, Korean, Japanese, Russian, Dutch, Gaelic, and Hebrew, among many others (see Figure 33-3).

Figure 33-3. Chat in any language in The Bistro.

Open the Bistro window with Keyword: **Bistro**. Click any language along the side of The Bistro main window to reveal the resources for that language. Each resource window offers a chat room for the same language, in addition to other resources, such as links to recipes or the international area of the country where that language is spoken.

To locate any languages not listed along the side of the window, such as Gaelic or Persian, click the Other button. Additional chat room links appear in the item list. These links lead you to individual chat rooms for the various languages.

Also look for foreign language chats in the worldwide AOL services. These foreign AOLs offer many chat rooms in different languages, especially if you access a service whose native language is something other than English. To visit an international service, follow these steps:

1. Click the International channel button along the side of the Welcome/Channels window. The International channel window opens.

2. Click the Europe button on the world map to visit one of the European AOLs, or click the North America button to see AOL Canada.

3. Click the button that corresponds to the international service you want to visit. A Terms of Service window opens.

4. Click the country's flag to access the service. The international AOL service loads, and you see a welcome window or channel window, as shown in Figure 33-4.

Figure 33-4. Drop into the Chat area and shoot the breeze in German.

To practice German and its variants, visit AOL Germany, AOL Switzerland, or AOL Austria. For French, visit AOL France or AOL Canada (click the Français channel).

The People Connection offers a selection of chat rooms for speaking Japanese and a couple for Canadian French and Spanish (AOL Brazil). To find them, do the following:

1. Click the People Connection button on the tool bar, and select Find a Chat from the drop-down list that appears. The Find a Chat window opens on screen, with the created by People Connection tab active.

2. Highlight the Canada, Brazil, or Japan category.

3. Click View Chats. A selection of chat rooms appear in the chat room item list, as seen in Figure 33-5.

4. To visit any of the rooms, double-click its name.

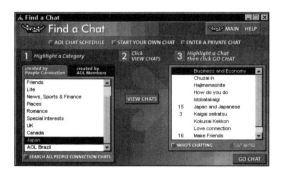

Figure 33-5. In addition to popular chats in English, the People Connection also offers chats in Japanese and French.

Coming Up Next . . .

Increase your general well being with a few resources from the next chapter. Whether you're looking for a few healthy recipes, a place to purchase vitamins and herbs, or a support group with people who've been there, you can find it online.

Chapter 34

Staying Healthy and Fit

Your health. It's one of the most important things you have. When it's good, you can visit interesting places, do exciting things, and enjoy it all. Well, okay — you enjoy most of it. Keep hold of your current healthy lifestyle, and even enhance it, by exploring some of the many online resources dedicated to your health.

From herbal remedies to healthy recipes, look to this chapter for places you can gain information, meet others who live the way you do, and even garner support when you need it.

Eating Healthy

Healthful diet means more than munching rabbit food for the rest of your life. If your idea of healthy cuisine means carrot sticks and raw broccoli, then the online food areas for the health-conscious will open your eyes.

The Dieting and Nutrition area (at Keyword: **Dieting**) leads you to some excellent collections of low-fat and generally healthy meal suggestions online. Click the Nutrition tab to see folders on nutrition and health, kids' nutrition, healthy fast food, and more. As with every other change in your life, healthy eating means making decisions each and every day. Grabbing the carrot sticks soaking in the fridge instead of that half-empty bag of potato chips qualifies as a decision — and a good one, at that. Link-up to several healthy food areas online with Keyword: **Healthy Eating**. Many of the individual forums (especially the women's areas) offer a small health and diet section. And through the Healthy Eating window you can visit them all, without memorizing a host of keywords to get you there (see Figure 34-1).

Look for an amazing number of vegetarian recipes at Veggies Unite, www. vegweb.com.

Prevention's Healthy Ideas site, at www.healthyideas. com, offers recipes, weight loss tools, and more.

34

Staying Healthy and Fit

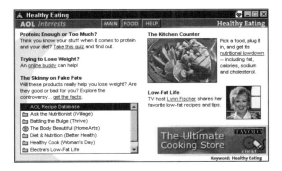

Figure 34-1. Find those hidden health areas through Healthy Eating.

If you want more than introductory information, and if you're looking for meals that steer you toward the healthy side of life, Keyword: **Vegetarian** opens the Vegetarian Resources and Recipes area. Even if you have no intention of becoming a vegetarian, you'll find many ideas here for that occasional (if not several times weekly) meatless meal.

Exercising Well

A healthy balance exists somewhere between *couch potato* and *fitness fanatic*. You can find a way to exercise that lets you move, but doesn't make you feel like you're training to join the Green Bay Packers. Well-chosen exercise helps you to feel better, move more easily, and greet the day with more energy.

Visit the Fitness forum, at Keyword: **Fitness**, to find out about various fitness options. In addition to folders that discuss fitness for children, seniors, men, and women, the Fitness window also offers help for people thinking about bicycling, walking, running, or weightlifting. While you're here, click the Tools tab and work through the Exercise Match to see which exercise really fits what you like to do. In a few screens, it matches your personality with exercises ranging from jump roping (the ultimate solo sport) to rugby.

Thrive Online's Weight area even plans your fitness program for you, if you like two of the nine exercise options it proposes. In addition, this area links you to Web-based exercise assistance, such as planning and sticking with a walking program, hopping on that indoor cycle, and stretching tips. Keyword: **Thrive Weight** opens the window; click the exercise button for the fitness goodies (see Figure 34-2).

Figure 34-2. Weight loss and exercise tips abound at Thrive.

Taking Supplements and Herbals

When good food and exercise don't seem to be enough to bolster energy or drive away that sniffle, many people turn to vitamin supplements and herbal remedies for a little extra boost. Learning which vitamin to take, or which herb to brew into a tasty tea, requires a knowledge base all its own. Accelerate your end of the learning curve by visiting a couple of online information areas designed to point you in the right direction.

AOL's Alternative Medicine forum, at Keyword **Alternative Medicine**, gives you a large collection of herbal facts in one place (see Figure 34-3). Why would you take St. John's Wort? How much Echinacea should you take to boost your immune system? Find the answers to these questions and many more when you click the Herbal Remedies tab and open one of the herbal folders in the list. From Aloe Vera to Valerian, look up those herbs you're curious about here.

Find It Online

Prevention's Healthy Ideas Web site contains some excellent information on herbal remedies and vitamins. Find it at www. healthyideas. com/healing.

34

Staying Healthy and Fit

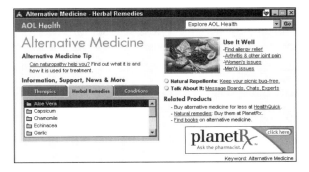

Figure 34-3. Learn about herbal remedies in Alternative Medicine.

If you find an herbal remedy you'd like to try, the Alternative Medicine window also contains a couple of links that open online alternative health stores. Purchase vitamins, herbals in capsule or tablet form, minerals, and other products online.

Find It Online

Track down a dentist close to you with The Accessible Dental Directory, at `http://dentalinks.com`.

Find It Online

Use the Doctor Directory, at `www.doctordirectory.com`, to find a doctor in your area

Find It Online

Looking for a Chiropractor? Try Chiropractic.com, at `www.chiropractic.com`.

Finding a Practitioner

No matter what you try, that ache won't go away. Whether it settles in your tooth, your back, or somewhere else, you might need to see a medical professional. Short of driving up and down the neighborhood looking for the Doc in a Box sign, or thumbing through the Yellow Pages, where do you turn?

Try the AOL Yellow Pages, at Keyword: **Yellow Pages**. Type the kind of practitioner you need into the text box, enter your city, select your state, and click the Find button to see the results. In addition to names, addresses, and phone numbers, the online directory generally offers you a map and driving directions so you can actually get there.

Online Support Groups

Whether you're struggling with an illness yourself or you're concerned about the health of someone you love, AOL offers a whole collection of chats, message boards, and experts versed in every conceivable malady or concern. From cold sores and colic to Chronic Fatigue Syndrome, connect with someone else who understands — whether you do it through a message board or you attend one of the weekly (and sometimes daily) scheduled chats.

Keyword: **Health Talk** opens the Health Talk window, which hosts these support chats and boards (see Figure 34-4). If you read through the message boards and still have questions, click the Experts tab to find an expert in your area of concern. You can ask your question online of a real doctor, and get an answer, even outside office hours. In addition, these sites provide additional information about a whole host of health questions and concerns.

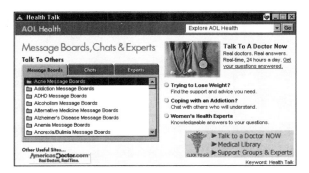

Figure 34-4. Find a support group chat or talk to an expert in Health Talk.

Coming Up Next . . .

Who do you share your home with? If you're thinking of
adopting a furry, fuzzy, or scaly roommate, the next chapter
gives you the pros and cons of pets — whether your idea of
the perfect partner is a lemur or a lynx.

34

Staying Healthy and Fit

Chapter 35

Deciding on a Pet of Your Own

You're ready to share your life with something cuddly and warm. Perhaps it prickles a bit when it's scared, like a hedgehog. Maybe it slithers a little when you let it out of its cage. Regardless of your idea of the perfect pet, use online resources to track it down, purchase a healthy one, and keep it kicking — or jumping, or running, depending on what it does best.

Deciding on Your Perfect Pet

Should you add a dog, cat, or iguana to your life? Each animal brings pros and cons with it — if you're allergic to dog and cat hair, perhaps the iguana becomes the best choice. On the other hand, if temperature-controlled cages leave you cold, then settle for one of the warm fuzzies.

Pet Match Guides

Use America Online's Match Guides to assist with the selection. If you're torn between several types of animals, open the Pet Match window with Keyword: **PL Pets**, a shown in Figure 35-1.. This guide allows you to compare specific pets side by side, or to view a list of potential pets according to your personal preferences. Pets in the database include dogs, cats, ants, mice, ferrets, hedgehogs, and llamas. Find the unique pet that matches you.

Figure 35-1. Reach the Pet Match window with Keyword: **PL Pets**.

If you already know you've narrowed the choices to *a dog* or *a cat*, but you aren't sure which one to give your love, use Keyword: **PL Dogs** or **PL Cats** to open the Dogs (or Cats) Match. These guides, much like the Pet Match, allow you to sort through a list of breeds — large ones, small ones, long-haired ones and short-haired ones. You answer a series of

Tip

If two or more of the breeds you selected show large discrepancies in behavior or needs (one dog requires a huge back yard while the other prefers life as a lap dog, for instance), the software highlights that text in yellow so that you notice it.

questions about your likes and dislikes, and the guide then presents a whole list of possible choices.

To narrow your choices to one or two dogs or cats from a select few, use the Dog Match or Cat Match Compare feature:

1. Use Keyword: **PL Dogs** or Keyword: **PL Cats** to open the correct animal Match window.

2. Click the Compare button. The Compare screen appears, ready for your selections.

3. Select the first letter of the dog's name. A listing appears for that alphabet range.

4. Select the dog's name from the list. Information about that dog fills the screen in a column format, along with a Choose Another Dog (Cat) link.

5. Click the Choose Another link to repeat the process and select another animal from the list.

6. The second animal's statistics appear next to the first listing. See Figure 35-2, which shows the Compare Dogs screen.

7. To add a third animal to the comparison list, click the Choose Another link and select another breed.

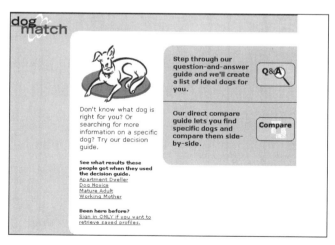

Figure 35-2. Shall we buy a Scottish Deerhound or an Afghan Hound?

Pet Care Resources

Drop into the Pet Care forum to take a look at the best dog, cat, and small mammal breeds, along with various fish and reptile species. First, use Keyword: **Pet Care** to open the Pet Care window, and then click the button that corresponds with the pet you want to learn about. In the animal's main window, look for a Breed Showcase or Species button.

Click the button to open a window full of information about various breeds or types of animals. From raising crickets to calling a Chartreux cat your own, you'll find some good data about each animal in the lists. The Pet Care forum also includes message boards where you can find out what other members like (and perhaps dislike) about various breeds.

Exotic Animals

If the Pet Match guide marks you as an exotic animal lover, you might want to check out the HomeArts Exotic Pets section. Research potential pets such as flying squirrels, sugar gliders, ferrets, prairie dogs, and hedgehogs. Each animal's write-up includes a list of pros and cons for the prospective owner, as well as a list of top ten traits every owner should have for each animal.

Here's how to read about some of these sweeties:

Use diagram to illustrate path.

1. Browse to www.homearts.com. HomeArts opens in the browser window.
2. Click the Family button. The HomeArts Family section opens.
3. Click the Just Pets graphic, and Just Pets blazes to life.
4. Finally, click the Exotic Pet Review text to open the exotic animals section.
5. Click any animal's name to open that critter's description (see Figure 35-3).

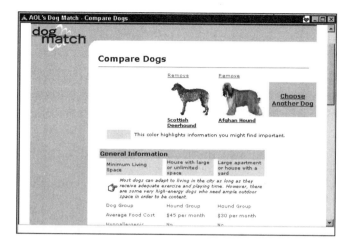

Figure 35-3. Find the exotic animal of your dreams.

Locating Your New Pet

Once you decide whether you want to cuddle a lemur or a Lhasa, how do you find one to call your own? Depending on your choice of a pet, opening the Yellow Pages might not provide a whole lot of choices. Online resources, however, bring you a world's worth of animal breeders right to your computer screen.

Several pet Web sites supply the names and addresses of breeders, in addition to general pet advice. Some of the larger sites include the following:

- ▶ **CyberPet:** Click the Cyber Dog or Cyber Cat to delve into breeder lists, articles, pet products, and Web links. Click the Breeders Showcase button to find a breeder; each breed of cat or dog appears as a link, which then leads to a breeder for that particular type of animal. Visit the CyberPets at www.cyberpet.com.

- ▶ **PlanetPets:** Whether you find yourself wanting a horse, llama, reptile, bird, or another type of companion, PlanetPets, at www.planet-pets.com, offers advice, breeder contact info, products, and some animal history about the pet you love.

▶ **Cat Fanciers:** Join the cat lovers of the world at `www.fanciers.com`, and use the Fanciers Breeder Referral List to locate a breeder for that cat that makes your heart flutter.

▶ **Birds n Ways:** Track down a breeder for that parrot or exotic bird you've always wanted at `www.birdsnways.com`. Birds n Ways specializes in bird stuff — locate clubs, supplies, chats, trainers, and more, all dedicated to the ways of birds (see Figure 35-4).

Tip

If you want to play a part in pet rescues, take a look at the Pet Rescue Clearinghouse at `www.homearts.com`. (Look in the Family section's Just Pets screen for the link.) Pet Rescue Clearinghouse organizes pet rescue organizations by state; click your state's link to find your closest shelter.

Figure 35-4. Locate birds, their supplies, and kindred spirits at Birds n Ways.

Another rescue listing appears at Planet Pets (`www.planet-pets.com`). Click the Pet Rescues button to see the list of rescuing agencies by state.

Adopting an Animal

You've found the perfect finch or ferret, and you even located a breeder. Now, on your way to pick the little critter up, you realize the need for some advance information — and maybe a name idea or two.

If Poopsie and Miss Muff don't appeal to you, turn to the Pet Name Encyclopedia at HomeArts for a comprehensive list of names that go far beyond Fido and Fluffy. Browse through the

35

Deciding on a Pet of Your Own

names yourself at www.homearts.com; use the Family button, and then the Just Pets link, to open the Just Pets window. From there, click the X Marks the Spot graphic to enter the Pet Name Encyclopedia.

Tell the software whether the name goes to a dog, cat, or other animal and whether you want the name to be distinctly male, distinctly female, or you don't really care. Then select the name's beginning letter, if it's important to you, and click any categories you want to pull names from — arts and literature, history, cartoons, science, and so on. When you're finished, click the Find Your Pet Name button to see the list of possibilities that the site recommends. From Beatrix to Darling and Geisha to MacBeth, the site returns plenty of names to choose from (especially if you select more than a couple possible name categories). Happy selecting!

If your new housemate comes without printed instructions — and most of them do — you might want to purchase a pet book or two from sites like Planet Pets or CyberPet. Most of the larger sites sell pet manuals in their products sections. These books give you a basic overview of the breed, along with any personality quirks — such as the American Eskimo's tendency to be skittish around anyone outside the immediate family. Even when an animal's potential behavior doesn't deter you from bringing the animal home, knowing what you're getting into can save headaches later.

As a nod to the "forewarned is forearmed" school of thought, you also might want to check out one or two online vet sites such Veterinary Hospital (go to Keyword: **Pet Care** and then click the Veterinary Hospital button) or NetVet's Electronic Zoo (http://netvet.wustl.edu/e-zoo.htm). Veterinary Hospital, written for animal owners, gives you current articles about animal health in addition to a link to the VetQuest vet search service. Electronic Zoo, which includes resources for vets as well as owners, offers information on the species, health issues, and various related site links for virtually any animal species. Click the Electronic Zoo graphic to begin your adventure (see Figure 35-5).

Figure 35-5. Research any animal under the sun with the Electronic Zoo.

Coming Up Next . . .

Taking your treasured animal's photos out of the box and placing them online makes them available to friends and family. The next chapter tells you how to combine the online world and your pictures for maximum enjoyment by all.

CHAPTER

36

SNAPPING AND SWAPPING
YOUR BEST PHOTOS

Chapter 36

Snapping and Swapping Your Best Photos

Pictures keep us in touch with one another like little else. Phone calls are nice, and e-mail catches us up with the details, but a good snapshot conveys the entire flavor of an event in one moment. With an e-mail account or Web page and access to digitized photos, you can show Grandma your two-year-old dressed up in his or her latest finery or your best live sports shot from summer Little League.

You can jump onto the digital bandwagon in one (or more) of several ways: Put your new pictures online, scan your old pictures onto your hard drive, or join the digital photography revolution.

Setting Up You've Got Pictures

When you sign on to AOL, you see a You've Got Pictures button on the Welcome screen. It looks like a little film canister. That button is your link to sharing your new shots with friends and family via e-mail.

To use the You've Got Pictures feature, you process your film the way you always have, using a photo retailer that participates in the You've Got Pictures program. You drop the photos off and pick up your prints and negatives as usual (or use a mail order firm such as Mystic Color Lab or York Photo — for more details see the front page of the You've Got Pictures area). The difference is that now those pictures also appear in your online You've Got Pictures storage area (Keyword: **Pictures**).

When your pictures hit your account, the You've Got Pictures button changes. Just like the mailbox shows a letter when you have e-mail messages waiting, the film canister shows a photo rolling from it (see Figure 36-1).

Note

If you get your pictures back from the developer and you still don't see the photo in the You've Got Pictures button, open the You've Got Pictures window and click the link under Looking for Pictures. Then enter your Roll ID number and Owner's Key from the claim card inside your prints envelope to see your prints online.

Tip

When holiday and gifting time comes around, order additional prints and photo gifts right from your AOL account.

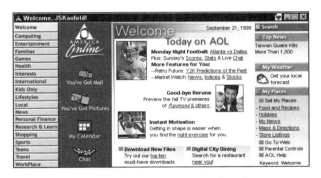

Figure 36-1. You've Got Pictures! Your new online photos await.

Unless you save the pictures, they expire from your account in 30 days. Save them by downloading them to your hard drive or saving them online in the Saved Pictures section. You can save up to 50 prints in your Saved Pictures storage space for free; after that, you can purchase extra space to store your photos. Stored pictures have no expiration date; they're there as long as you want them.

36

Snapping and Swapping Your Photos

Displaying the Best Online

Use the saved pictures in your You've Got Pictures Saved tab to create online photo albums, share individual snapshots with friends via e-mail, or send and receive full photo albums among your online buddies.

Click the My Albums tab, as shown in Figure 36-2, to start creating your own picture masterpieces. Then follow these steps:

1. Click the Saved Pictures tab to start creating your own picture masterpieces. Your saved pictures appear, as seen in Figure 36-2.

2. Select the pictures you want to include in the new album, and then click the Create New Album button.

3. Select a picture and then click the Create Caption button to include a caption for that photo.

4. Type in a caption, and click Next Photo or OK when you're done.

5. Use the Choose Background button to select a background color, and the Rename Album button to give your album a descriptive title.

6. When you've made all the changes you want to the album, click the Save button to make it your own.

Figure 36-2. Use your own pictures to create a great photo album.

When you create an online album, you can jazz it up a little:

- ▶ Select the pictures from your online collection that tell the story best.
- ▶ Create a title for your album, such as *Christmas at Nana's*, *Our New Darling*, or *Home Styles We Love*.
- ▶ Select a background color that brings out the colors in your photos.
- ▶ Write captions for the pictures that give more information — *Sean hated to leave the slopes* tells more than *See Sean ski*.

Tip

When other members send you their online albums, look for them in the Buddy Albums section of your You've Got Pictures area.

Once your album is created, share it with others by clicking the Share button. In just a few moments, your album pages wing their way across the Internet to friends and family, complete with your captions and descriptions.

View your own albums any time you like by clicking the My Albums tab. Then select the album you want to see, and click the View button to open it. Figure 36-3 shows what your hard work will look like.

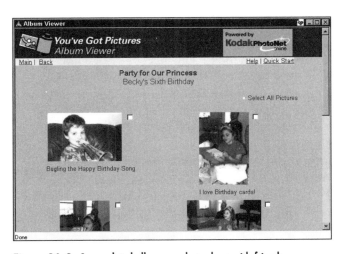

Figure 36-3. A completed album, ready to share with friends

Friends who receive the albums you send can save pictures they like into their Saved Pictures area, incorporate your pictures into an album that they create, and download your pictures into their computers. You can do the same with Buddy Albums you get from friends and family members. And if some-

36

Snapping and Swapping Your Photos

For you frequent flyers out there, digital cameras pass through airport security just like computers. X-rays don't hurt them a bit.

one sends you a picture that you want to frame, you can order prints directly from your Buddy Album page — no more waiting until your friends have the time to send an additional photo order to the processing plant.

Diving into Digital Photography

No more negatives to catalog. No more waiting until the pictures come back from the developer. Have you reached utopia? Not exactly — you just entered the realm of the digital photographer.

Digital photography allows you to take pictures that are stored as electronic images on a disk inside the camera. Then you attach a special cable from the camera to your computer (you find it in the camera box), and upload the images from the camera to your hard drive.

Once the pictures are stored on your computer, you can do any or all of the following with them:

▶ **Print them.** Either use special Kodak photo paper, which makes them look really nice, or print a gray-scale copy on your regular old laser or inkjet printer paper.

▶ **Drop them into documents.** Include a digital photo in your next letter to Grandma. Use one as a backdrop for a special greeting card you create with greeting card software.

▶ **Include them on Web pages.** Design a Web site specifically to show off your vacation pictures to friends and family. Create a page and rotate the pictures so that everyone can keep up with the changes in your life.

▶ **Create scrapbook pages.** Using a layout and design program such as Microsoft Publisher, design pages for that scrapbook you've been working on and print them on nice inkjet paper from your color printer.

In the last couple of years, prices for digital cameras have fallen at the same time that functionality has risen. No longer considered a "techie toy," digital cameras are moving into the mainstream. See the Digital Camera forum at Keyword: **Digital Camera** for further details. There you'll find articles about digital photography, links to some camera reviews, and buttons that lead to Beyond.com and CNet, where you can buy a camera for yourself (see Figure 36-4).

Figure 36-4. Which digital camera fits your lifestyle?

Scanning Precious Photos

One option — and a good way to get all those old pictures online — is to purchase a scanner and upload the images to your hard drive. From there, you can post them to a Web page, send them to friends via e-mail, or even print them in the yearly family newsletter.

The scanner should come with software that helps you manipulate and organize the images; depending on the type of scanner you get, you'll pay anywhere from $80 to $400 to add a scanner to your computer gizmos collection.

To try the whole scanned photo thing, ask about scanning services at your local photo developer. To dive into it with both feet, buy a scanner.

Want to scan some text and other things (like the dog)? Go for a full page scanner.

Find photo and full page scanners online at Keyword: **AOL Shop Direct**, or www.cnet.com.

Coming Up Next . . .

If you rank photography as one of several hobbies, turn to the next chapter for tips on connecting with crafting buddies on AOL and elsewhere on the Internet. Drop into a hobby chat room, locate patterns and instructions online, and join a focused mailing list to keep your enthusiasm high and your fingers busy.

Chapter 37

Crafting with Online Friends

Unless you belong to a quilting guild, sewing circle, or stained glass club, crafting can be a solitary business. Share your passion with others and swap tips, patterns, and ideas through online message boards and chat areas — not to mention an occasional mailing list to add spice and chatter to your mailbox.

Meeting Like-Minded Crafters

Getting to know others who enjoy the same things you do rekindles your crafting interest during the waning seasons. Creative people tend to brainstorm together; gathering with a small group to share ideas, whether it happens in person, in a chat room, on a discussion board, or through a mailing list, helps you over those creative humps and bouts of boredom.

America Online offers discussion boards for quilters and woodcrafters, paper crafters, cross stitchers, and rubber stampers. To drop into the message boards, use Keyword: **Crafts** to open the main Crafts window, and then click any of the subject links to open that specialty's message board, as shown in Figure 37-1.

Figure 37-1. Delve into your favorite craft with the resources here.

The Crafts window also links you to other cool crafting areas throughout America Online. Visit the U.K. Craft Corner for British project ideas and message boards (you can also go there directly with Keyword: **Craft Corner**), or spend a little time in the Moms Online Creative Pursuits area and learn to make colored bubble bath, puzzles, lamps, and much more, with project ideas contributed by other online crafters. Double-click the Arts & Crafts (Moms Online) text to thread your way to the Creative Pursuits window.

To meet and mingle with other crafters, drop into one of the People Connection chat rooms. Located in the Special Interests chat list, People Connection offers these crafty chat rooms for members:

Tip

If you want to know the ins and outs of turning your crafting flair into a business, use Keyword: **CraftBiz** to visit the Crafts Business Forum (see Figure 37-2), which offers weekly scheduled chats, specialized discussion boards for the business of crafting, and a large collection of articles of interest to the business crafter. Learn about pattern copyright, pricing your wares, and business write-offs as they apply to the crafts business.

▶ Crafts Chat

▶ Crafts Crochet

▶ Crafts Fabricrafts

▶ Fiber and Needle Art

▶ Hobby Shop

▶ Needlework Corner

To visit the Quilting chat room, use Keyword: **Quilting** to open the Quilting window, and then click the Quilting Chat button.

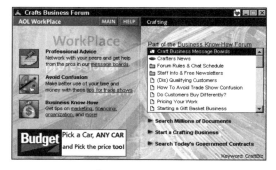

Figure 37-2. Get the scoop on starting your own craft business.

Ranking right behind chat rooms, where members drop in day after day to discuss current projects and ask questions of other crafters, mailing lists offer the next-greatest chance to really get to know other craft and hobby aficionados. When you sign up for a mailing list, messages drop directly into your e-mail box.

Use a couple of the big mailing list search engines to locate a list or two. These lists discuss one or two particular subjects in depth, and members tend to get testy if the topics stray too far from the stated list goals. If you really enjoy lacemaking and woodworking, your best bet is to find two mailing lists (one for each passion) rather than joining one or the other and attempting to "broaden" the other members' horizons.

The Publicly Accessible Mailing Lists database, at www. neosoft.com/internet/paml, archives lists of mailing lists that anyone can join. If you've heard of a list, use the Index to track it down. This also works if you want to browse the mailing lists by subject. On the other hand, if you want to search for a specific list or group of lists, use the Search button. Searching takes a lot longer than browsing the Index. The Index Crafts entry contains links to lists for everything from beadwork to knotwork, and from soap making to wood carving.

ONElist, another searchable mailing list compilation, (at `www.onelist.com`), offers nearly 400 craft mailing lists and over 1,600 hobby mailing lists (see Figure 37-3). Click the Recreation link to see the Crafts and Hobby links. As you browse through the ONElist mailing lists, a few of the lists show *restricted* next to their list names. This means that they aren't open to all; they require some type of qualification and approval before you can join. Sometimes, the qualification is to join another related mailing list offered by the same list moderator. You then express interest in the more restrictive list, and they sign you up.

Tip

Your best bet, when exploring mailing lists for the first time, is to choose one or two to begin with. Some lists inundate your mailbox with new messages several times a day, whereas other lists may send you only a few messages each week. Although your America Online mailbox holds up to 1,000 new messages at a time, you certainly don't want to sit down and read that many each day — even 150 new messages each day gets old very quickly.

Figure 37-3. Tap into ONElist to find that cadre of crafters.

Patterns and Tools Galore

The online world provides one of the best places to track down patterns and project directions. Between craft stores on the Web that offer patterns for sale, craft TV shows that print project directions, and passionate crafters who post their own

Tip

Although PAML and ONElist both archive a huge number of lists, you might stumble across one occasionally that isn't part of the database. Online buddies who share your interests might mention a mailing list or two that sounds interesting. If the list intrigues you, go ahead and sign up — just because it isn't listed in the search engines doesn't lessen its usefulness.

patterns on their Web pages for any fellow craft lovers to freely download and use, the Internet teems with more projects than you could complete in three or four lifetimes.

Craft Stores

If your favorite craft store or craft store chain offers a Web site, you might be able to buy your materials online and save driving time. Plus, it's fun to wander through pages of projects and craft materials.

Your best bet to find online craft stores is to conduct a search for your particular interest. Typing **Craft Supplies**, **Needlework Supplies**, or **Craft Patterns** into the browser bar and then clicking the Search button reveals a hefty number of sites to explore. To save you some time, you might want to try a few of these sites for patterns and materials:

▶ **Craft King:** This catalog company specializes in beads, jewelry, and similar crafts. Find them at `www.xmission.com/~arts/ck/items.html`.

▶ **Grandma T's:** Purchase knit and crochet patterns, yarns, kits, latch hooks, embroidery thread, and other needle craft supplies from `www.grandmats.com`.

▶ **Aunt Annie's Crafts:** Delve into the world of computers and paper crafts with Annie's craft software. Puppets, airplanes, games, flowers, and more paper projects await you at `www.auntannie.com`.

▶ **Fascinating Folds:** Explore paper crafts, from origami to quilling and beyond, at `www.fascinating-folds.com`. This company sells all kinds of papers from all over the world.

▶ **Lark Books:** One of the premier craft book publishers, Lark Books carries instructions for glass bead making, Japanese tamari balls, knitting, sewing, and more. Also look here for Folkwear ethnic and historical clothing patterns, which Lark now publishes. `www.larkbooks.com`.

Looking for a particular designer? Try typing that designer's name into the browser bar text box and using it as a search term. I found knitted doll patterns from a Scottish designer that way, and saved myself the trouble of ordering them from England or Scotland.

TV Shows

When you see a craft show that really interests you, and the instructions flash by a bit fast, turn to some of the show Web sites to unearth the missed, or other equally intriguing, project instructions.

Here are a few Web sites to get you started. If the show you want isn't listed here, use AOL Search to find its Web site:

> ▶ **Home and Garden Television:** Find areas devoted to individual craft shows on HGTV, such as the Carol Duvall Show, Sew Perfect, and Simply Quilts. The address www.hgtv.com opens the site, looking a lot like Figure 37-4.

> ▶ **Aleene's Creative Living:** Aleene provides free instructions for featured projects from the Creative Living show. Use www.aleenes.com/projects/ to open the site, and then click the Free Project Instructions link to see what's available.

> ▶ **Hands On:** Check out these projects, designed especially for kids. From a Paper Crazy Quilt to Milk Carton Birdhouses, these projects involve kids in the joys of creation. See the site at www.crafts4kids.com.

Find It Online

If you want something particular, try searching for it on eBay. Keyword: **eBay** opens the site; then type a term that describes the pattern or tool into the search text box and click the Search button.

Figure 37-4. Explore several craft show offerings through Home and Garden Television.

Crafters' Stashes

▲ Find It Online

Visit Hometown AOL, America Online's member Web page area, for some nifty craft patterns. Use Keyword: **Hometown** to open the site, then click the Hobbies & Interests link. When the Hobbies & Interests area appears, look in the Creative Pursuits section for pages devoted to ceramics, flower arranging, painting, textile & needle arts, woodworking, and other pursuits.

Individual crafters who also happen to be Web denizens often place their own pattern selections on the Internet for other craft lovers to download and use. Although these patterns generally carry the copyright of the designer (most likely the Web page owner), you can download these designs and reproduce them for your personal use and as gifts. Making them to sell, without permission from the designer, is a no-no unless the designs specifically state that they are copyright free — and some of them do.

Begin your foray into downloadable patterns in the Crafts Community window, which you'll find listed in the Crafts window item box. Open the Crafts window with Keyword: **Crafts**, and then double-click the Crafts Community folder to see a list of message boards and libraries for each crafting subject.

The libraries include projects, references, and some instructional material for crochet, knitting, cross stitch, jewelry, miniatures, papercraft, woodworking, and more. Open a library window by double-clicking on it, and then double-click any item to read its description. If you decide you want the pattern, click the Download Now button to bring a copy into your computer. Most of these files are small text files, so they download pretty fast.

To find other pattern sites on the Web, type your specialty into the browser bar text field, as in **Crochet Patterns** or **Knitting Patterns**. When you click the Search button, the Web sites listed all offer some type of pattern on their site. Although some of these patterns are for sale, you can find enough free downloadable patterns to keep you busy for many long winters.

Coming Up Next . . .

Now that you have all the patterns and instructions you'll ever
need for those favorite crafts, turn your eyes to the kitchen.
The next chapter tells you where to download recipes to fill
your file boxes, even if you prefer dessert as a main dish or
want a different ethnic meal every night.

CHAPTER

38

FINDING RECIPES TO ENTICE THE PALATE

Chapter 38

Finding Recipes to Entice the Palate

IN THIS CHAPTER

Locating special cuisines

Finding menus free for the downloading

Choosing recipes for every day

Even the most accomplished cook longs for new recipes every now and then. Whether you star in the kitchen or you consider yourself a stark beginner at meal preparation, this section guides you to some of the best online areas. Turn here when you're stumped for an idea for that next meal, you want a dish or two to make the upcoming holiday really special, or you'd like to prepare a meal that hails from faraway shores.

Serving Your Specialty

What does everyone clamor for when you bring food to festive gatherings? Whether your main dishes melt in the mouth or you make pies that defy description, you'll find plenty to strengthen your strong suit here. These online areas and Web sites contain thousands of recipes. Find a few that tickle your palate and print them out to try the next time the creative urge hits.

Use Keyword: **Food** to open the AOL Food & Recipes window, as shown in Figure 38-1. In addition to timely articles on food preparation and a few starring recipes, the window also contains buttons that open other food areas online.

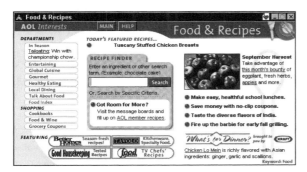

Figure 38-1. Find a new special recipe here.

From here you can visit the Better Homes & Gardens Online Kitchen, which presents seasonal recipes with flair. Read feature articles on topics such as holiday entertaining and planning family reunions, and locate and print recipes from the site. The site even offers a menu planner, which you can use to select the recipes that interest you and then print the recipes, a shopping list, or both. Use the print button on the toolbar to print your selections.

Click the Food Network button to load FoodTV.com into the browser. The Food Network supplies recipes from your favorite TV chefs. Whether you live for Emeril's cooking shows or you love the Two Fat Ladies and their British cuisine, you'll find biographies, show synopses, schedules — and recipes — here.

Several sites scattered around the Web offer excellent recipe collections as well. These sites do a particularly good job of offering a large selection of recipes in almost any conceivable category:

▶ The Recipe Network (www.allrecipes.com) features general recipes of the day, in addition to separate sections devoted to baking, soups, chicken, seafood, pasta, and vegetarian. Each section provides an extensive collection of goodies to try.

▶ Look for kids' favorites, ethnic selections, fast meals, and healthy options (in addition to all the standard categories) at The Recipe Place, www.recipeplace.com. Also take a look at the Submit a Recipe link if you want to contribute one of your favorites to the cause.

▶ Veggies Unite, at www.vegweb.com, contains over 3,000 vegetarian recipes. Turn here for meatless options, help with weekly meal planning, and a glimpse at the Recipe of the Week. The site includes a collection of quick recipes for the vegetarian on the run.

Dishes from Around the World

Spice up your cooking with a few international recipes. Either add one or two new dishes to your repertoire, or jump into the international spirit and create an entire meal from another country. Getting the family (or roommates) into the act with group cooking or homemade decorations adds even more to the fun.

The Global Gourmet, at Keyword: **GG**, lists recipes from Argentina, Austria, West Africa, and many nations in between. Whether you're interested in recipes to explore a culture or you want to trace the tastes of your family's past, begin with the Global Gourmet (see Figure 38-2). Click the Cookbook graphic for a window that groups recipes by country. The Destinations graphic leads to a window offering a short introduction to each country, along with several Web links for additional information and national food glossaries.

Figure 38-2. Tour the world with recipes from Global Gourmet.

If you want to hop on the Web in your international search, try the World from Your Kitchen International area. Here's how to reach International Recipes:

1. Type **www.creative-homeliving.com/World_ Kitchen** into the browser bar text field, and click Go.

2. Once the WYK Recipe Index page loads, scroll to the bottom of the page.

3. Click the International Recipe Links link. The page becomes blank except for a One More Click link.

4. Click the One More Click link.

5. Hurrah — the International Recipe Links page loads, looking a lot like Figure 38-3.

6. Click any continent on the world map to see that continent's recipe list. The site highlights several countries with Cuisine Tours, which offer cultural information in addition to recipe links and cooking Web sites for that country. Scroll down any continent's page to see various recipe and cooking site links for the countries of any continent that don't already have their own Cuisine Tour.

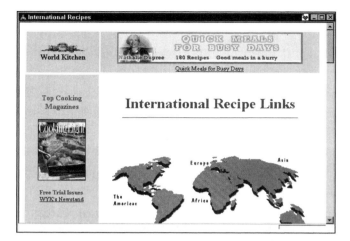

Figure 38-3. Select a continent and browse through international recipes galore.

Holiday Fare

To track down holiday dishes, begin by using the upcoming holiday as a keyword, such as **Christmas**, **Kwanzaa**, or **Passover**. The special holiday windows always contain a button or link to holiday recipes. Often these recipes are family favorites that other members share. Try some of these sites for additional holiday dishes:

▶ Christmas Recipe.com (www.christmasrecipe.com) offers holiday recipes for appetizers, main dishes, desserts — you name it. The site even offers a vegetarian section. For a quick overview of the types of recipes on this site, click the Recipe Roulette link, as shown in Figure 38-4. A Christmas wreath appears. Each time you click the wreath, a different recipe link hops to the screen. You could use this site to find foods for many different holidays; it's definitely not limited to Christmas.

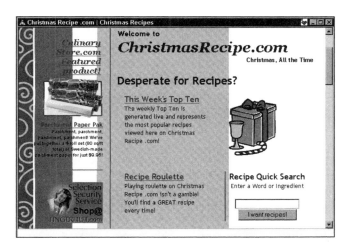

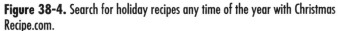

Note

Visit Keyword: **Kwanzaa** for traditional African American holiday recipes.

Figure 38-4. Search for holiday recipes any time of the year with Christmas Recipe.com.

▶ Visit Holiday Living from World in Your Kitchen and browse a huge number of holiday recipes gleaned from around the Web (www.creative-homeliving.com/ World_Kitchen/holidayliving/holidayliving. stm). Here you can browse through recipe collections for St. Patrick's Day, Cinco de Mayo, Guy Fawkes Night, and Canada Day, plus the holidays you expect to see. In addition to the recipe collections, this site offers ideas to help you celebrate each holiday in style.

Daily Dinner Help

If you're like me, dinnertime comes as a shock each and every day. Thankfully, the online world comes to the rescue with several recipe areas tailor-made for busy cooks. To begin your journey, use Keyword: **Recipes** to open the Recipes window on AOL. Near the top, you'll see Today's Featured Recipe, which changes every few seconds. If you find one you like, click it, then, click the Print button near the bottom of the text box.

38

Finding Recipes to Entice the Palate

To browse further, click one of the links in the window:

▶ The AOL Member Recipes link leads to recipe message boards. These contain recipe categories for special diets, low fat, kosher, and vegetarian in addition to the general appetizer-to-dessert options.

▶ The Recipe Finder saves time for busy cooks. What kind of cuisine do you want? How much time do you have to prepare it? Which course do you have in mind? To answer these questions and find several recipes to fit your time and your refrigerator, click the Custom Results button and begin to check your choices for cuisines and courses, ingredients, and recipe sources.

At the iVillage Recipe Finder site (see Figure 38-5), you click to specify the main ingredient, and then mark any special options or food allergies. Select the amount of time you have to prepare the meal (ranging from ten minutes to an hour) and click the Find My Recipes button. The search engine then gives you several options for dinner.

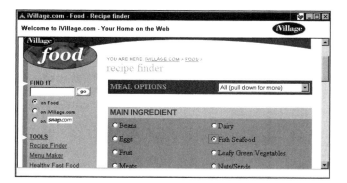

Figure 38-5. Find the recipes that fit your pantry with a little help from iVillage.

Keyword: **iVillage** opens the main iVillage window. Click Food in the channels list to open the iVillage Food section, and then click Recipe Finder under Interactive Kitchen to get to the iVillage Recipe Finder.

Coming Up Next . . .

Dive into the world of games in the next chapter. Whether you prefer crossword puzzles or chess, you can find instructions, interactive games, and other players to share your passion online.

CHAPTER

39

GAMING AND PUZZLING
THE HOURS AWAY

Chapter 39

Gaming and Puzzling the Hours Away

It's Friday evening and nothing's on the tube. Your month-long quilling project sits abandoned while you struggle with a general sense of ennui. Instead of feeling sorry for yourself, hop online and spend the evening in one of the many online trivia areas. Whether your taste tends toward the fast-paced and competitive, or if you'd rather test your wits via e-mail or message boards, or even if you prefer a plain vanilla (but by no means simple) crossword puzzle, America Online offers a game or a puzzle for you.

Let's start with trivia games. With many games running 24 hours a day, you can play online trivia whenever you like. Try a few and join in the fun.

Interactive Trivia

One of the coolest things about the online world is that it's interactive. You can play against people you've never met simply because they happen upon the game at the same time you do. Or you can schedule a specific time to meet in a game with a few AOL buddies and slug it out as a group.

Many of the trivia games on AOL are computer-generated. They all use the same visual layout, so when you learn one you know how to play them all. The topics and questions, however, differ radically.

NTN

NTN Trivia, the granddaddy of them all, provides the backbone behind the computerized trivia games on AOL, in addition to offering many different trivia games in the NTN online area itself. Whether you want to play sports trivia, kids' trivia, entertainment trivia, or an extra-challenging version, NTN is the place to visit.

Keyword: **NTN** opens the main NTN window, as seen in Figure 39-1. From here, you can choose kids games, sports, or general trivia. Sports trivia includes games for such specific categories as baseball, football, soccer, tennis, and hockey. The Kids games include Kids Trivia, Kids Sports Trivia, and Cranial Crunch (the hard version). The Games section houses general trivia, with games such as Retro*AcTiVe, a TV trivia game; Brainbuster, for players who really know their stuff; and Entertainment Trivia.

Note

Keyword: **Games** also opens up a whole world of games, in three huge categories: Game Shows Online (card games and board games), the Game Parlor (game shows), and Xtreme games (strategic games promising even more action and adventure).

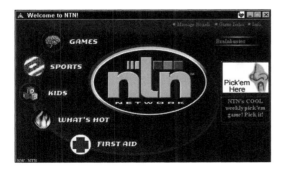

Figure 39-1. Choose any category to begin the online trivia experience.

A click on the Games window Entertainment button reveals the Entertainment Game Index, with links to the other NTN games hidden around AOL. Use this window to explore other interactive trivia options online, such as Trekkie Trivia, MTV's Krank Trivia, or Movie Trivia.

To open any NTN trivia game, click the game's button or double-click its name in an item list. Once the game opens, you'll see a window much like the one in Figure 39-2. Along the left side, five buttons list possible answers to the trivia question. Read the question that appears in the top-left corner and click your answer. As you play, you compete against other players for points. The quicker you click the correct button, the more points you receive for that question. A screen name list on the right side of the window keeps a running tally of the top five or so players and their point totals. Your screen name and current total appear above the name list.

The upper-right corner lists hints as the question progresses. Each hint that appears lowers the total points you receive for answering that question correctly. If you decide not to answer it at all, you receive zero points for that question — but you don't lose any points. If you attempt a question and score an incorrect answer, you lose 250 points, every time.

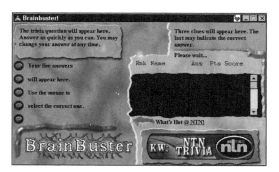

Figure 39-2. Stretch your muscles with Brainbuster trivia.

International Trivia

Play NTN Trivia, international style. This window leads you to international versions of the popular trivia games.

To play International Trivia, follow these steps:

1. Use Keyword: **Trivia** to open the Trivia Online window.
2. Double-click the International Trivia folder in the Online Trivia Links item list. The International Trivia window opens, showing a list of available games.
3. Double-click any trivia game to open it. The national flag in front of each entry in the box identifies the game's country of origin; each game uses that country's native language.

Tip

Use International Trivia to brush up on foreign language skills in French or German, or study Canada with Canadian Trivia.

Live Trivia

Not all the online trivia games are computer-generated. Several online areas sponsor live trivia, which takes place in trivia chat rooms. Players compete to see who knows the correct answer and how quickly they can send it to the chat room window. All these areas post weekly game schedules, and some of them are extremely popular, which might tell you how fun they are. You might want to arrive early to avoid the rush.

Games Paradise

A marriage of two separate trivia areas on AOL, Games Paradise offers live chat room games featuring a wild assortment of topics. A quick romp through the weekly game schedule shows Country Music Trivia, TV Trivia, Make The Grade (trivia by category), Disney Trivia — you name it. Different trivia games appear various days during the week, and players gather in one of five different game chat rooms to play. Because they're played live, the trivia games take place from 8 p.m. or so until the wee hours of the morning. Check the Paradise Game Schedules folder to find out where you need to be and when. Keyword: **Paradise** opens the Games Paradise window, as seen in Figure 39-3.

39

Gaming and Puzzling the Hours Away

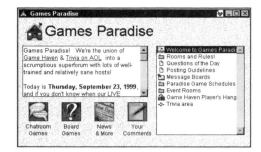

Figure 39-3. Live trivia games thrive in Paradise.

SpeakEZ Trivia

Relax each evening and visit the trivia room. From 9 p.m. to 1
a.m. ET, the SpeakEZ team brings you music, sports, quotation,
general, advanced, and other trivia topics, seven days a week.
Check the SpeakEZ Schedule to see what's on tap for the current week. Use Keyword: **Trivia** to open the Trivia Online
window, and then double-click SpeakEZ in the item list to
open the SpeakEZ area.

Inner Circle Trivia

Try your hand at advertising jingles, alphabetizing, identifying
mystery people, and more in the Inner Circle Trivia Games
Room (Figure 39-4). These live trivia games take place every
night of the week, offering trivia with a tinge of culture. Since
these games begin at regular hours, be sure to check the
schedule so you know what game plays when. Use Keyword:
Trivia to access the Trivia Online window, and then select
Inner Circle from the item list.

Figure 39-4. Answer cultural questions and meet new friends in the Inner Circle
trivia games.

Off the Beaten Path

As you browse through America Online, you might stumble across some of the games listed below. Hidden away in various online areas, these selections offer some of the most interesting trivia online. Rather than trying to meet the demands of a general trivia-playing public, each of the games in this section focuses on a particular trivia topic. How challenging you find them depends a lot on how well you know the subject at hand. If you've already memorized every chapter in the Old Testament, for example, Old Testament Trivia will be a breeze. However, if you've only recently discovered science fiction, you're bound to find quite a bit of challenge in the Zealot Sci-Fi Trivia game.

Antagonist Trivia

Antagonist Trivia offers trivia with an edge. If the question itself isn't provocative, look for a snappy comment after the answer appears. Designed for young (and older) adults and covering history, media, music, sports, geography, and several other subjects, this game gives trivia an attitude. If your feelings are easily offended, you might want to skip this one. If not, you'll probably get a good laugh as you play this game. Find it at Keyword: **AT**.

Gut Instinct

Think of Gut Instinct as a trivia game standing on its head. This game focuses on situations found in the workplace — but with a catch. Instead of answering the questions with the correct answer, your challenge is to answer the question the way the majority might answer it. Some of the questions are factual, such as "What is the average household income of a family in Rhode Island?" Other questions, like "What's your favorite evening workday activity?" require a bit more insight into the collective consciousness. Hop over to the game with Keyword: **Gut Instinct** and try it yourself.

Jewish Trivia Question

If Jewish trivia interests you, look for it in Jewish Community Online. Each day, the staff posts a document called (*date*) On This Day. The bottom of the document lists the daily Jewish Trivia Question, along with the previous day's answer. Here's how to get there:

1. Use Keyword: **JCOL** to open the Jewish Community main window.
2. Click the button next to This Day, which opens the This Day window.
3. Look in the item box for a listing of On This Day documents. Today's date appears at the top of the list, and they go progressively backward.
4. Double-click any On This Day file to open it; scroll down to the bottom of the document to see the Jewish Trivia Question.

NTN Old Testament Trivia

How much do you really know about the people and events of the Old Testament? This trivia game focuses on general questions — for example, it won't ask you to identify the topic of the 59th chapter of Isaiah. However, it does ask questions like "Who was turned into a pillar of salt?" and "Which one listed was *not* a son of Jacob?" As with all the NTN games, you choose from five possible answers. Get there with Keyword: **CO Fun**, and then click the Old Testament Trivia button to open the Old Testament Trivia window.

Parent Soup: The Game

Tickle your funny bone and try your hand at parenting trivia at the same time. Which foods are rich in calcium? What stops diaper rash? Which first name is most common in nursery rhymes? Answer questions like these and show your parenting prowess. To get there, use Keyword: **PS Fun** and then click the Parent Soup Trivia Game button. The Parent Soup — The Game window opens. Click the button marked Click here to play the PS Trivia Game and join the fray.

Sports Trivia Forum

Unlike the computer-generated NTN sports trivia games, the Grandstand Sports Trivia Forum operates a live chat-based trivia room, poses a Question of the Day, and presents Sports Match Trivia. Each evening of the week, the Sports Trivia chat room hums with general sports trivia, baseball trivia, and other specialized trivia chats. Get there by using Keyword: **GS Trivia**. Once the Sports Trivia Forum window opens, as seen in Figure 39-5, click the Live Trivia link.

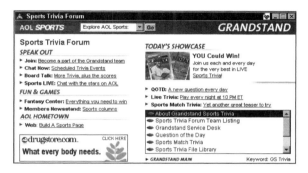

Figure 39-5. Maximize your knowledge in the Sports Trivia Forum.

Question of the Day and Sports Match Trivia are both e-mail trivia games. To play Question of the Day, follow these steps:

1. Open the Sports Trivia Forum window by using Keyword: **GS Trivia**.

2. Double-click Question of the Day in the item list. The Question of the Day window opens.

3. Double-click the dated entry in the item list. It should say something like "Here is the August 1 Question."

4. Read the current question. If you know the answer, close the window and then click the Answer Here button to open the Grandstand Trivia Question dialog box.

5. Type your answer into The Grandstand Trivia Question's text box and click Send. Your answer wings its way to the Grandstand's Trivia department.

6. Correct answers get points. Members who collect the highest number of points for the month see their screen names posted in a monthly winners' document.

The method for playing Sports Match is much the same. Instead of answering one question, though, your goal is to match the correct player with his position, past accomplishments, award, or whatever the general question asks. Think of it as a voluntary matching quiz on one of your favorite topics. Look for the Sports Match item in the Sports Trivia Forum item list to get started.

Zealot Sci-Fi Trivia

Test your mastery of science fiction and fantasy knowledge with Zealot Sci-Fi Trivia. Answer queries about classic sci-fi flicks, mythology, TV shows, and literature. If you find you excel at Zealot Trivia, you might want to join one of the four Zealot teams to enhance your fame and fortune (plus win redeemable tokens if you triumph at the trivia games). Use Keyword: **Z** to visit the general Zealot Trivia window and navigate your way from there.

Playing Online Crossword Puzzles

In the remainder of this chapter, you'll find links to crossword puzzles and other word games. Like many of the games described earlier, some puzzles can be played online. You need to print other puzzles out and sharpen your pencil to solve the mystery. Still other options include playing word games against other players in live chat rooms. Pick your method, and have a sleuthfully good time.

You can find several crossword puzzles online. Play a few, or play them all. Print one or two for the road, and do them over lunch. No matter how you solve them, the crosswords here provide plenty of fun.

My News Daily Crossword

Each day delivers a new crossword to your own customizable news area on AOL, My News. You can solve the puzzle online, save the puzzle to your computer, print it to take with you, or print the puzzle's solution. If you miss a day's crossword, look for it in the archive of past puzzles.

Visit My News Daily Crossword by using Keyword: **My News**. Once My News loads into your Web browser (it's part of AOL.com), look for the crossword link under the Essentials section. You'll find Essentials along the left side of the window, about halfway down. Click the link and My News Daily Crossword loads, looking a lot like Figure 39-6.

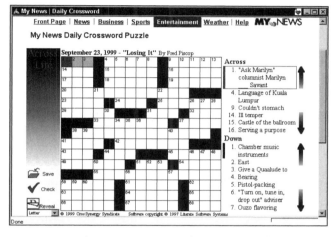

Figure 39-6. Solve away — a new puzzle appears every day at My News.

Read the clues along the right side of the screen, and type in your answers. To navigate inside the puzzle, use your mouse or the arrow keys. To change from across clues to down clues, use the arrow keys or click the appropriate clue.

If you're in the midst of working the puzzle and need to stop, click the Save folder along the puzzle window's left-hand side and follow the steps to save the puzzle to your hard drive. The software saves your puzzle where you left off, so you don't need to retrace any steps (or re-solve part of the puzzle) when you have time to finish it. If you shut the puzzle down without saving it and then reopen it later online, it appears just as blank as the first time you laid eyes on it. Oops.

Puzzle Zone

Flexicon offers a new twist on crosswords. Their versions are made up of several levels. As shown in Figure 39-7, you click each square to reveal the clues and grid for that level. Running through all the small crossword pieces, one large word or group of words provides the answer to the overall clue — in a tongue-in-cheek way.

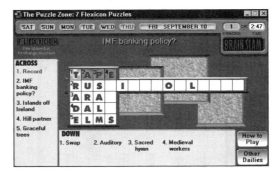

Figure 39-7. Try your hand at the multidimensional Flexicon puzzle.

To play the Puzzle Zone, you first need to download the Puzzle Zone software. Use Keyword: **Puzzle Zone** to open the online area, and then click any puzzle in the window. The system searches for the software; and if the system doesn't find the software, it offers to download that software for you. Once you download the software for the first time, it takes only a moment or two to update each daily puzzle. Best of all, if you miss a day or two, you can click any of the daily buttons along the top of the Flexicon window to load that day's puzzle.

As you solve the puzzle, Flexicon offers you a hint if it senses you might be stuck. However, the hint applies to the long word that answers the *overall* clue, and *not* to any particular clue you might be trying to solve. Use the spacebar to change direction from across to down, and vice versa, as you solve the puzzle.

New York Times Crosswords

If you're a New York Times crossword lover, you have three options: First, for $9.95 a year, you can subscribe to New York Times' Premium Diversions service and have access to all the daily puzzles on the site, *including* the Sunday puzzle. (If you love crossword puzzles, getting the Sunday Times puzzle qualifies as a Big Deal.) Second, subscribers to the seven-day print version of *The New York Times* get the online puzzles for free.

Premium Diversions subscribers, in addition to the weekly crossword puzzles, also have access to archived puzzles they might have missed, as well as monthly available-to-subscribers-only puzzles. Generally these monthly puzzles have some kind of month-appropriate theme.

The third option, for members who aren't ready for a daily dose of New York Times puzzles or who want to introduce the kids in their lives to crosswords, is to print the monthly children's puzzle. Available at no cost, it's part of The New York Times Learning Network, the Times' educational Web site.

Visit The New York Times site on America Online by using Keyword: **NYT**. Click the Diversions department button to sign up for Premium Diversions; also click the Diversions button to see the link for the Learning Network crossword.

Chicago Tribune, AOL Edition Puzzles

Dip into the Chicago Tribune Web site for the paper's daily crossword puzzle, scanned from the print version for your daily solving pleasure. You download these puzzles (which have been saved as GIF files) and then print them. Unlike most of the other puzzles, these can't be completed online. But they offer two advantages: Because you've downloaded them to your hard drive, you can always print them later, and since the puzzle is a scanned image of the original Tribune puzzle, it contains the previous day's answer with nothing else to download.

To get to these puzzles, do the following:

1. Use Keyword: **Tribune** to open the Chicago Tribune AOL Edition main window.

2. Open the Site Index in the Chicago Tribune AOL Edition window.

3. Scroll to the bottom of the Daily Sections portion of the Site Index window.

4. Double-click the Puzzles folder to open the Puzzles window.

5. Double-click any dated puzzle in the Stories and Information item box. This opens a dialog box that explains how to download and view the puzzle.

6. Click the Download Puzzle button to begin the download. When the puzzle is finished downloading, it appears in a window on screen.

Tip

If you're new to New York Times crosswords, you might want to begin with the Monday puzzles. The puzzles get increasingly more difficult as the week wears on, ending with a triumphant (and incredibly difficult) Sunday puzzle.

Tip

The Chicago Tribune area suggests that you download an extra graphics viewer and use it to display the puzzle before you print it. If you don't want to go to that trouble, AOL's built-in graphics viewer automatically opens the puzzle after you download it; I tried this and found the daily puzzles quite readable when I printed them directly from the AOL screen. The Sunday puzzle, however, might benefit from a different graphics viewer. The Chicago Tribune crossword download area links you to the free graphics viewers online so you can find one that works with your system, download it, and install it.

7. Click the Print toolbar button to print the puzzle so you can solve it.

Stretching Your Mind with Word Games

Language-oriented adventure awaits you online when you visit some of the word game areas and explore their contents. Try the interactive computerized word games, or jump into the live-action chat room puzzlers to try one of a dizzying number of word game choices.

Puzzle Zone

In addition to the Flexicon crossword, the Puzzle Zone (Keyword: **Puzzle Zone**) also presents Clink, Strip Search, and Elvis Lives. Each one is a different type of word game; for example, Strip Search is a word search in which you look for words that fit into a category, like *astronomers* or *celestial bodies*. The trick is that you search for the words without a word list to guide you. In order to see the words, you need to click the Show Words button at the bottom of the Strip Search window. As you locate the words and highlight them with the mouse, they take their place in the word list.

To play Clink, you drag words as they appear at the top of the screen to their definitions in the playing board. As you can see in Figure 39-8, most of the words fit in more than one place. Drag a correctly placed word to a highlighted area elsewhere on the board, and let it go. If it fits there, a copy clinks into place.

Unscramble mixed words in Elvis Lives. Each puzzle focuses on a different celebrity name, along with three scrambled words that describe (or help to identify) that person. Unscramble the words and the name before the timer runs out.

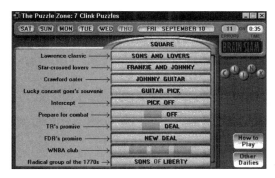

Figure 39-8. Complete the word definitions one part at a time in Clink.

Games Paradise

Visit the Games Paradise live chat rooms to play word games galore. From false definitions in Dictionary to guessing the secret word in You Don't Say, this area hosts nearly 90 live word games each week across five chat rooms. Use Keyword: **Paradise** to visit the area, and then spend some time reading through the Paradise Game Schedules folder to see what games are available at any given time.

Taking an Identity in a Role Playing Game

Spend the evening looking at the world through someone else's eyes. Defeat evil forces, track down UFOs, or solve a mystery in a game where you follow the clues and help play out the story line. You choose the scenario and you create the character. In some cases, you also create the story.

Playing a Role

In a role playing game, you play in a fantasy world, usually set far back in the past or way off in the future. You assume the identity of a character that fits in with the story line — you don't want to be an elf in a futuristic space society, and a medieval warrior might not exactly match the genre either. Each game's guidelines generally tell you what types of

Tip

Premium role playing games are created by game software companies and charge members $1.99 per hour to play. The Premium games include a couple of classics, such as Legends of Kesmai and Multiplayer BattleTech, along with some newer titles like Cosrin and Darkness Falls.

characters are acceptable, whether human, elven, magical, or something entirely different.

Just like in real life, your character gets a name and an America Online screen name of his or her own. To be polite, as well as to help the other players, members create online profiles or Web pages to describe their characters. Like real people, these imaginary characters have strengths and weaknesses, which you usually determine as you create the character by rolling dice in a chat room (Keyword: **Dice** opens the Dice Roller window). You then join the game and act out the plot under the direction of a game director whose function is to guide the action of the game.

For more information about role playing online, along with a list of games available on AOL, use Keyword: **Gaming** to open the Role Playing Forum window. From there, the Colosseum button leads to information on two online role playing games, The Arena and Parthos. Find out how to create a character and join in the fun.

Use the RPG Chat button to scope out the current game schedules and find out which ones need new players. For a list of Premium Role Playing Games, click the Premium RPGs button.

You can also find some top-notch role playing games on the Web. To play other interactive gaming systems, try these:

- ▶ **Asheron's Call:** Look for this popular sword and sorcery game at www.asheronscall.com.
- ▶ **Everquest:** Become a warrior, bard, or shaman and join a group that gathers to seek adventure and gather treasure. Find this game at www.everquest.com.
- ▶ **Ultima Online:** Create a character, develop a set of skills — even adopt an animal or two. Ultima Online (at www.ultimaonline.com) gives you adventure with or without the blood — your call.

These games usually require a CD-ROM copy of the game itself. Then you pay a monthly fee to access the game system and play against other characters online.

Simming Around

Simulations function a little differently than role playing games. In a simulation, or sim, the experience is more like acting in a play. Although a role playing game could be described as a loosely legislated free for all, a simulation follows specific rules and uses a definite set of characters. In a role playing game, no one notices an extra dwarf, but one extra alien in a sim could upset the ecobalance.

In a simulation, you act in a world with parameters, as in a play. Simulations make you one of the team, whereas a role player can go it alone and create his or her own adventure. Sim players also follow a scripted plot. Looking up into the sky and shouting "Look! A dragon!" would be a less-than-applauded behavior in a space exploration simulation game, for example.

To reach the Simming Forums on America Online, use Keyword: **Gaming** to open the Gamers Forum, and then click the Simming button. The Simming Forums window blazes to life, as seen in Figure 39-9.

Figure 39-9. Find a simulation game to join in the Simming Forum.

Check the Simming Schedules in the Game Rooms window, or check out the individual simulations which sport buttons in the Simming Forum window. Diaspora is a science fiction adventure, while Space Fleet and Space Wars voyage through galaxies on space ships far, far away. For a dip into midnight fantasy, Dark Gothic invites you to join a world of vampires, changelings, and werewolves.

If you had something a little more earth bound in mind, click the More Sims button to explore a paranormal simulation, a Victorian mystery game, and more.

Finding Classic Online Strategy Games

Locate an online game that you love and compete live against people around the world. Strategy games make you think — they rely more on logic skills than wrist flexibility. The classic games, such as hearts, poker, and bridge, also reside in their own Net niches. Tour one or two of these online gaming sites, find the games you like to play, and enjoy.

On America Online, The Game Parlor offers everything from backgammon and chess to virtual pool. You play in real time against other members. Part of the Premium Games service, these games cost $0.99 per hour to play. The Game Parlor (at Keyword: **Game Parlor**) offers the following:

Backgammon	Jack Nicklaus Online Golf
Bridge	Online Casino
Casino Blackjack	Poker
CatchWord	Spades
Classic Cards	Splatterball
Cribbage	Tetris: Head 2 Head
Gin	USCF Chess
Hearts	Virtual Pool

Look for strategy games (and others) at the larger online gaming sites. These sites offer chess, Go Fish, mahjong, pinochle, and more:

▶ **Yahoo Games:** Visit games.yahoo.com to compete one-on-one in card games or strategy games (see Figure 39-10).

▶ **Excite Games:** This portion of the Excite search engine hosts trivia games, bingo, and arcade games in addition to the usual chess, checkers, and bridge. Find it at www.excite.com/games.

▶ **MSN Gaming Zone:** Play strategy games or retail games such as Scrabble or Age of Empires at Microsoft's Gaming Zone, found at `zone.msn.com`.

Figure 39-10. Pick your favorite game and play online.

Coming Up Next . . .

Whether you take your sports as a spectator or you prefer to get your fingertips dirty by managing a fantasy team, you'll find plenty of online sports resources in the next chapter. Find your favorites, draft your own team, or explore your favorite sport's beginnings, all through your online connection.

CHAPTER

40

JUMPING INTO
ONLINE SPORTS

Chapter 40

Jumping into Online Sports

There's more to the online sports world than stats, figures, and polite arguments over whose team will rank the highest at the end of the season. Although you can find all of this online, as well as general articles that introduce you to sports that may be unfamiliar, you can also use your online connection to do much more. Create and manage a sports team of your own. Locate specifics about your favorite teams. Trace the history of golf or baseball.

This section leads you to some of the more interactive, as well as interesting, sports areas online.

Playing Fantasy Sports

You always wanted to be the one calling the shots. Live the dream by managing a fantasy sports team of your own. Whether your blood beats for baseball, basketball, football, golf, or hockey, fantasy sports allow you to cheer wildly for your very own team — or groan in despair, depending on how your players perform.

Note

Keyword: **Sports** offers up-to-the-minute scores for major sports events, plus additional sports info.

In a fantasy sport, you sign up for a team, give the team a name, and then assemble your players from a list of available names. As the season progresses, you manage the team's statistics and watch their progress against other teams in the league. Your team battles against other league players for the top spots, game by game. Victories throughout the season might bring prizes to top teams and players, depending on the league you join.

You have a choice of four different fantasy sports providers on America Online. Each provider offers something a little different; the following paragraphs tell a little about the various fantasy opportunities online. Reach the Fantasy Sports Center window, shown in Figure 40-1, with Keyword: **Fantasy Sports**.

Figure 40-1. Join a fantasy sports team and race for the pennant.

CBS Sportsline Sports

CBS Sportsline Fantasy Games runs a variety of games, and their site gives you several fantasy options. If you already run a fantasy league of your own, and would like some assistance with statistics and league management, take a look at their Sportsline Commissioner software. Office pool managers should take a look at the free Office Pool Manager that helps you run a pool online.

40

Jumping into Online Sports

In the fantasy sports realm, you can join a league that competes in baseball, basketball, cricket, football, hockey, and soccer. Major League Baseball Fantasy Challenge is free to play; most of the other games cost $19.95 per season. Click the CBS Sportsline Fantasy Sports button in the Fantasy Sports Center window to open the Sportsline site.

STATS Fantasies

Play a variety of fantasy baseball, basketball, football, and hockey games at STATS. The games vary in their level of realism, and they also vary in cost. Diamond Legends, a baseball simulation, lets you select from a roster of historical players and compete on the Internet. Several fantasy sports leagues cost $9.95 per season to play; the cost rises to $99.95 for Diamond Legends.

To see the STATS Fantasy Sports window for yourself, click the STATS button in the Fantasy Sports Center window or use Keyword: **STATS Fantasy** to open the site directly.

Grandstand

The Grandstand, one of the America Online sports areas, sponsors fantasy teams in baseball, football, basketball, and hockey. The Grandstand Fantasy Sports window, in addition to links to the various leagues, also contains links to a fantasy sports chat room, the Grandstand Fantasy e-mail newsletter, and league message boards. Open the Grandstand Fantasy Sports window, shown in Figure 40-2, by clicking the Grandstand Fantasy Sports button in the Fantasy Sports Center window.

Figure 40-2. Grandstand Fantasy Sports offers several different fantasy games you can play.

Each Grandstand Fantasy team costs $34.95 for the season; double-click any Grandstand Fantasy text in the item box to open that sport's individual fantasy window. Then click the Sign Up to Play button to begin the signup process. If the game currently accepts registrations, it leads you through several signup screens. If, on the other hand, registration is closed for the season, a window appears telling you such.

NTN

NTN, the online trivia magnate, offers a free fantasy game or two in addition to a couple of games that add spice to sports viewing. DiamondBall (Keyword: **DiamondBall**) and QB1 (Keyword: **NTN Playbook**) spur members to call the plays just prior to the actual calls during live professional games. If you'd rather play in a fantasy team game, check the NTN Fantasy Baseball window (**NTN Full Count**) or NTN Fantasy Basketball (Keyword: **NTN Hoops**) for further information.

Finding a Favorite Team

When you check the stats and rosters for your pet sport, you don't always want to wade through every current sport or every team to get to the good stuff. Although dropping into the Sports channel or going directly to The Grandstand (Keyword: **Grandstand**) leads you to some interesting forums, you have a couple of other options to locate exactly what you're looking for.

First, try using the team's name or nickname as a keyword. If the team maintains some type of area online, with stats, rosters, articles, and other data, this works every time. Keyword: **Maple Leafs** opens the Toronto hockey team's window, Keyword: **Braves** gives you the Atlanta baseball team forum, Keyword: **Knicks** (not Knickerbockers) gives you the New York basketball franchise.

Tip

The general NTN Sports window, which leads to interactive trivia games in addition to the current fantasy game, can be found at Keyword: **NTN Sports**.

Find It Online

Search the Web for a glimpse of your favorite team. Type the team name, or the team's league (National Football League, National Basketball Association, and so on) into the browser bar text field and click the Search button. The Web results should show you links to fan pages, official team sites, and top news stories.

Tracing Sports History

Who threw the first basketball? Where did golf truly come from? Find out the answers to these burning questions and discover the origins of various sports while you're at it. Sports history sites tell about beginnings and endings as well as milestones and mishaps.

Delve into the history of your favorite sports with a few of these sites:

▶ **Hickok's Sports History:** No matter what type of sports history interests you, this site provides a good story — along with some historical sports cards you can send to friends via e-mail. See Figure 40-3 for an example, and check out the site itself at `www.ultranet.com/~rhickok/sendcard.shtml`.

Figure 40-3. Read history tidbits or send an electronic greeting card from Hickok's Sports History page.

▶ **Baseball History:** Alexander Doubleday started it all in Cooperstown, NY. Did you also know that Doubleday went on to become a captain in the Civil War? For a brief look into baseball history, check out A Short History of the Hall of Fame in the About the Hall of Fame section (`www.baseballhalloffame.org`).

▶ **Basketball History:** Delve into the history of hoops at the Hooptown, USA Web site. This site contains a link that tells how Springfield, MA, the town where the Basketball Hall of Fame is located, became the birth-place of the sport. See for yourself at `www. hooptown.com`.

▶ **Football History:** What would a collection of sports history Web sites be without a football site? Visit the Pro Football Hall of Fame, at `www.profootballhof. com`, to read about football history decade by decade, or to peruse individual team histories.

▶ **Golf History:** Historical articles, a list of the oldest courses, and a timeline of golf history awaits you at the GOLFonline history page, at `www.golfonline. com/history`.

▶ **Hockey History:** Drop into the Hockey Hall of Fame Web site (`www.hhof.com/index.htm`) and see photos of some of the hockey greats. Find them in the Resource Centre section.

▶ **Wrestling History:** SLAM! Wrestling provides Worldwide Wrestling Federation history, as well as wrestling biographies and a link to the Canadian Hall of Fame at their site, `www.sunmedia.ca/ WrestlingHistory/home.html`.

Index

G

continued

continued

Notes

Notes

Notes

Notes

Notes

Notes

Notes

Notes

Notes

Notes

Notes

Notes

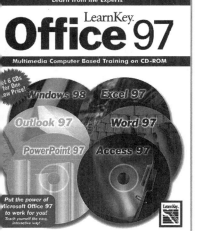

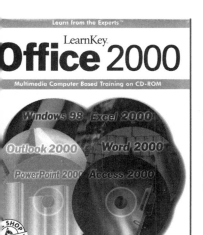

AOL Selects the Best

Increase Your Computer's Productivity!

Order Today!
1-888-299-0329

AOL's PowerSuite Deluxe

Seven powerful utilities to help you work smarter and make your computer work harder for you! The programs on these CD-ROMs will help you perform tests and diagnostics to help your computer work at peak performances, give your computer more open space safely and easily, keep your software up-to-date with the help of AOL and the Internet, index Web sites quickly and easily, and stay organized and on schedule!

$39.95 (s&h $5.60)   #0010372N 10141

So easy to use,
no wonder it's #1

AOL Selects the Best

Get the Most Out of Your Computing Experience!

AOL Shop Direct Upgrade Shop

In general, when accessing AOL and the Internet - and uploading or downloading pictures, files or information - the speed and performance of your computer are tied to three primary components:

--The central processing unit (CPU)
--The memory capacity (hard drive and RAM)
--The modem speed

AOL is dedicated to help you have the best online and computing experience. In AOL's Upgrade Shop we have devoted an entire area on "Quick Tips," handy information and popular computing terms to better aid and assist you in upgrading your computer. In addition, we have tested, selected, and priced the best products to turbo-charge your system.

So easy to use, no wonder it's #1

Go to AOL Keyword: Upgrade Shop

AOL Selects the Best

Send and receive email anywhere, anytime!

AOL Mail For Palm™ Organizers

AOL Mail represents a significant first step toward bringing the full convenience and ease of use of AOL to Palm™ handheld devices. For the first time, AOL members can leave their PCs and laptops behind and continue to enjoy the AOL experience. All you need to get going is a compatible Palm™ device*, a Palm™ snap-on modem, and an AOL account. AOL Mail connects members directly to AOL using their regular screen names and passwords. Leveraging AOL's global network of access numbers, AOL Mail allows members to connect with the service from just about anywhere. AOL Mail requires a Palm III, IIIe, IIIx, V, VII, or an earlier Palm that has been upgraded to Palm III compatibility, and 425K of free RAM.

Coming Soon... AOL Mail for Windows CE Palm-Size PCs

AMERICA *Online*

So easy to use, no wonder it's #1

CD-ROM Installation Instructions

Windows

1. Insert the AOL CD into your CD-ROM drive.
2. If installation does not begin automatically, click Start on the taskbar (Windows 3.1 users click on the File menu of your Windows Program Manager), then select Run.
3. Type **D:\SETUP** (or **E:\SETUP**) and press OK. Follow the easy instructions and you'll be online in minutes!

Macintosh

1. For AOL 4.0 for Mac, insert the AOL CD into your CD-ROM drive.
2. Double-click on the Install icon.
3. Follow the easy instructions and you'll be online in minutes!

Cert: 4A-3642-7681

Password: COEVAL-LANCET